Advocacy Across Borders

Advocacy Across Borders

NGOs, Anti-Sweatshop Activism, and the Global Garment Industry

SHAE GARWOOD

Kumarian Press
An Imprint of Stylus Publishing

Advocacy Across Borders: NGOs, Anti-Sweatshop Activism, and the Global Garment Industry
Published in 2011 in the United States of America by Kumarian Press, 22883 Quicksilver
Drive, Sterling, VA 20166 USA.

The text of this book is set in 11/13 AGaramond.

Editing and book design by Joan Marie Laflamme, jml ediset.
Proofread by Kathryn Owens.
Index by Robert Swanson.

Bulk Purchases
Quantity discounts are available for
use in workshops and for staff
development.
Call 1–800–232–0223

∞ The paper used in this publication meets the minimum requirements of the American
National Standard for Information Sciences—Permanence of Paper for printed Library Materials, ANSI Z39.48–1984

Library of Congress Cataloging-in-Publication Data

Garwood, Shae, 1974–
    Advocacy across borders : NGOs, anti-sweatshop activism and the global garment
industry / by Shae Garwood.
        p. cm.
    Includes bibliographical references and index.
    ISBN 978–1–56549–454–1 (pbk. : alk. paper) — ISBN 978–1–56549–455–8
(casebound : alk. paper) — ISBN 978–1–56549–456–5 (library ebook) — ISBN 978–1–
56549–457–2 (consumer ebook)
    1. Anti-sweatshop movement. 2. Clothing trade—Moral and ethical
aspects. 3. Non-governmental organizations. I. Title.
    HD2337.G37 2011
    338.8'8787—dc22

                                                                        2011016030

For Amaya and Zadie

Contents

Tables and Figures

Acknowledgments

I owe a great deal to the many people who helped make this book possible, but especially to the activists and scholars who generously shared their time with me and responded to my many requests. Roderic Pitty and Jie Chen at the University of Western Australia helped me find my focus, stay on track, and complete the thesis from which this book has grown. Bruce Stone and Linley Hill made sure that I had access to the resources I needed to conduct the research and dedicate time to writing. Kanishka Jayasuriya, Robert J. S. Ross, and Nicola Piper provided valuable feedback on the thesis, which strengthened the book. Friends and colleagues engaged in lively discussions and commented on earlier drafts. I especially want to thank Sky Croeser, Kate Riddell, Liza Beinart, Christalla Yakinthou, Kelly Gerard, Michelle Hackett, Janaka Biyanwila and Karen Soldatic. The Bluestocking Institute for Global Peace and Justice allowed me to share my work and connect scholarly debates with NGO practices. Jim Lance, Erica Flock, and Alexandra Hartnett at Kumarian Press shepherded the book through the publishing process. I received travel and research funding from an Australian Postgraduate Award, the UWA Graduate Research School, and the School of Social and Cultural Studies.

I am deeply indebted to my family for their love and unwavering support. Through their actions, my parents, Mary and Griff Garwood, taught me the importance of doing our part to make the world a little better. My sister, Anna Garwood, is an inspiration for her dedication to living her principles and following her dreams. As a scholar and activist, my husband, Ethan Blue, made this project possible through his intellectual engagement, willingness to listen, and unconditional support. For this and everything else, I am forever grateful.

Abbreviations and Acronyms

AABTC	Action-Alert-Branding-Targeting-Campaign
ACFID	Australia Council for International Development
AFL-CIO	American Federation of Labor—Congress of Industrial Organizations
AMRC	Asia Monitor Resource Centre
ARA	Australian Retailers Association
ATC	Agreement on Textile and Clothing
ATNC	Asian Transnational Corporation Monitoring Network
ATO	Australian Tax Office
AWID	Association for Women's Rights in Development
BFC	Better Factories Cambodia
CAFTA	Central America Free Trade Agreement
CCC	Clean Clothes Campaign
CITA	U.S. Committee for the Implementation of Textile Agreements
CLR	Campaign for Labor Rights
DR-CAFTA	Dominican Republic–Central America Free Trade Agreement
DSP	Designated Suppliers Program
EPZ	export processing zone
EU	European Union
FFI	Fibre & Fabric International
FLA	Fair Labor Association
FWF	Fair Wear Foundation
GATWU	Garment and Textile Workers' Union
GRWU	Gina Relations Workers Union

ICFTU	International Confederation of Free Trade Unions
IGO	intergovernmental organization
ILO	International Labour Organization
ILRF	International Labor Rights Forum
IMF	International Monetary Fund
IOC	International Olympic Committee
IRS	Internal Revenue Service
ITGLWF	International Textile, Garment and Leather Workers' Federation
ITUC	International Trade Union Confederation
JO-IN	Joint Initiative on Corporate Accountability and Workers' Rights
MFA	Multifibre Arrangement
MOU	memorandum of understanding
MSI	multi-stakeholder initiative
MSN	Maquila Solidarity Network
NGO	nongovernmental organization
NLC	National Labor Committee
NTEE	National Taxonomy of Exempt Entities
OECD	Organisation for Economic Co-operation and Development
SACOM	Students and Scholars against Corporate Misconduct
SAI	Social Auditing International
SEWA	Self-Employed Women's Association
SITRAIMASH	Union of Workers of the Maquila and Similar Industries Honduras
STEYY	Yoo Yang Enterprise Trade Union
TAN	transnational advocacy network
TCFUA	Textile, Clothing and Footwear Union of Australia
TNC	transnational corporation
USAID	U.S. Agency for International Development
USAS	United Students Against Sweatshops
USLEAP	U.S. Labor Education in the Americas Project

WFSGI	World Federation of the Sporting Goods Industry
WRAP	Worldwide Responsible Accredited Production
WRC	Worker Rights Consortium
WTO	World Trade Organization

Introduction

NGOs and advocacy networks as transnational political actors

The clothing and textile industry employs more than 29 million people around the world, mostly in export processing zones in Asia and Central America. Workers frequently face long hours and inadequate wages and are often subjected to harassment and abuse. Many workers resist such conditions by participating in protests and joining labor unions. In many parts of the world, however, workers are unable to form independent unions, and the unions that do exist have found it difficult to deal with manufacturers who move from one site to another in search of lower production costs and a compliant workforce. Because of these challenges, garment workers have reached out to allies across political borders in order to apply pressure on garment manufacturers.

In the 1990s a group of NGOs emerged that focused on the role consumers could play in improving industry standards. Constraints on traditional labor movements forced these NGOs to develop alternative strategies to improve conditions for garment workers. The unique structure of the garment industry, with power concentrated among large retailers reliant on branding, gave consumer-oriented NGOs an opportunity to exert influence on retailers from the consumption side of the industry. The emergence of the anti-sweatshop network in the 1990s is illustrative of an alliance-building process and of the constraints on, and successes of, such alliances in effecting political and social change for the betterment of workers' rights and conditions.

Anti-sweatshop activists focused on changing the behavior of retailers in addition to conventional forms of political advocacy aimed at the state. One of their most effective strategies was to link high-profile brands with particularly egregious labor abuses in factories where those goods were produced. Anti-sweatshop NGOs linked brands with cases of child labor, physical abuse, and indentured labor in the industry. Activists were able to do

I

this because increasing consumer demand and branding opened up new points of leverage for consumer activism and political action. As a result of the anti-sweatshop campaigns in the 1990s and early 2000s, retailers began to disclose their factory locations and adopt codes of conduct, and some even joined multi-stakeholder initiatives (MSIs) aimed at monitoring abuses in the industry.

Nevertheless, problems remain. Despite the gains made by the anti-sweatshop network over the past fifteen years, working conditions have not drastically improved. Moreover, the anti-sweatshop network is at a critical point because shifts in its operational terrain have necessitated new approaches to activism. Sweatshops are no longer a hot topic among the media. Advocates are now at the stage of working more closely with targeted corporations through MSIs, dealing with the challenges of maintaining public interest in the issues, and since late 2008, coping with the global financial crisis that has led to the closure of many garment factories around the world.

This book investigates the ways in which NGOs and the anti-sweatshop network influence the garment industry, given significant structural challenges of complex supply chains and concentration of power among retailers. It provides a glimpse into an advocacy network at a particular point in time and conceivably at a critical juncture in its evolution. It also includes case studies of four Northern NGOs in the network. The four cases provide opportunities for comparative analysis of specific NGO activities as well as analysis of these NGOs as a group with distinctive characteristics. The focus on small, Northern-based NGOs is owing to the prevalence of these types of organizations in the anti-sweatshop network and the absence of adequate analysis of such organizations in the study of international relations.

NGOs and their networks in international relations

While NGOs have long been a part of international politics, the number of NGOs is growing steadily, with a reported fifty-nine thousand international NGOs in existence as of 2004 (Anheier, Kaldor, and Glasius 2005, 320). This increase in number and visibility has led to a growing interest among scholars in investigating the relative significance and influence of NGOs in international politics. Scholars from various fields including international law, development studies, and sociology have all taken an interest in the ways that NGOs interact with society. Although each discipline offers insights into the function and form of NGOs, they have not fully addressed how NGOs operate as political agents and the ways in which they interact across national boundaries. Locating NGOs in an international relations framework provides a way to examine NGOs and their connecting networks as political actors and to analyze the ways that they exercise power and influence in international politics.

The discipline of international relations has traditionally focused on states as the primary unit of analysis. Within realist or neo-realist perspectives NGOs are viewed as domestic pressure groups, relevant insofar as they influence state behavior. Even the label of non-state actor within international relations illustrates the orientation of the field because entities as diverse as transnational corporations, criminal gangs, epistemic communities, and NGOs are categorized together. Traditional international relations scholarship defines these diverse entities in opposition to the state, prompting comparisons between states and non-states. Although these comparisons can be useful, conceptualizing all non-state actors as a unified category obscures the diverse and complex interactions among NGOs, corporations, and other non-state actors.[1]

Several theoretical streams in international relations have begun to include NGOs within the realm of study. Much of this has come out of the growing influence of constructivism in international relations. With its emphasis on the place of ideas and norms in shaping global politics, constructivist perspectives contribute to understandings of the political role of NGOs. Constructivist literature has helped illuminate how those with relatively little power are able to participate in global debates by influencing cultural changes, ideas, and norms. It also recognizes non-state actors alongside states and acknowledges the importance of ideational structures as well as material ones. By rejecting a sole focus on the state, constructivism entails viewing the international political arena as an increasingly complex sphere where multiple interests are expressed, norms are created and dispersed, and increasingly transnational interactions complicate conceptions of international politics as exclusive states interacting with one another.

While the literature on NGOs in international relations has contributed significantly to the field, analysis of NGOs within international relations has largely been focused on the influence of large NGOs on states or intergovernmental organizations. A focus on large NGOs is not surprising because the field of international relations has its roots in macro-analysis of large entities (states) and formal politics.[2] Although valuable, insights related to large NGOs are not necessarily applicable to the thousands of small organizations that do not have the same resources.

Along with a growing interest in NGOs in international relations, there has been a growing interest in networked politics. Kahler (2009) points out that literature on international politics approaches network analysis in two ways. One approach focuses on networks as structures that "influence the behavior of their members, and, through them, produce consequential network effects" (Kahler 2009, 4). The second approach focuses on networks as actors whereby networks are particular forms of coordinated collective action aimed at influencing international outcomes. Kahler notes that both approaches are needed to explain certain international outcomes.

Piper and Uhlin (2004) argue that most research on transnational activism has not significantly addressed power. More specifically, Hurrell (2005) criticizes literature on NGOs' roles in global governance for ignoring four types of power: state power, power within transnational civil society, power within weaker states, and power in particular parts of the international system that favor the values and interests of Northern states and societies. Such criticism speaks to the need for scholarship on NGOs and international politics to move out of the realm of theorizing about the transformative potential of NGOs and into developing analysis that accounts for multiple aspects of power.

This book seeks to contribute to the analysis of NGOs in international politics by incorporating two aspects of power. Following Piper and Uhlin, such an approach combines "a thorough investigation of how the structural power of the state system and the capitalist economy shape transnational activism" with "a nuanced analysis of discursive power and the complex entanglements of power on a micro level" (2004, 8). Combining analysis of the structural inequalities of power with the micropolitics or communicative power of NGOs provides a way to analyze NGOs as political actors in a particular time and place rather than in an idealized world devoid of such structures and inequalities. It shows how both aspects of power constrain and facilitate transnational antisweatshop advocacy. Throughout the book I draw upon constructivism and critical theories in international relations, as well as pertinent scholarship in social movement studies, feminist theories, and development studies, to weave together analysis of anti-sweatshop NGOs, their roles as political actors, and the ways in which material and discursive power shapes their abilities to advocate on behalf of garment workers.

NGOs, networks, and social movements

Josselin and Wallace (2001) argue that focusing on non-state actors presents two main challenges for the study of international relations. First, it challenges state-centric approaches. This book seeks to expand the object of analysis and scope of inquiry beyond states and formal politics found in state-centric approaches to international relations. This is particularly important for the garment industry because much of the political activity surrounding it takes place outside the realm of states. Second, focusing on non-state actors challenges approaches that would regard structure as the prime locus of power and change. Uvin remarks that "what makes NGOs important is not their power in terms of the economic and military resources states have but rather the power of their ideas and the capacity to spread these ideas" (2000, 23). It is through this ideational realm that NGOs can influence the public, government institutions, and the private sector.

There is significant confusion about the term *nongovernmental organization*. The lack of consensus on how to classify NGOs has impeded understandings about the sector (Vakil 1997). The term is often used interchangeably with *nonprofit organization, charitable organization,* or *voluntary organization,* although these can represent quite different entities. As part of the Johns Hopkins Comparative Nonprofit Sector Project, Anheier and Salamon (2006, 95) define nonprofit organizations as exhibiting the following characteristics: organized, self-governing, nonprofit distributing, and non-compulsory. NGOs are a subset of this broader category of nonprofit organizations that, put simply, are "geared to improving the quality of life of disadvantaged people" (Vakil 1997, 2060).

NGOs are often viewed synonymously with social movements, yet not all NGOs are involved in social movements, and those that are, are often just one type of actor within movements. NGOs involved in social movements are sometimes referred to as social movement organizations in order to distinguish them from other types of NGOs (Smith, Chatfield, and Pagnucco 1997). Along with networks and coalitions, NGOs can be seen as mobilizing structures within social movements that act as vehicles through which people engage in collective action to bring about social change (McAdam, McCarthy, and Zald 1996). The relationship between NGOs and social movements is important because NGOs alone do not constitute a movement, even though they can play a significant role in coordinating actions within movements. NGOs exhibit more structure than movements and therefore are often able to access official decision-making channels. However, this level of formality also comes with limitations such as restrictions on lobbying government officials or rigidity that might exclude some actors.

Social movements and NGOs operate within the realm of civil society. Kaldor defines civil society as "the medium through which one or many social contracts between individuals, both women and men, and the political and economic centers of power are negotiated and reproduced"

(Kaldor 2003, 44). This sphere is separate from the state and from the private, for-profit sector, but it is in constant dialogue with those political and economic centers of power. While none of these categories is separate from the market and the state, defining a distinct sphere helps to open up space for alternative forms of politics beyond those targeting the state.

As social and political actors, NGOs rarely act alone. The NGOs profiled in this book exist within a transnational advocacy network (TAN) of individual and organizational actors aimed at improving working conditions in the apparel industry. Keck and Sikkink (1998) describe TANs as loosely organized sets of global actors aimed at promoting causes, principles, and norms involving people advocating policy changes that may not be directly related to their interests or have a direct benefit to themselves. Although activists are drawn to their work for a variety of reasons, networks of activists are primarily motivated by the centrality of principled ideas or values in forming the network, rather than profit or personal gain. This is one of the factors that distinguishes TANs from other transnational networks such as professional or trade associations.

Keck and Sikkink refer to networks, as opposed to social movements, in order to convey the structured and structuring relationships of these agents. Collective action aimed at improving the garment industry fits the description of a transnational network as its underlying structure, with increased coordination for specific campaigns. Figure Intro–1 depicts the relationship among civil society, TANs, social movements, and NGOs. In practice, TANs can involve some government actors that may not be firmly in the realm of civil society. Nevertheless, the figure represents the basic relationship among the overlapping bodies and how the concepts relate to one another. Anti-sweatshop NGOs reside in the area where social movements, NGOs, and TANs overlap.

NGOs and world civic politics

In his study of environmental organizations Wapner demonstrates how environmental NGOs engage in what he terms "world civic politics," which are actions aimed at influencing societal attitudes and behavior as opposed to targeting the state directly. Like the transnational environmental groups he observes, the anti-sweatshop NGOs in this book are keenly aware that "states do not hold a monopoly over the instruments that govern human affairs but rather that nonstate forms of governance exist and can be used to effect widespread change" (Wapner 1996, 2, 7). This recognition, along

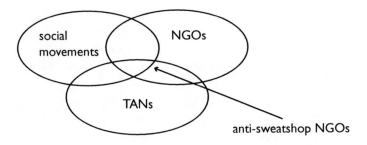

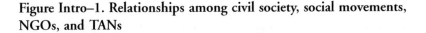

Figure Intro–1. Relationships among civil society, social movements, NGOs, and TANs

with a lack of access to formal political institutions in many cases, has led anti-sweatshop groups to focus on consumers and retailers directly in an attempt to transform the culture of the industry.

A further aspect of this research is informed by Young's definition of politics as activities in which "people organize collectively to regulate or transform some aspect of their shared social conditions, along with the communicative activities in which they try to persuade one another to join such collective action or decide what direction they wish to take it" (2004, 377). The important aspect to note here is the inclusion of communicative activities, which include debates and struggles within organizations, within networks, and within movements. It is through these communicative activities with opponents, supporters, and allies that NGOs are able to influence cultural change.

NGOs seek to shape norms directly by persuading corporate executives and policymakers to change official policies indirectly by altering public perception of government and businesses activities (Florini 2000). NGOs often have been more effective in achieving change by influencing cultural shifts than by their efforts to affect government policies directly. The goal of anti-sweatshop campaigns is to reveal how the production and consumption of clothing are a social relationship among people, not simply an exchange of money and objects. By applying a definition of politics that reaches beyond formal political activities to include broader collective actions aimed at social change, this book captures some of the ways in which those without formal political power engage in transnational politics as workers, activists, or trade unionists.

Micheletti, Follesdal, and Stolle (2006a) refer to the range of activities that promote responsibility through market channels as political consumerism, arguing that as people's identities become forged with their consumption habits, the market becomes a viable arena for political engagement. They suggest that "by viewing businesses as political actors and as new alternatives to political parties and interest groups, citizens articulate and promote their interests to society, businesses, and government through the market" (2006a, xi). It is debatable whether businesses are alternative political actors or whether they provide alternative political arenas for political change. In either case the politicization of the market in this way is the result of globalization, a growing dissociation from public life, and changing relationships between consumption and citizenship. This site of political activity shows how people's actions as consumers differ from traditional notions of how citizens interact with states. Consumer activism represents an emergent form of political activity in and across national borders that state-centric approaches in international relations often overlook. Campaigns focused on changing consumers' buying habits aim to capitalize on this changing relationship and imbue the buying process as a political act, with the market as a political arena.

Northern-based NGOs and advocacy

The advocacy relationship between NGOs and those they aim to benefit is complex, especially when reaching across language, cultural, and political boundaries. Challenges within advocacy relationships are present even when the distance between constituents and advocates is limited, but it is especially challenging in transnational contexts. NGOs based in the global North occupy a distinct location in transnational advocacy networks. In theory, their strength comes from "simultaneous access to grassroots experience in the South, and to decision-makers in the North" (Edwards 2002, 98). In practice, though, that position can be problematic. The location of these NGOs close to the centers of power means that they are often a long way—spatially and ideologically—from the marginalized (Diokno-Pascual 2002, 3). This position is partly strategic in order to gain greater access to decision makers. However, this distance can also result in Northern-based NGOs excluding people from decision-making processes, including those who will be most directly affected by such decisions.

Transnational advocacy does not take place in an abstract and idealized global sphere; rather, these relationships take place in geo-political contexts that are shaped by histories of empire, racism, privilege, and power.

Advocacy relationships are often developed as a counter-hegemonic force, but they are not separate from the very systems and structures that they aim to change. While power is an ever-present factor in such relationships, advocacy relies on at least two parties, both of whom depend on each other and necessarily shape the other side. In other words, advocacy relationships are not simply one group offering charity to another or one group using another but are interdependent relationships whereby complex negotiations take place embedded in social, political, and economic structures.

NGOs as rooted cosmopolitans

In recent years scholars have begun to examine the global aspects of civil society. Some refer to this as "transnational civil society" (Florini 2000), while others prefer the term *global civil society* to acknowledge its "counterweight to globalization" (Anheier 2001, 16). Kaldor, Anheier, and Glasius further define global civil society as "a sphere of ideas, values, institutions, organizations, networks, and individuals located between the family, the state and the market, and operating beyond the confines of national societies, polities and economies" (2005, 2). This is a useful definition, although it is arguable whether any civil society actors are truly operating beyond nation-states.

While engaged in transnational advocacy, the organizations included in this book are not acting *beyond* national boundaries but are instead strategically positioned *within* national contexts, working *across* those boundaries. Instead of breaking free from national constraints, these NGOs embody what Tarrow (2005) refers to as rooted cosmopolitanism, galvanizing support domestically for international causes. These organizations cannot accurately be relegated to either the global or the national political sphere, suggesting that global civil society is not "free floating" beyond national boundaries but is rather part of the process of engagement among local, national, and global political arenas.

As rooted cosmopolitans with ties to places, identities, and ideologies, anti-sweatshop NGOs interact with numerous layers of political institutions and systems. These structures include formal political structures such as intergovernmental institutions and their ability, or lack thereof, to enforce laws and agreements. Also relevant are the regulatory powers of various states regarding NGO activities. Smith, Chatfield, and Pagnucco make the distinction between the "high politics" of social movement activities in explicitly political arenas and the "deep politics" of shaping individual beliefs and actions (1997, 70). Deep politics take place within the realm of extra-institutional contexts, which include values, beliefs, and patterns of behavior. These are the intangible, less formal aspects of societies and culture that influence NGOs and their abilities to create change. While both the formal and informal structures influence the modes of advocacy available to social movements and NGOs, neither is immutable or unchangeable. Combining accounts of material power and communicative power highlights the particular role of NGOs as political actors and the aspects of power that facilitate and constrain transnational advocacy.

Methods and sources

A variety of qualitative research methods was used in conducting the research for this book. In addition to providing analysis of the anti-sweatshop network, this study also includes case studies of four NGOs within the network. The cases were chosen after an extensive search of NGOs engaged in anti-sweatshop advocacy through web searches and in dialogue with activists and scholars in the field. The four NGOs studied are relatively small, with two to seven full-time employees and annual budgets from US$76,000 to US$1.2 million.[3] The case studies were chosen to reflect the broader group and to highlight a range of Northern-based NGOs in the anti-sweatshop network.

The case studies include the Clean Clothes Campaign (CCC), United Students Against Sweatshops (USAS), STITCH, and FairWear. The CCC and USAS are obvious candidates for case studies since they are two of the best-known anti-sweatshop NGOs and are often cited by activists. CCC generates significant resources and information used by others in the network, while USAS is often noted as a source of inspiration by anti-sweatshop activists for its organizing strategies and tactics. The other two organizations are less well known. They are smaller and more focused on specific populations, but they differ in their relationships to their constituents and structures of governance. STITCH works closely with union women in Central America, while FairWear advocates on behalf of homeworkers in Australia and is beginning to address the needs of garment workers abroad producing for the Australian market.

In addition to collecting campaign materials, corporate documents, and NGO reports, I conducted interviews with activists, scholars, targeted retailers, former garment workers, trade unionists, factory inspectors, and participants in student and consumer groups. These interviews took place in several locations where people are engaged in political action to improve conditions in the industry.[4] By conducting research in multiple locations, this book contributes to the growing body of multi-sited research in anthropology, sociology, and political science (Hannerz 2003). Beyond a traditional comparative approach, each location is seen as a node in an interconnected network. With multi-site research a variety of qualitative methods is applied to examining global processes at work in localized sites. Yet, multi-site research does not imply viewing NGOs as isolated units subsumed under national and global processes. Drawing on Marcus (1995), Fisher suggests, "Unpacking the micropolitics of NGOs is dependent upon placing these associations within larger contexts, understanding them not as local wholes subsumed within larger national and global political contexts but as fragmented sites that have multiple connections nationally and transnationally" (1997). With this in mind the book emphasizes the transnational and relational aspects of NGO advocacy and politics, along with comparisons among NGOs and differing national contexts.

Workers' voices and critiques of NGOs are not prominently featured in this book.[5] In a few cases I include workers' words, mainly drawn from other scholars and NGOs. I acknowledge the ways in which my own position as a researcher, relying on such mediated messages, can replicate the problems that Northern-based NGOs face in fulfilling their political responsibilities to workers. Highlighting Southern workers' perspectives of anti-sweatshop advocates is needed and would complement the focus of this study.

Organization of the book

Chapter 1 highlights the global context in which anti-sweatshop advocacy takes place and outlines the changing political economy of the garment industry. It defines the issues advocates aim to address and seeks to answer why some of the channels of political change are unavailable to activists. This chapter establishes how the structure of the industry affects activists' abilities to influence powerful actors and the conditions in the industry that enable and hinder certain types of politics.

Chapters 2 and 3 introduce the agents involved in anti-sweatshop advocacy and their responses to the political economy of the industry. Chapter 2 explains the origins and key players in the anti-sweatshop network and shows the developments of the anti-sweatshop network over the past fifteen years alongside the economic and political changes outlined in the previous chapter. With each change activists have adapted their strategies to encourage retailers to take greater steps to improve working conditions in their supply chains. Chapter 3 introduces USAS, STITCH, FairWear, and the CCC as case studies of Northern-based anti-sweatshop NGOs. It argues that these NGOs embody forms of cosmopolitanism with ties to places, identities, and ideologies that influence their ability to improve working conditions in the global garment industry.

Chapter 4 considers the institutions that govern the behavior of the anti-sweatshop NGOs. It analyzes the structures of governance that influence NGOs' abilities to create change and argues that NGOs interact with multiple governance structures that include states, international institutions, and private regulatory initiatives. Each of these structures shapes the NGOs' abilities to influence targeted actors in particular ways.

Chapter 5 examines the strategies activists use in anti-sweatshop campaigns. The chapter includes a detailed analysis of each of the case-study organizations, its campaigns, and its patterns of advocacy. The chapter argues that as activists applied pressure to universities, retailers, and governments, they used multiple forms of politics with varying degrees of success. The chapter concludes by comparing the patterns of advocacy in terms of points of leverage, movement across political arenas, and the role of states and intergovernmental organizations. It shows the ways that activists have sought to change the industry, the factors affecting their success, and the difficulties they have encountered in different campaigns.

The next two chapters focus on the implications of agents' political actions. Chapter 6 examines the accountability of NGOs as they become increasingly important actors in international politics and addresses the extent to which anti-sweatshop NGOs are accountable to the workers they aim to benefit. The chapter contends that, along with accountability to garment workers, political responsibility to adhere to an organization's stated values in its day-to-day activities is crucial for anti-sweatshop advocates' legitimacy as political actors. Chapter 7 assesses the extent to which anti-sweatshop advocacy has been effective at improving conditions in the industry. It investigates why, despite achievements in some political arenas, activists have been unable to secure lasting, structural improvements in working conditions in the industry.

The conclusion, Chapter 8, reviews themes that emerged throughout the book, including NGOs and world civic politics, factors that facilitate or constrain NGOs' actions as transnational political actors, opportunities and limitations of consumer campaigns, agency and power in the garment industry, and developing alternative forms of governance. By studying small NGOs as political agents, along with the opportunities and limitations of various forms of political action, the book aims to provide insight into the challenges facing non-state actors in an increasingly transnational civil society.

Chapter 1

Political economy
of the garment industry

Over the past forty years the size and distribution of the garment industry have changed dramatically. The garment industry was dominated by the United States and Europe until the mid-twentieth century, but developing countries now produce over half of the world's textile exports and almost three quarters of the world's apparel exports (UNCTAD and Appelbaum 2005). Many factors have influenced this shift, including technological developments; lowering transportation costs; shifts toward lean, just-in-time production; consolidation of power among retailers; the search for cheaper labor costs; and easing trade restrictions.

The international political economy of the garment industry is discussed in this chapter to situate the actions of NGOs in the anti-sweatshop network in the broader structures of the garment industry. The first section examines the changing sites of production in the garment industry. It discusses the growth of export processing zones and defines sweatshops. The second section focuses on the political and economic structure of the garment industry. It describes how buyer-driven supply chains created historically new power configurations in the garment industry. It also explains how the Multifibre Arrangement (MFA) and subsequent quotas shaped the industry. The third section analyzes the impact that the political economy of the industry has had on workers. It outlines labor standards and working conditions in the industry, union membership, the feminization of labor, and ways that workers have responded to these conditions. The fourth section details new developments in the industry with regard to the global financial crisis that began in 2008. The chapter concludes with how the political economy of the garment industry shapes political action to improve working conditions and standards.

13

Globalization and changing sites of production

While some skeptics debate the extent to which the current wave of globalization constitutes a significant departure from previous periods of economic interdependence and cross-cultural interaction, most agree that since the 1970s economic, social, and cultural interaction across political borders has increased dramatically. Castells notes that capitalism has undergone profound restructuring in the past three decades, characterized by the following features:

> greater flexibility in management; decentralization and networking of firms both internally and in their relationship to other firms; considerable empowering of capital vis-à-vis labor, with the concomitant decline in influence of the labor movement; increasing individualization and diversification of working relationships; massive incorporation of women into the paid labor force, usually under discriminatory conditions; intervention of the state to deregulate markets selectively, and to undo the welfare state, with different intensity and orientations depending upon the nature of political forces and institutions in each society; stepped-up global economic competition, in a context of increasing geographic and cultural differentiation of settings for capital accumulation and management. (Castells 2000, 1–2)

While there has been much written about "globalization from above" referring to the influence of transnational corporations (TNCs) and international finance, many scholars and activists have begun to tout the potential of "globalization from below" (Brecher, Costello, and Smith 2002, 4), noting that cross-cultural interaction, communication across borders, and connections among marginalized peoples are also facilitated by an increasingly globalized world. Those engaged in civic action, political organizing, and social movements across borders are also a part of the globalization process, particularly through their use of information technology and networked campaigns. Like their counterparts, they are purposeful actors who make decisions and create alliances.

The garment industry has been particularly affected by globalization due to the low cost of market entry, ease of transportation of goods, and favorable push and pull regulations and incentives encouraging Northern retailers to outsource production (Hale and Wills 2006). The industry is characterized by what some term a "race to the bottom" (Chan 2003, 41) with competition based on low wages and a largely non-unionized workforce. In many ways the garment industry has become emblematic of globalization, providing a stage where conflicting interests clash and hegemony is reestablished through multiple forms of material and ideological power. It is in this context that export processing zones were developed in the 1970s and garment production relocated to lower-cost production sites, which has shaped the current form of the industry.

Export processing zones

In the 1960s and 1970s the IMF and World Bank embarked on a program of structural adjustment. These structural adjustment packages included requirements upon a number of countries to privatize many state services, cut state spending, open up markets, and move toward export-oriented production. The emphasis on export-oriented production resulted in the establishment of numerous export processing zones (EPZs) throughout the global South. In 1970 only ten countries had EPZs. By 2006, 130 countries had EPZs employing 66 million workers, with 40 million of those in China alone (Boyenge 2007). Governments offer foreign investors extensive incentives to locate in these special zones. For example, in 2008 the Export Processing Zones Kenya website enticed foreign investors by claiming that foreign companies in Kenyan EPZs are exempt from various regulations that normally apply to businesses in Kenya, including exemptions from payment of customs and from corporate taxes for ten years. Foreign companies located in EPZs are also often given exemption from certain labor laws. For example, in Bangladesh unions are prohibited in EPZs. In Mexico company-based unions are encouraged in EPZs to help employers control workers, and in China independent unions are prohibited altogether (Quan 2007).

The demographics of cities that grow up around EPZs are changing the face of urban centers. For example, many EPZs draw migrants from rural areas. Along the U.S.-Mexico border, the assembly factories draw migrants displaced by structural adjustment policies and market forces from rural Mexico in search of employment. In China many women in the countryside come to Guangdong or other provinces where factories are located in order to make money to send back to their families. Internal migration from the countryside to urban centers presents a number of challenges for the individuals who make the journey as well as for those left behind in villages. Further, once factories shut down, as has happened in recent years, few garment workers return to their villages, leaving government officials in a quandary about how to sustain a large unemployed urban population.

Defining sweatshops

The U.S. General Accounting Office defines a sweatshop as "an employer that violates more than one federal or state labor law governing minimum wage and overtime, child labor, industrial home work, occupational safety and health, workers compensation, or industry regulation" (Ross 1997, 12). While this definition specifically relates to conditions in the United States, it is widely cited by academics and activists elsewhere as a baseline for determining whether employers in developing countries warrant the label of sweatshop. The term has long been associated with the garment industry with its reliance on layers of subcontracting and minimum requirements of capital to enter the market (although an abundant supply of labor is needed).

In *Sweated Work, Weak Bodies* Bender traces the discourse about sweatshops in the United States. He argues that the word *sweatshop,* with its connotations of cramped and unsanitary conditions, was connected to "larger anxieties about the effects of industrialization and immigration" in the early 1900s in New York City (2004, 3). Early anti-sweatshop campaigns relied on evocative images of immigrant workers in unclean workplaces toiling for low wages. These images provided powerful tools for anti-sweatshop campaigners but also reified categories of difference, playing on middle-class Americans' fears of contagion and an immigrant underclass.

In addition to advocating for an adherence to existing labor laws, many activists in the contemporary anti-sweatshop movement consider existing standards, particularly minimum wages, to be insufficient. They believe that labor standards in the industry should include provisions for a living wage. The International Textile, Garment and Leather Workers' Federation (ITGLWF) argues for a living wage based upon a "basket of goods" approach by which trade unions in each country would determine the living wage depending on the local price of food, housing, medical attention, transport, education, and 10 percent for savings or discretionary spending (ITGLWF 2008). This sets a higher standard than that often included in national or international labor standards.

Some activist organizations such as USAS go further. According to the "Principles of Unity" stated on its website in 2007 it defines sweatshops as "not limited to the apparel industry as traditionally conceived; sweatshop conditions exist in the fields, in the prisons, on our campuses, in the power relations of a flawed system. Thus, we consider all struggles against the systemic problems of the global economy to be directly or by analogy a struggle against sweatshops." By applying a broader definition of sweat-shops, USAS activists argue that sweatshops are not an anomaly in an otherwise just system, but rather that they have become ubiquitous and symptomatic of broader trends of neoliberalism and economic globalization, and that to struggle for better conditions in the garment industry is by extension a struggle against corporate power in the global economy.

Garment industry politics and markets

In 2007 the global textile and clothing sectors had a combined value of over US$583 billion. Over 29 million women and men work in the garment industry worldwide. This includes those employed in the formal sector as well as informal workers who are involved in a wide range of tasks, including piece-rate work performed in the home. In 2007 clothing and textiles represented 2.5 percent and 1.7 percent, respectively, of total world exports (WTO 2008). Although clothing is considered to be a separate industry in trade statistics, the two are often categorized together, and the terms *clothing, garments,* and *apparel* are used interchangeably here.

The growth in the sector has been accompanied by several major shifts in the production of clothing since the mid-twentieth century, beginning with a shift from Western Europe and North America to Japan in the 1950s and early 1960s. With the implementation of quota systems in 1974 (described later in this chapter), production spread to Mexico and Central America. In Asia, production moved to Hong Kong, Taiwan, and Korea (Gereffi 2002). Once these countries maximized their quotas in the 1990s, production moved to other developing countries in Latin America, Southeast Asia, and Sub-Saharan Africa. This movement, from South to South, meant that Korean-owned factories, for example, relocated to El Salvador, Cambodia, and Indonesia in order to take advantage of unmet quotas in those countries. In Cambodia, for example, only 9 percent of the 248 clothing factories located near Phnom Penh are Cambodian owned. The remainder are owned by companies based in Hong Kong, China, Taiwan, South Korea, and Malaysia (Ferenschild and Wick 2004). One of the effects of this is that much of the income generated from garment factories leaves the country, a practice that is hardly mitigated by increased tax revenues, as governments commonly give tax concessions to foreign companies for locating their EPZs.

While the second half of the twentieth century saw a relocation of garment production from North to South, another shift is taking place, with increasing production in China and, to a lesser extent, in India. These shifts are due to changes in the global economic structure, consolidation among retailers, and easing of quota restrictions. China, for example, increased its share in world exports of clothing from 9 percent in 1990, to 18 percent in 2000, and to 31 percent in 2006. The current global financial crisis, as well as increasing costs of production in China, may result in slowing down the shift of production to China, but for the present China remains the primary exporter of the world's clothing.

The clothing and textile industry accounts for a significant portion of some countries' exports. For example, the garment industry is responsible for 83 percent of merchandise exports in Bangladesh, 70 percent in Pakistan, and 55 percent in Sri Lanka (UNCTAD and Appelbaum 2005). This represents a large portion of the workforce in these countries. In Sri Lanka, garment workers make up 33 percent of the total workforce. In Bangladesh garment workers are 40 percent of the workforce (Hale and Burns 2006). Such a high percentage of exports coming from one sector can create a high degree of vulnerability to shifts in the industry among workers. Moreover, changes in sourcing decisions can have a significant impact on entire national economies, not to mention on the individuals who depend on the sector for their livelihood.

The structure of the garment industry is the result of particular negotiations among competing interests through the various stages of production and consumption of clothing. In the United States, for example, there is a number of industry lobbying groups, including the American Manufacturing Trade Association, American Apparel and Footwear Association, American Apparel Manufacturers Association, and the American Knitwear Association. Similar special interest groups exist in Australia and Europe, along with groups representing certain sections of the industry such as the World Federation of the Sporting Goods Industry. These groups represent powerful interests aimed at opening foreign markets, protecting domestic industries, minimizing tariffs and taxation, and attracting subsidies.

Buyer-driven supply chains

There are several features that characterize the garment industry and shape its structure, working conditions, and prospects for change. One of these features is the configuration of supply chains whereby legal liabilities are severed through lengthy subcontracting. Gereffi (2002) distinguishes between the various actors in apparel supply chains. Manufacturers are those entities responsible for designing, cutting, and assembling clothing. Retailers are those who sell the final product to the customer. Some companies act as branded marketers; they may not act as the final retailer, yet they rely heavily on their brand recognition to sell their products through third parties. Gereffi also makes the distinction that branded manufacturers, unlike branded marketers, control the manufacturing of clothing rather than subcontracting this function.[1]

In the 1970s American and European retailers began shedding their manufacturing role to concentrate on design, branding, and advertising. Lengthy supply chains, often using fabric from one country assembled in another and shipped to a third for sale, came to characterize the industry. Unlike more traditional producer-driven chains, commodity chains in the garment industry are buyer driven (Gereffi 2002). Buyer-driven supply or commodity chains exist where large retailers and manufacturers play significant roles in setting up decentralized production networks in numerous countries. In such networks large buyers have significant control in selecting suppliers in different parts of the world. These buyers exhibit more power than those who produce the goods, partly due to the separation of functions and also to their sheer size and buying power.

Gereffi contrasts buyer-driven chains with producer-driven commodity chains that are controlled by large manufacturers at the point of production. He suggests that "companies that develop and sell brand-named products exert substantial control over how, when, and where manufacturing will take place, and how much profit accrues at each stage of the chain" (2002, 3). Gereffi refers to these companies, such as Walmart, Nike, and Gap, as manufacturers without factories.

In addition to the big retailers, several large manufacturers primarily based in Asia exert significant power in the industry. These "first tier" manufacturers are less widely known than retailers, yet they play an important part in managing supply chains. These include companies such as the South Korean Dada Group and South China Garments, a cartel that controls production in Lesotho, Zambia, and Madagascar (Conroy 2007, 230). Another such company is Tainan Enterprises, worth US$17.65 million, with factories in China, Cambodia, Indonesia, and Taiwan (Quan 2007). Another powerful corporation is Li and Fung, which contracts with ten thousand suppliers in over forty countries. These large sourcing agencies and manufacturers are involved in every aspect of the industry, including developing patterns, ordering fabric, cutting and sewing, assembly, and shipping. By contracting with one of these first-tier manufacturers, retailers are able to offload much of their risk (Quan, personal communication, December 12, 2008). Although these companies do not have the same name recognition and brand vulnerability that big retailers do with consumers in global North, they are increasingly important players in the industry.

At one end of these lengthy supply chains are many small manufacturers, while consolidated retailers dominate the other end of the chain. For example, with an annual turnover of nearly US$118 billion, Walmart is able to exert considerable influence over suppliers that are reliant on its orders to survive. Conroy (2007) notes that Walmart has considerable "monopsony" power, indicating that through its size and the volume of its purchases it is able to demand lower prices from producers. The problem extends beyond Walmart, with almost two-thirds of all clothing in the United States being sold through the ten largest clothing retailers (Hurley and Miller 2006, 21). Such powerful buyers are able to control prices, turnaround times, and terms of subcontracting because they control such a large segment of the market.

For example, according to Vincent Tse, regional manager of Adidas's Social and Environmental Affairs department, the Adidas group sources finished products from one thousand factories, with six to eight times that many subcontractors producing some part of a shoe (personal communication, October 6, 2008). The vastness and complexity of such networks mean that retailers wield significant power to set prices and determine terms of sales, yet they are unable (or unwilling) to monitor subcontractors adequately.

Increasingly complex supply chains and more widespread use of subcontracting have presented traditional trade unions with significant challenges. Traditionally reliant on bargaining between two parties, trade unions have been unable to adapt quickly to global production networks in the garment industry (Wills and Hale 2006). In her study of garment factories in the United States and Mexico, Collins (2003) shows how subcontracting and "casualization" of the workforce eroded workers' abilities to make claims on their employers. Unions have also been "unable to challenge the impact of subcontracting beyond their workplaces" (Wills and Hale 2006, 7). These challenges have opened up space for NGOs to influence retailers while unions target direct employers and manufacturers.

The Multifibre Arrangement

The Multifibre Arrangement came into effect in 1974. Its purpose was to protect American and European textile manufacturers. The MFA constructed an elaborate quota system that limited the quantity of clothing and textiles that forty different countries could export to the United States, Canada, and Europe. Quotas limited the amount of clothing that could be produced in any one country, thereby limiting production in countries that would have otherwise developed a large sector. As a result, the industry spread out to dozens of countries. Despite the quotas, manufacturers in the United States and Europe still could not remain competitive with other countries, and therefore many manufacturers moved to countries with lower production costs.

The application of the MFA reflects competing interests within the countries concerned. For example, the U.S. Government restricted the importation of Bangladeshi goods through the MFA at the "behest of a protectionist domestic lobby" but also offered a proposal to the Bangladeshi government through the U.S. Agency for International Development (USAID) to get around the quota system (Kabeer 2000, 10). This kind of policy incoherence offers an insight into the complex and contradictory position of various actors within the United States about the purpose of the MFA and its dissolution.

The MFA itself ended in 1994, replaced by the Agreement on Textile and Clothing (ATC), which lays out procedures for the gradual phasing out of quotas on textile and clothing exports to Northern markets by January 1, 2005.[2] The ATC was designed to align the textile industry with the rules of the World Trade Organization (WTO). Unlike the MFA, which applied only to imports to Canada, the European Community, Norway, and the United States, the ATC applied to all member countries of the WTO. The ATC stipulates a gradual process of lifting quotas. As a result of United States and European Union lobbying, the ATC also includes provisions for transitional safeguard measures, reciprocal market access, and rules of origin to prevent the falsification of labeling.

Much of the discussion at the international level has been about which countries will be the winners and which will be the losers from the fall out of the MFA. Hale and Burns (2006) note that such discussions center on national interests rather than workers' rights and conditions. They claim that the discourse of national economies as winners and losers assumes that what benefits a country benefits a population. Since much of the determination of where production relocates is based on a country's comparative advantage in terms of low wages and a non-unionized workforce, there are no guarantees that workers' rights will be respected or that wages will increase, even in countries that are slated to gain from the end of quotas. While employment in the garment sector is expected to increase in India and China, labor standards are not necessarily going to improve in these countries. After all, the main incentives for production to increase in these countries are low labor costs and workforces constrained in their abilities to organize.

Quotas after the phaseout of the MFA

Even before the MFA ended on January 1, 2005, lobbyists in the United States sought protections against Chinese imports. In 2004 a coalition of domestic manufacturers and unions filed a preemptive petition with the U.S. Committee for the Implementation of Textile Agreements (CITA) to restrict Chinese imports based on the threat of market disruption. They were able to do this because of the provision for safeguard mechanisms in the ATC, although such threat-based petitions were unprecedented since such restrictions were intended to come into effect once market disruption or dumping could be shown (Martin 2007).[3]

CITA never made a ruling on the petition because in the meantime the United States and China signed the memorandum of understanding (MOU) between the governments of the United States of America and the People's Republic of China concerning Trade in Textile and Apparel Products (U.S.-China MOU). The U.S.-China MOU was part of a deal struck in the U.S. Congress to get Republicans in textile states to agree to the Central American Free Trade Agreement (CAFTA). In particular, it was used to get support from Robin Hayes, a Republican from North Carolina. In exchange for his CAFTA vote, "Hayes requested and received assurances from the administration that a 'comprehensive' agreement would be negotiated with China to limit textile and apparel exports to the United States" (Rivoli 2005, 217). The European Union enacted similar measures in June 2005 with the EU-China MOU limiting Chinese imports that were considered sensitive to the European textile industry.

Through the ATC negotiations and these bilateral agreements with China, the United States and the European Union were able to maintain some level of control of the liberalization regime. For example, according to Hale and Burns (2006, 215), the offer to remove the MFA was used by the United States and the European Union as a bargaining tool to persuade India, Pakistan, and other countries to lower their tariff barriers. Rosen refers to the way U.S. trade negotiators have used the industry in trade negotiations as textile politics. She notes that in some cases maintaining this control was not necessarily done to protect domestic industries, which were waning, but was used as a point of leverage to be used in various negotiations. Textile politics has been used to exercise influence against many countries. In particular, Rosen claims, it is a way for the United States to influence China on issues beyond the garment industry (Rosen 2002, 209).

In WTO trade negotiations, U.S. and EU representatives were able to offer to lift quota restrictions because they no longer needed them. This was because, with the advent of the MFA, the industry had changed dramatically. In the 1970s small- and medium-sized manufacturers produced clothing for national retailers. Since then—and in part due to the MFA—there has been significant market concentration and a shift to outsourcing through lengthy supply chains. As a result of the MFA, North American and European companies began sourcing their goods elsewhere in order to avoid the high cost of domestic manufacturing. At the same time Asian producers in Hong Kong and Korea, for example, who had already maximized their own quotas, subcontracted to suppliers in countries that had not yet met their limits. In either case large manufactures were the only ones who could manage these transnational processes (Hale and Burns 2006). In other words, what began as a protectionist measure in the North contributed to the power of large retailers in the industry through market concentration and the need to manage complex supply chains.

In some ways these changes signify a disregard for national boundaries as capital moves across borders. At the same time, national boundaries were an essential part of the quota system that forced manufacturers to move across political borders in order to circumvent the quota system. Like many aspects of globalization, the production of clothing has become a process of increasing borderlessness as TNCs traverse political borders. Simultaneously, however, governments are reinforcing those borders through trade negotiations, immigration policies, and selective implementation of international norms and standards.

Impacts on workers

Labor standards

The International Labour Organization (ILO) outlines basic rights in the workplace in the Declaration on Fundamental Principles and Rights at Work (also known as the core labor standards), adopted in 1998 (see Table 1–1). Although the ILO has no enforcement capabilities, the language from the declaration is enshrined in domestic labor legislation in many countries and is referenced in many corporate codes of conduct. While widely recognized, some countries, including the United States, have refused to ratify some of the core conventions. For example, of the conventions making up the declaration, the United States has ratified only two, one on the abolition of forced labor and another addressing the worst forms of child labor. Although U.S. reports to the ILO assert that U.S. laws are generally in conformance with the conventions aimed at freedom

Fundamental principles	ILO Conventions
Freedom of association and the effective recognition of the right to collective bargaining	**C87** Freedom of Association and Protection of the Right to Organise Convention, 1948 **C98** Right to Organise and Collective Bargaining Convention, 1949
Elimination of all forms of forced or compulsory labor	**C29** Forced Labour Convention **C105** Abolition of Forced Labour Convention, 1957
Effective abolition of child labor	**C138** Minimum Age Convention, 1973 **C182** Worst Forms of Child Labour Convention, 1999
Elimination of discrimination in respect of employment and occupation	**C100** Equal Remuneration Convention, 1951 **C111** Discrimination (Employment and Occupation) Convention, 1958

Table 1–1. Fundamental principles and rights at work

of association and collective bargaining, U.S. representatives claim that actually ratifying the conventions would amount to "back door" amendments to U.S. labor law (Compa 2003, 29). Nevertheless, under the Declaration of Fundamental Principles and Rights at Work, all ILO member states are obligated to meet certain basic standards, including freedom of association and collective bargaining, even if a particular state has not ratified the conventions. Whether they actually do so is another matter.

The ILO standards are also incorporated in many national labor laws in countries where garments are produced. The difficulty local labor organizers face is the lack of implementation of such laws in the face of steep competition to produce goods both cheaper and quicker than competitors. In 2008 China enacted a new contract labor law aimed at stabilizing employment relations. Among other things the new law requires employers to provide long-term contracts to employees with more than ten years of service, limits overtime, and provides compensation to employees who are dismissed. Local provinces have found ways to minimize claims by implementing statutes of limitations. According to Li Qiang (2009) of China Labor Watch, the new contract labor law is an improvement in the protection of Chinese workers' rights, but it is inadequate to protect workers fully.

Anti-sweatshop activists often use existing labor laws as a starting point but aim to achieve conditions above and beyond bare minimums, believing that a minimum wage, for example, is often insufficient to maintain a decent standard of living. For example, the code of conduct of the Worker Rights Consortium (WRC), which applies to clothing produced for the North American collegiate market, stipulates that workers should be entitled to a living wage as opposed to a minimum wage. The WRC often extends its goals beyond factory walls, recognizing the interdependence of social and economic factors influencing the well-being of individuals, their families, and their communities. As an example of this, the WRC code (discussed in Chapter 7) includes a section on contingency plans for children displaced from jobs as a result of bans on child labor. Furthermore, it includes language acknowledging women's multiple roles and the double burden of productive and reproductive labor.

Along with the ILO standards, the WRC code also includes provisions for workers to join an independent union. The ILO and WRC standards can be divided into those standards aimed at improving working *conditions* in relevant factories, and the extent to which workers have been empowered through securing the *right* to join an independent union. Working conditions—also referred to as protective rights—pertain to issues such as wages, health and safety, and overtime. Freedom of association and the right to collective bargaining are enabling rights (Elliot and Freeman 2005). While some NGOs tend to focus more on conditions versus rights, anti-sweatshop activists understand that any improvements in working conditions cannot be sustained without ensuring workers' rights to organize (Connor and Dent 2006).

Working conditions

Even when labor standards exist, governments often lack the political will or ability to implement them. This results in exploitative working conditions ranging from low wages to non-payment of wages, forced overtime, discrimination, forced labor, and insufficient health and safety protections. Inadequate wages, whether legal but low or unpaid, are a constant source of concern in the industry. While a variance in wages is to be expected, at issue is whether the wages are sufficient to provide workers with a decent standard of living. Garment workers in Indonesia, for example, reported finding it difficult to afford accommodations and basic staples such as rice, vegetables, and drinking water on their hourly wage of five thousand Rupiahs or U.S. fifty-five cents (Connor and Dent 2006). Workers in one Indonesian factory, Tae Hwa, reported relying on overtime to compensate for base wages too low to allow workers to meet basic needs and send remittances home. Researchers found that overtime at Tae Hwa was compulsory and far exceeded legal limits in Indonesia. Workers, however, did not support a reduction in overtime unless it was accompanied by an increase in standard wages, since the workers depended on the overtime income to supplement their base pay (Oxfam, CCC, and Global Unions 2004).

Even though wages are an important factor in locating production facilities, wages only make up a small percentage of the overall cost of clothing, particularly branded clothing and footwear. For example, an athletic shoe sold in Europe for €100 is made up of the following costs:

production costs €1.5
material €8.5
profit subcontractor €3
labor costs workers €0.50
transport and tax €5
labor cost retailer €18
publicity retailer €2.5
rent/stocks retailer €12
profit brand name €13
research €11
publicity brand name €8
value added tax €17 (CCC 2008e)

Factory (or home work) labor in this case accounts for a tiny fraction of the overall cost of production, while retailers are able to make a 13 percent profit on each shoe.

Clearly for most retailers low wages are an important factor in sourcing decisions but not the only factor. Production costs, transportation costs, lead time, and costs associated with monitoring contracts with suppliers are also significant (Nordas 2005). Another significant factor is the flexibility of the workforce. In particular, the prohibition of independent unions in some countries provides retailers and subcontractors with added stability and flexibility. In many countries where unions are legally permitted to exist, workers fear that joining a union will cause them to lose their job and even face intimidation or violence (Oxfam, CCC, and Global Unions

2004). Countries that do not permit independent unions at all, such as China, provide an ideal environment for manufacturers who do not want to deal with the presence of independent unions.

Several studies have been conducted recently on the state of working conditions in the garment industry.[4] Nonprofit social-auditing firm Verite conducted several studies into working conditions in the Chinese garment industry. Based on interviews with over 750 workers, Verite found that overtime commonly exceeded international labor standards and Chinese labor laws. In 133 factories (93 percent of those surveyed) workers' hours exceeded legal limits (Verite 2004). Chinese law dictates a maximum of thirty-six hours a month of overtime, while many TNC codes state that overtime should not exceed twenty hours a week, itself a violation of Chinese law. Workers reported the necessity to work overtime for financial reasons as well as the assumption that it was not voluntary. Verite researchers also found several instances in which factories maintained two sets of payroll records, one to show to auditors and the other for internal purposes.

In Cambodia, the ILO reports a starkly different picture. Through the Better Factories Cambodia (BFC) project, the ILO monitored 277 factories encompassing over 325,000 workers, 93 percent of whom are women. It found that 95 percent of the factories were in compliance with the minimum wage, and 68 percent of the factories were in compliance with paid sick leave. It also showed significant improvements in the rates of compliance related to maternity benefits since 2006. For example, in 2006, 68 percent were in compliance with maternity benefits. By May 2007, 86 percent were in compliance (BFC 2007). The discrepancies between the ILO's findings in Cambodia and studies conducted elsewhere may be due to several reasons. One reason could be the presence of the BFC project, which provides Cambodian manufacturers with greater access to U.S. markets if they meet certain labor standards. Another reason could be because the BFC project uses a lower set of standards than those set out in the WRC code. For instance, compliance of BFC is measured against Cambodian labor laws and ILO standards but may not reflect more-stringent codes that include extensive health and safety provisions.[5] Nevertheless, a high rate of compliance with national and ILO standards is still noteworthy and may provide a model for other countries.

One might expect Northern garment producers to be more compliant with international standards, but this is not the case. By the end of the 1990s the number of sweatshops in Holland grew to between eight hundred and one thousand (Sluiter 2009). In many of these small factories and home workshops, workers, made up mostly of Turkish immigrants, were paid well below the legal minimum wage. During the previous decade consumer prices decreased 60–70 percent. These decreases in retail prices were made possible by paying workers low wages and by tax evasion, since many of these shops operated illegally (Sluiter 2009). U.S. garment producers have also shown significant rates of noncompliance with domestic or international labor standards. For example, a study conducted by the U.S. Department of Labor of garment factories in Los Angeles found that more than half of the garment shops were out of compliance with local labor laws (Esbenshade 2004, 85). This particular study was conducted in 1996, yet more recent studies conducted by the California Division of Labor Standards and Enforcement and NGOs show that the situation has scarcely improved. The Garment Worker Center and Sweatshop Watch (2004) in Los Angeles reported that its clients worked an average of fifty-two hours a week and received an average of US$3.28 an hour, well below the federal minimum wage. These figures are ignored in official statistics since most of these workers are engaged in home work or work in facilities that are not registered with the state.

Inadequate wages are not the only problem that workers face. Poor health caused by inhalation of dust, chemicals, and repetitive tasks is also a serious issue. Some women have reported experiencing irregular menstrual cycles once they began working in the garment factories. Labor activists are in the process of designing a survey to assess women's health issues in the industry (Labor advocate Sanjiv Pandita, personal communication, October 8, 2008). Health concerns extend beyond the shop floor to workers' living arrangements. Following interviews with 369 workers in the Katunayake and Biyagama free-trade zones in Sri Lanka, Marcus et al. (1998) found that many garment workers in Sri Lanka face a range of health and safety issues. Employers provided workers with accommodation, but it consisted of a small room (10'x12') that was shared by ten to twelve workers. Although some factories offered medical facilities, many did not and workers were hesitant to access medical care for fear of losing their jobs or losing wages.

Workers are often not provided with adequate safety gear or protection from chemicals and dangerous equipment. A spate of fatal fires swept through garment factories in recent years, reminiscent of the Triangle Shirtwaist factory fire in 1911 that killed 141 workers in New York City. In 2006 garment workers in Bangladesh took to the streets to demand better enforcement of safety standards following several deadly fires. In the Pearl River Delta of China, where many export-oriented factories are located, there have been several fires, including one in the Yue Xin textile plant in June 1994 that killed 76 people and injured 160. Manufacturers and retailers responded to these events by making improvements in particular factories. However, not all companies have followed suit, leaving millions of workers at risk.

Labor advocate Sanjiv Pandita argues that occupational health and safety are often inappropriately framed as technical issues (Pandita, personal communication, October 8, 2008). In an interview he explained that a technical approach de-politicizes the issue and creates specialists who are trained to break down and itemize health and safety checklists. Pandita gave the example of chemicals in a factory. The traditional approach views workers' attitudes as the problem and seeks to find ways to get workers to wear masks instead of questioning why those chemicals are in the factory in the first place or analyzing the social implications of exposure. Labor activists throughout Asia are working to "bring politics back in" to the field of occupational health and safety. The Asia Monitor Resource Centre (AMRC) provides training for workers outside factories and works with unions, NGOs, and workers to promote the idea that occupational health and safety is a right, not a privilege (Pandita, personal communication, October 8, 2008).

In terms of documenting workers' rights to organize, the International Trade Union Confederation (ITUC) collects data on violations of trade union rights each year.[6] In 2000 it noted 140 deaths worldwide of trade unionists (not limited to the garment industry) (ICFTU 2000). ITUC collects data on harassment, torture, and imprisonment of trade unionists as well as unfair dismissals. In each category the numbers of incidents are either consistent between 2000 and 2007 or have increased. In 2005, 115 trade unionists were murdered, one thousand were victims of violent crimes, and nine thousand were arrested worldwide. In the same year ten thousand workers were fired for their involvement in union organizing (ICFTU 2006). In 2007 there were 144 reported deaths (ITUC 2008). The data are collected from affiliated trade unions and human rights organizations. It is unclear whether the figures indicate an increase in violence against unionists or the methods of data collection and reporting have improved. Therefore, the exact numbers are less significant than the broad understanding that in the past ten years there have not been any major discernable improvements in reducing violence against trade unionists.

Arguments about working conditions for garment workers rarely focus on low wages, precarious employment, or substandard health and safety standards. The point of debate is often whether these jobs are better than the alternatives—and whether corporations can justify high earnings while claiming that they are unable to pay living wages. Jagdish Bhagwati and other economists wrote a letter to university presidents criticizing the anti-sweatshop network for its attempts to seek higher wages for garment workers in the global South, claiming that their efforts are misguided and will ultimately harm those they intend to help (Collins 2003). Activists contend that retailers and manufacturers could pay more and improve conditions without closing down factories. They question the logic of maintaining high profits at one end of the chain while claiming that increases in wages for workers would make the company collapse.

In an article that caused much public outcry, liberal-left economist Paul Krugman (1997) wrote in praise of sweatshops, arguing that, although the wages are low and working conditions are poor in export-oriented manufacturing, these jobs provide much-needed income for workers with few alternatives. Many anti-sweatshop activists agree with Krugman that these jobs are often more desirable than locally available alternatives. However, they do not agree that this justifies poor working conditions in the production of branded clothing. On the contrary, activists argue that more needs to be done to improve the number and quality of jobs available across sectors.

Collins points out that critics of the anti-sweatshop network often ignore the role that labor movements have played in improving working standards elsewhere. For example, she notes that "advances such as the forty-hour week, the minimum age, and health and safety rules did not simply evolve in the industrialized nations, and they were not the result of the largesse of industry leaders. They resulted from workers' protest and national dialogue about what was right and fair" (Collins 2003, 187). Labor movements and civil society actors were instrumental in achieving these changes. The main difference now is that local negotiations between labor and management are complicated by the power of retailers and sourcing agents, who can easily relocate production across national and political lines.

Union membership

Trade union membership has been on a steady decline for several decades. Only 150 million of the 2.9 billion wage earners worldwide are members of some form of trade union (Waterman and Timms 2005). International union bodies such as ICFTU have made clear commitments to international solidarity; however, the tension between protectionism for domestic workers and global solidarity among workers has not been reconciled within most national unions. Unions deal with these competing interests in different ways. Some unions, like the American Federation of

Labor—Congress of Industrial Organizations (AFL-CIO), once considered arch-conservative and pro-imperialist, has reoriented itself toward internationalist perspectives and more inclusiveness among domestic workers (Munck 2002, 17). The AFL-CIO has also begun to work closely with anti-sweatshop NGOs, most notably the Solidarity Center, which it helped establish in 1997.

Although union membership worldwide has declined over the last three decades, union membership is still one of the primary ways for workers to represent themselves in domestic and international political arenas. The ITGLWF represents 217 affiliated organizations in 110 countries. Although it lends rhetorical support to local labor struggles, it does not have the resources or mandate to mobilize its members on a grand scale. In addition to providing direct representation and services to workers, many unions have been crucial in supporting the development of labor rights NGOs.

Feminization of labor

In Cambodia 89 percent of garment workers are women, and in Bangladesh 80 percent of garment workers are women. The percentage tends to be lower in Central America but still remains high compared to other sectors (ILO 2005). Young women are often hired because of employers' assumptions about their inherent skills at dealing with repetitive tasks and their reluctance to demand better working conditions and higher wages. The terms under which women are hired are often based on gender, cultural, and racial stereotypes.[7] Many employers believe that women make more desirable employees, because they are thought to be more malleable, less likely to organize, and can be paid less than their male counterparts. Yet women also gain income and a new degree of independence from their participation in the formal labor market. In many countries there are few opportunities for women to work outside the home in formal employment, and garment work can provide new opportunities for independence.

The gender dynamics of the industry after the phaseout of the MFA have yet to be fully explored. Hale and Burns ask:

> If the industry collapses, what will happen to these women? It is questionable whether they will be able to reintegrate back into their villages. Their lives in the factories go beyond the bounds of what is traditionally acceptable for a future wife. In Sri Lanka, for example, marriage adverts announce "factory girls need not apply." In

Bangladesh, where garment workers have transgressed the boundaries of Islamic tradition, the stigma is even greater. But if they stay
in the city, how will they survive? And what will the impact of their
loss of earnings be on the poor rural areas they come from? Similarly, for working-class urban families, women's income from garment work has been vital for family and community survival, so it
is not just workers themselves who will suffer. (Hale and Burns
2006, 222)

While garment work has the potential to provide income for thousands of
women, the industry is structured in a way that takes advantage of the
many social and economic disadvantages many women face. In other words,
women's disadvantages in terms of bargaining power and wages are seen as
their comparative advantage in the market place.

Workers' responses to poor working conditions

The strength and characteristics of labor movements vary throughout
the global South. Katie Quan, a former union organizer and current asso-
ciate chair of the UC Berkeley Labor Center, suggests that although unions
are weakening in the global North, there are signs that unions are getting
stronger in the South (Quan, personal communication, December 12,
2008). She gave an example of garment workers in Indonesia and Cambodia working in solidarity with workers in El Salvador. Workers at Tainan
factories in Indonesia and Cambodia pressured Tainan over the ways in
which it shut down its factory in El Salvador and the poor treatment of the
Salvadoran workers. This type of cross-national organizing is often difficult to achieve, but in this case, where workers were willing to show solidarity for one another, Tainan was forced to act. As a result of workers
organizing in Indonesia, Cambodia, and El Salvador, along with consumer
campaigns in the United States, Tainan reopened its factory in El Salvador
and reinstated dismissed workers (Quan 2007). This case shows the success of workers engaged in cross-border solidarity.

In many cases workers are prevented from engaging in direct action for
fear of losing their jobs or being subjected to violence. Despite the risks
many workers have resisted poor working conditions in the garment industry through large protests, including the one in Bangladesh in 2006,
when thousands of workers protested against unsafe factory conditions
and low wages in light of high levels of inflation. Following a series of
deadly factory fires in which over a hundred people were killed and scores

were injured, three thousand garment workers in Dhaka participated in street demonstrations demanding improved safety standards and wage increases. One such protest, in May 2006, resulted in two hundred factories being set on fire and police killing one garment worker. Although the garment manufacturers' association claimed it was the work of "miscreants" waging a war against the economy, Neil Kearney, general secretary of the ITGLWF, considered the protests to be the workers' way of acting out against the appalling health and safety conditions in the factories (ITGLWF 2006).

Workers have also gone on strike numerous times in Vietnam in recent years. For example, from January to September 2008, 112 strikes took place in the textile, clothing, and footwear industries in Ho Chi Minh City (Tuan 2008). Due to soaring inflation workers demanded higher wages to keep up with the rising costs of basic items. In April 2008 over twenty thousand workers at a factory producing Nike footwear went on strike. Workers returned after a week with a wage increase of 10 percent (Hookway 2008). Garment workers in Vietnam continue to struggle for increased wages and improved working conditions.

Workers differ in their approaches to transforming the industry. Some advocate for radical changes while others aim to reform the existing system. The Central American Network of Women in Solidarity with Maquila Workers used the campaign slogan, "Jobs, yes . . . but with dignity" (Mendez 2002, 132). Such messages clearly state these workers' intentions not to call for removal of the assembly plants but instead to advocate for better conditions within the given structure of the industry. In addition to coordinated protest activities some workers are involved in daily acts of resistance such as work slow downs and impromptu strikes (Peled 2006). Whether or not these acts are framed as direct critiques on working conditions, they can be seen as examples of the numerous direct and indirect ways that garment workers challenge exploitative conditions in the industry.

In a few cases workers have established worker-led cooperatives. For example, following the closure of a Bed and Bath factory in Thailand in 2002, workers set up The Solidarity Factory and produced clothing under their own brand name, Dignity Returns (Yimprasert 2006). After several years of subcontracting, the factory now receives all of its work through direct orders and is able to pay workers a living wage. In another case, workers established Just Garments, a unionized factory in El Salvador that produced goods for the fair-trade market in North America. After several years, however, the factory closed. The closure was described by one of its allies in a press release, "Despite Herculean efforts by the union and the plant administration that have come at great personal and professional cost, Just Garments was not able to overcome the opposition of local forces, the cut-throat nature of the apparel industry, the lack of development of the sweat-free market in the North, and its unique approach of essentially operating as a unionized cooperative" (USLEAP 2007). In the end the Just Garments factory was unable to survive in an industry that favors low wages, capital mobility, and a non-unionized workforce.

Global financial crisis

Some of the debates around working conditions in the garment industry have recently been eclipsed by the global financial crisis that began in late 2008. Toward the end of that year consumer spending was down in the United States from previous years. As a result, major retailers in the United States experienced significant declines. Gap saw a decrease of 12 percent, The Limited a decrease of 10 percent, and H&M was down 4 percent (MSN 2009). Consumer spending appeared to be moving from middle- and high-end retailers to discount chains like Walmart. Although Walmart did report an increase of 1.7 percent in sales in December 2008, this was less than its anticipated 2.8 percent. The full impact of decreased consumption in the United States and Europe is unclear, yet it is likely that these costs—and associated risks—will be passed on to suppliers and workers (MSN 2009).

As consumer demand decreased in 2008, growth in the garment sector in China was slower than expected, with many Chinese workers joining their counterparts in El Salvador and Honduras in finding themselves out of work. The full extent of the impact of the financial crisis on those employed in the industry is uncertain. It *is* clear that the financial crisis has led to lower wages and disrupted an already unstable industry in which TNCs hold tremendous power over subcontractors and workers.

Changes to export production in the past decade will make some countries particularly vulnerable. For example, India and China were not heavily affected by the Asian financial crisis in 1997 because both countries relied heavily on domestic production. Both economies are now more export oriented than they were in 1997 and will presumably be more vulnerable to the current crisis. Countries that are heavily dependent on exports, such as Thailand and Cambodia, are likely to be hit hard by the current crisis while demand for goods decreases and credit is scarce.

The financial crisis has also changed public perception of businesses in some countries. The Edelman Trust Barometer found that Americans' trust in business in 2009 plummeted to 38 percent, down from 58 percent the previous year (Edelman 2009). The survey found similarly low levels of trust in Australia (39 percent) and much of Europe. Sixty-five percent of respondents worldwide agreed that governments should impose stricter regulations across all industries (Edelman 2009). The growing distrust of businesses in the United States, Australia, and Europe may provide new opportunities for anti-sweatshop activists; campaign messages about the role of retailers in remedying labor abuses may resonate with Northern consumers more now than those same messages would have even a few years ago.

Pandita suggests that at a deeper level the financial crisis reveals export-oriented growth as a faulty model for development (Pandita, personal communication, October 8, 2008). Although the crisis is certain to cause disruption and difficulties for many people, it may also create some new opportunities. In an interview labor activist Kelly Dent suggested that it may open up conversations about unsustainable consumerism and corporate greed, two topics that until recently have not featured in the mainstream media (Dent, personal communication, January 13, 2009). The financial crisis may, in fact, encourage dialogue among activists, government officials, and industry representatives about ways that the industry can be regulated responsibly at the national and international level.

Conclusion

In the current debates on globalization garment workers are often portrayed as either victims or beneficiaries of a globalizing economy. The phasing out of the MFA in 2004 further entrenched the garment industry as an emblem of contemporary globalization. The industry is characterized by trade liberalization in some instances, such as the easing of some quota restrictions through the WTO, alongside the establishment of bilateral and regional agreements that allow the United States and the European Union to continue to exert influence over the industry. The North's disproportionate influence is sometimes used to benefit transnational retailers and large manufacturing cartels, but is also used by American and European trade representatives as a bargaining chip in trade negotiations that reach beyond the garment industry.

The production and consumption of clothing embodies the unevenness of globalization. While the nature and structure of the industry have been transformed by flows of information and capital across borders, the industry is still very much based in national economies. Workers have been unable to organize on a large scale because national borders are far less permeable for labor than they are for capital. Workers are further constrained by disjunctures between (1) national legislation and international labor standards, and (2) the influence of corporations on national political institutions.

Poor working conditions are not unique to the garment industry, nor are they new. However, since the 1970s the industry has gone through several transformations aided by the international financial institutions' push toward export-oriented production, the expansion of EPZs, and the ease with which global capital can move across borders. These shifts helped create an industry that is characterized by buyer-driven supply chains, a concentration of power among retailers, and a unique geographic distribution of manufacturing. This confluence of factors has led to low pay and hazardous conditions.

International labor standards do exist and are enshrined in ILO conventions, and most states have domestic labor laws. Yet widespread violations of these standards exist and, activists argue, have become routinized in the industry, where labor violations are the norm rather than the exception. In this context states lack power and political will to put additional regulations in place or even to enforce existing international or domestic standards. The most powerful actors in the garment industry supply chain are the transnational retailers that in some cases are larger in terms of annual profit than many countries' gross domestic product.

Workers have not passively accepted these changing political and economic structures. However, many workers' capacities to realize improvements are limited. Traditional labor movements aimed at factory owners and managers have been unable to effect significant change in the terms of labor. This is because retailers, who have the power to dictate prices and impose unrealistic deadlines on manufacturers, largely control the industry. Coupled with threats of physical violence and workers' economic insecurities about losing their jobs, garment workers have found few options for seeking improvements on a broad scale.

Constraints on traditional labor movements created a vacuum and enabled the consolidation of retailers' power. NGOs recognized an opportunity for alternative mobilization strategies on behalf of garment workers. These NGOs exert influence on retailers from the consumption side of the industry. Although states are not the primary targets of advocacy campaigns, states played important roles in structuring the contemporary garment industry through the establishment of the MFA and its dissolution and through bilateral trade agreements. As such, states are significant actors in the garment industry, although they have largely avoided their responsibilities to ensure that workers' health, safety, and basic needs are met. NGOs responded to these features of the industry by building a transnational anti-sweatshop network to address the complex issues workers face in the global garment industry.

Chapter 2

Development of the anti-sweatshop network

As the garment industry spread throughout the global South in the 1980s and 1990s, labor organizers and NGO advocates began to develop a transnational network aimed at improving conditions in the industry. In the United States, Australia, and Europe activists sought to raise awareness among consumers about working conditions in the industry. Their campaigns highlighted the role of retailers in contributing to the low wages, long hours, and use of child labor. In particular, activists launched several high-profile campaigns that garnered significant media attention, galvanized debate among government officials and labor advocates, and mobilized other activists to set up dozens of anti-sweatshop NGOs.

This chapter explores the contemporary anti-sweatshop network, traces the phases of its history, and outlines the relationships that constitute the network. It presents key actors in the network and the main phases of contemporary anti-sweatshop advocacy. It also analyzes anti-sweatshop activists and their tools of influence, especially the ways in which they manage and disseminate information. The purpose is to demonstrate how NGOs and networks behave as transnational political actors and the ways in which they engage with the structures of the global garment industry.

Activists involved in the anti-sweatshop network draw upon elements of what Keck and Sikkink refer to as information, symbolic, leverage, and accountability politics to varying degrees. Information politics refers to the ability to generate and disseminate politically usable information. Symbolic politics includes the "ability to call upon symbols, actions, or stories that make sense of a situation for an audience that is frequently far away" (1998, 16). Another type of politics used in consumer campaigns is leverage politics. TANs can seek leverage over more powerful institutions in two forms, materially and using morality. Material leverage links the issues to money. Moral leverage "involves what some commentators have called

39

the 'mobilization of shame,' where the behavior of target actors is held up to the light of international scrutiny" (Keck and Sikkink 1998, 23). Shame, of course, can also have material consequences for corporations, but it does not always have a clear causal relationship to money. The last of the tactics described by Keck and Sikkink is accountability politics, which means holding targeted actors to their previously stated principles. Participants in the anti-sweatshop network have used these types of politics at various times.

Overview of the anti-sweatshop network

The contemporary anti-sweatshop movement began in the 1990s as a reaction to the dispersal of garment production to hundreds of EPZs in the global South, the consolidation of capital among TNCs sourcing their products from multiple suppliers, and the absence of an overarching industry regulatory body. In countries as diverse as Mexico, Bangladesh, and China similar patterns emerged as migrants moved to urban centers in search of new opportunities in the garment sector. Activists in these locations began drawing connections among the mobility of capital, restrictions on labor, and the ways in which workers were recruited based on gender, racial, and ethnic categories. Young, single women became the preferred workers in the industry in Central America and Asia, while Asian immigrants, mostly women with children, were employed as home-based workers in Australia and the UK. In the United States, Asian and Latino immigrants made up the bulk of garment workers in New York and Los Angeles. Manufacturers seized upon existing social divisions to create highly exploitable pools of labor. Labor activists in these locations began to work within existing union structures as well as developing anti-sweatshop NGOs in order to address the changing conditions in the industry.

In the early 1990s activists and union organizers in Indonesia and Vietnam began collecting data for a worldwide campaign targeting Nike. At the same time, in Australia, union organizers were developing a campaign for garment workers as production moved away from factory-based work and into home-based work. In Europe, labor organizers and feminist activists launched a campaign against Dutch retailer C&A. At the same time labor activists in the garment industry in the United States were working with immigrants' rights organizations in Texas and California. Although there was some awareness about activities in other countries, none of these actions were part of a coordinated network. Instead, activists in each location were witnessing localized, yet connected, shifts in the industry with production moving to new locations and becoming increasingly oriented toward a "just in time," flexible regime.

The anti-sweatshop network gained momentum in the mid to late 1990s, taking on a slightly different character in each region; this has carried through to the present day. In Australia, Oxfam Australia launched the NikeWatch campaign to expose labor abuses in Nike factories in Asia, while FairWear began working with unions and churches to generate awareness about the state of homeworkers in the garment industry in Australia. Media coverage of homeworkers led to a Senate inquiry in 1996, which raised significant awareness about the exploitation of homeworkers in Australia and connected their conditions to sweatshop conditions abroad. Linking working conditions in factories in Asia with homeworkers in the domestic garment industry continues to be a central aspect of anti-sweatshop advocacy in Australia. Because of their connections to the Australian union movement, Australian labor rights NGOs emphasize the need for collective bargaining and freedom of association in both their domestic and international advocacy campaigns (Connor and Dent 2006; FairWear 2008 homepage).

The European NGOs have taken on a slightly different character, with strong links to local labor and feminist movements. Several of the anti-sweatshop NGOs also receive financial support from European governments and the European Union. European anti-sweatshop NGOs have focused on building networks, exposing the most flagrant labor abuses, and encouraging ethical sourcing practices among European retailers and governments. This has contributed to a significant market in Europe for products certified as having been made under ethical conditions.

In the United States, the anti-sweatshop network was shaped by several key events in the late 1990s that served to generate interest in the issue and raised awareness about exploitation in the garment industry. The first event was TV celebrity Kathie Lee Gifford's tear-filled apology on national television in 1996 following the revelation that child workers were used on a line of clothes that bore her name. Her apology followed a campaign by the National Labor Committee (NLC) that exposed labor violations including the use of child labor in the Global Fashion factory in Honduras where her clothing line was being produced for Walmart (Ross 1997). The reason that this campaign was so effective was because it contrasted Gifford, a wealthy, white, celebrity talk-show host, with images and stories of Honduran children toiling away on clothing carrying Gifford's name on the label. The NLC targeting Gifford was an effective strategy. The media attention it won laid the groundwork for future anti-sweatshop campaigns.

The second event in the United States was the large protest in Seattle in 1999, when thousands of people gathered outside a meeting of the WTO. Participants in the so-called Battle of Seattle included labor activists, environmentalists, and anti-corporate activists. The scale of the protests and the linkages among previously disparate movements contributed to an awakening among activists and the general public of growing discontent with the neoliberal orthodoxy as espoused by the WTO, World Bank, and IMF. Organizations involved in the anti-sweatshop network, including Global Exchange, STITCH, USAS, and the Third World Network, played key roles in organizing protest events in Seattle. Along with hundreds of other organizations they mobilized participation in the protest, disseminated organizing materials, and educated allies and the public (Smith 2005). The impact of these events can be seen in contemporary campaigns that aim to build coalitions across issue areas and that continue to employ public "shaming" campaigns as one of their primary tools of influence.

The legacy of these formative campaigns is important for organizations and networks because they are continually shaped by earlier campaign activities, even those that they do not control. This is partly due to the ways in which attitudes about present-day campaign messages are shaped by preconceived knowledge and sentiments toward previous messages. Unlike electoral campaigns, where many of the messages are controlled centrally, these campaigns involve many different voices at the same time. They most often reinforce one another, but they can be contradictory or cancel one another out. Despite the lack of tight coordination, the influence is collective and cumulative.

The anti-sweatshop network resembles what Diani (2003) refers to as a clique structure, where the nodes in the network interact through multiple links, lacking a central coordinating body. Tim Connor, coordinator of Oxfam Australia's NikeWatch campaign, suggests that the loose, decentralized structure of the anti-sweatshop network has "facilitated innovation and adaptive learning." Since activists do not need to seek permission from others before taking action, he notes that "this has freed individuals and organizations to experiment with new and potentially risky campaign activities without waiting for the approval of a slow-moving bureaucracy and without endangering the movement as a whole" (Connor 2005, 72). Connor points out that the lack of a clear path that targeted companies can take, however, gives them little incentive to take steps toward improvement, since there is no guarantee that activists will call off their campaigns once companies make changes.[1]

Actors in the anti-sweatshop network

Defining the boundaries of the network can be difficult. There is no formal membership and no centralized institution coordinating all of the various actors. Some of the organizations involved in the network may have formal membership processes, but the network as a whole is dynamic and lacks a formal structure. Organizations and individuals move in and out, and the network shifts over time. While there are several key actors, the fluidity of the network is a central aspect of its structure.

The types of actors in the anti-sweatshop network include NGOs, unions, workers, and intergovernmental organizations (IGOs). Small NGOs make up the framework of the anti-sweatshop network and act as the driving force behind the network, doing much of the day-to-day work that keeps the network active. Despite their small size and limited budgets, these NGOs mobilize significant numbers of supporters to take action— writing letters, signing petitions, or attending protests. In a request for funds the NLC website proclaimed in 2006, "Perhaps you imagine that the National Labor Committee is a large and well-funded organization. It is neither. We are a small staff of five people working on a shoestring budget. A lot of what we do is 'smoke and mirrors,' but we work very, very hard to make the most of the small resources available." The "smoke and mirrors" the site refer to are the online campaigning and media attention aimed at projecting an image of a large, well-resourced organization.

The size of NGOs engaged in anti-sweatshop advocacy is significant because it is often assumed that the large, institutionalized NGOs are the ones becoming global political actors and shaping global governance. Yet small organizations are important actors in transnational politics surrounding the garment industry. The number of NGOs involved in transnational anti-sweatshop advocacy grew significantly over the past three decades, with a dramatic increase in the number of NGOs engaged in transnational anti-sweatshop advocacy in the mid-1990s. Most of these organizations report annual revenue of less than US$2 million and fewer than ten employees.

The growth of these NGOs coincided with declining union membership. While NGOs work alongside unions and often share their goals, the two types of entities differ in important ways. Braun and Gearhart suggest that NGOs and unions relate differently to political power. NGOs' legitimacy rests on remaining outside of formal politics, while unions often desire to become political insiders. Braun and Gearhart explain that NGOs seek to influence policymakers' thinking without endorsing candidates or putting up their own candidates, as many unions do. They note that many center-left parties around the world trace their origins to labor movements. Braun and Gearhart also differentiate between unions driven by members' particular interests and NGOs driven by a set of principles or ideals. Since NGOs have different relationships to the state than unions do, and are not usually bound by members' interests, NGOs are able to act in ways unavailable to traditional unions (Braun and Gearhart 2005).

The relationship between NGOs and unions is not always harmonious. Since NGOs are not direct membership organizations, many unions fear that NGOs are not representative of workers' views and that they may undermine unions by negotiating directly with management (Connor 2005; Eade and Leather 2005). NGOs must raise funds from external sources, which can create the potentially incompatible need to satisfy both workers and funders (Freeman, Hersch, and Mishel 2005). Despite the strained relationships between some NGOs and unions, there are many examples of cooperation, particularly when NGOs are engaged in activities that unions are unable to do or in industries where unions are weak or nonexistent.

In fact, some NGOs focus on strengthening local labor movements. For example, in an interview Sanjiv Pandita, director of AMRC, critiqued the model of the NGO-led consumer campaigns. Instead, AMRC focuses on strengthening labor movements in Asia and promoting a system of equal exchange among labor activists in the North and South (Pandita, personal communication, October 8, 2008). Similarly, Tony Fung, China field director of the WRC, suggests that local labor movements must be in control of campaigns, with Northern-based organizations acting as providers of resources. He said in an interview that the tools Northern anti-sweatshop NGOs have at their disposal—to pressure retailers to adopt codes of conduct, to conduct investigations, and to push for greater monitoring—are valuable only if they complement local actions (Fung, personal communication, October 8, 2008).

NGOs in Hong Kong deserve special mention because of their unique position in the anti-sweatshop network.[2] NGOs in Hong Kong are particularly important for their role in linking Asian NGOs working directly with garment workers with NGOs in the United States, Europe, and Australia. Some of these NGOs include the AMRC, Students and Scholars Against Corporate Misconduct (SACOM), Oxfam Hong Kong, the Christian Industrial Committee, and Labour Action China. These organizations constitute vital nodes in the network, conducting research on supply chains, developing analysis of the consumer campaigns and the labor movement, and applying pressure to sourcing agents in the industry.

Labor rights NGOs in Asia gained momentum after a series of deadly fires in the early 1990s. The fires contributed to the already growing awareness among labor activists in the region of the impact of globalization and flexible accumulation on working conditions. Another formative event in Asia was the exposure of child labor in the production of Nike-branded goods in Indonesia. Following widespread media attention on the issue of child labor, Asian labor rights NGOs raised questions about the appropriateness of banning child labor when institutions were not adequately in place to support those children and their families. Although there is considerable coordination among labor rights NGOs in Asia, there are debates among the organizations regarding various strategies to address labor issues throughout the region and the most appropriate role of Northern-based organizations and consumer campaigns.

In addition to the advocacy-oriented NGOs, numerous organizations provide services for garment workers. Some of these, such as the Self-Employed Women's Association (SEWA) in India, provide services to home-based women workers and others in the informal sector. Services include loans, childcare, and legal aid in addition to advocating on behalf of women in the informal sector (SEWA 2007). Many organizations developed innovative methods for contacting workers and providing them with essential services. The Chinese Working Women Network uses a "mobile support unit," a bus that has been converted into a resource center; the bus visits workers in three industrial towns each week (CCC 2005a). Another example is the Institute for Contemporary Observation, an NGO in Shenzhen, China, that provides advice to garment workers through a telephone hotline and chatrooms on QQ, a popular instant-messaging site in China. Other organizations in the network include religious groups and shareholder activists engaged in garment-industry advocacy. These other organizations, like those described above, do not act as a unified voice and may have quite different, and even conflicting, ideological or strategic positions, but they are all involved in advocating for change in the global garment industry.

Within the UN system, the ILO is actively engaged in setting standards and convening representatives of unions, business leaders, and government officials. International labor standards, such as the ILO's Fundamental Principles and Rights at Work described in Chapter 1, are widely used by NGOs involved in the anti-sweatshop network. The ILO also plays a role in setting standards and raising the profile of some types of workers. For example, in 1996 the ILO adopted a convention on home work. The convention expanded the meaning of worker to include home-based workers, who had previously been excluded from categories of workers. The ILO convention on home work was the result of an international coalition of organizations dedicated to homeworkers led by SEWA. There was significant debate among homeworker advocates about the representation of such workers. Many labor leaders portrayed homeworkers as helpless victims, lacking skills and in need of protection. Homeworker advocates, on the other hand, "conceded that homeworkers were exploited but insisted that they could take fate into their own hands, that they had the power to act" (Prugl 1999, 205). Such debates illustrate the role of the ILO both as a standard-setting body and as a site for international debate about changing ideas about workers and workers' rights.

The ILO, however, is limited in its scope. The agency is notoriously under-resourced and lacks the mandate to enforce international labor standards. This is one of the reasons for the reliance on voluntary codes of conduct and piecemeal monitoring by third parties. Unlike the ILO, the WTO does have enforcement powers, although its jurisdiction currently does not extend to labor laws.

Phases of anti-sweatshop advocacy

Since the 1990s anti-sweatshop activists have used a variety of campaigns and strategies in their attempts to improve working conditions and ensure workers' rights. Table 2–1 describes the phases of anti-sweatshop advocacy. Each phase of transnational advocacy took place in tandem with political changes and changes in the distribution of manufacturing. Activists' actions elicited different responses from targeted corporations, which in turn led activists to change their tactics. These changes demonstrate the power and resilience of political and economic structures in the garment industry, where each time NGOs achieved some influence, targeted companies were able to absorb activists' criticism and make minor adjustments without making major changes to their sourcing practices. The series of negotiations between actors in the anti-sweatshop network and corporations in each phase resulted in compromise and cooperation at times, as well as conflict and cooptation at others.

The early "name and shame" campaigns did have some notable successes, especially when conducted in conjunction with legal action. Chie Abad, an anti-sweatshop activist with Global Exchange and a former garment worker, lived through one such campaign. She was involved in a

Phase I: Name-and-shame campaigns
(1995–1998)

Policies: Phaseout of quotas begins (MFA ends, ATC implemented).
Production: Production increased in Asia and Central America.
NGOs: Launched name-and-shame campaigns, exposed celebrities and high-profile retailers with poor labor conditions, especially child labor.
Corporate responses: Targeted retailers denied any responsibility for working conditions in supply chains and refused to disclose factory locations.

Phase 2: Corporate social responsibility
(1999–2004)

Policies: 80 percent of quotas were still in place by end of 2005.
Production: As quotas were met in Korea and Taiwan, Taiwanese- and Korean-owned factories increased production in Central America, Indonesia, and Vietnam; China became the major supplier for the American, European, and Japanese markets.
NGOs: Developed model codes, pushed for factory disclosure, researched supply chains of major retailers.
Corporate responses: Targeted retailers began to acknowledge some responsibility for supply chains, first by developing individual codes, and later by joining MSIs; companies producing university apparel agreed to disclose factory locations, on a limited basis.

Phase 3: Post MFA
(2005–present)

Policies: MFA/ATC ended January 1, 2005; new quotas placed on China through the U.S.-China MOU and EU-China agreement, both phased out by the end of 2008; global financial crisis affected consumer demand and access to credit.
Production: Increased concentration of manufacturing in China and India; factory closures in Central America, Bangladesh, and Indonesia.
NGOs: Activists sought severance payments for retrenched workers, developed procurement policies, and engaged with MSIs.
Corporate responses: Codes of conduct became widespread; industry leaders and those producing for the university market disclosed factories, conducted internal audits, and expanded participation in MSIs.

Table 2–1. Phases of anti-sweatshop advocacy

landmark lawsuit against U.S. corporations in Saipan in 1999.[3] As a result of the lawsuit, workers were paid US$20 million in back wages. However, even before the verdict was decided, SAKO, the Korean corporation that owned the factory where Abad worked, made some significant changes. After having been forced to live in company dorms, workers were finally allowed to live wherever they wanted. SAKO also offered workers medical benefits, decreased recruitment fees, and reduced hours to sixty hours a week (down from one hundred hours per week) (Abad, personal communication, December 12, 2008).[4] These changes were due to the threat of legal action along with negative publicity in Saipan and on American television.

Since the late 1990s and early 2000s (and phase two of anti-sweatshop advocacy) most major retailers have implemented codes of conduct and regularly conduct internal audits. However, audits alone are insufficient to ensure compliance. According to Kaiming Liu, executive director of the Institute for Contemporary Observation, which works on improving corporate social responsibility and labor rights in China, many factories know how to evade auditors (Liu, personal communication, October 7, 2008). He explained that many factories maintain false documents and train workers in how to answer auditors' questions. Liu reported that there are even consulting firms available in Shenzhen that help factory owners get around such audits.

Although companies may not acknowledge the influence the anti-sweatshop network has had on their operations, many have changed the way they approach responsibility to improve working conditions. Retailers' responses to campaigns vary; however, in general those that have been targets of campaigns and come under greater scrutiny now have more thorough social auditing systems in place. Such changes can be seen in how Adidas, a frequent target of anti-sweatshop campaigns, implemented its social auditing program. A report in 2007 by the Adidas Group included on the inside cover the statement that since the establishment of its Social and Environmental Affairs Team in 1997 "we have established an extensive program for managing workplace issues in our supply chain, founded on the principle that although we have outsourced the manufacture of our products, we are still responsible for how our products are made" (2007a). The acceptance of responsibility for labor conditions in supply chains by retailers is limited and relatively new—and a significant departure from the period before the anti-sweatshop advocacy era. Only since the third phase of anti-sweatshop advocacy has begun have the major retailers acknowledged their responsibility for working conditions in suppliers' factories, published results of their findings of factory conditions, and joined MSIs.

Bill Anderson, head of Social and Environmental Affairs (Asia Pacific) for the Adidas Group, said in an interview, "If we are protecting the rights of workers, then ultimately we are managing the brand reputation. If we are failing to protect the rights of those workers, then the brand reputation won't stand for much" (Anderson, personal communication, October 6, 2008). Social-compliance departments in some big companies are part of their public relations departments, which indicates how compliance fits into image management. In contrast, the Adidas Group's approach is more technical and legalistic. Consequently, according to Anderson, the Social and Environmental Affairs department has significant clout within the company.[5] Anderson acknowledges that auditing alone is insufficient: "I think nearly every program that has had resources and expertise and personnel has learned early on that the success of an auditing-based program is relatively little" (Anderson, personal communication, October 6, 2008). He said that that is why the Adidas Group links commercial decisions with compliance performance. For example, before a factory can be contracted to produce goods for Adidas, the Social and Environmental Affairs department must be satisfied that it meets basic requirements. These basic requirements, known as zero-tolerance issues, relate mainly to health and safety. Other issues, referred to as threshold issues, are those that Adidas staff note and give factories time to bring into line with Adidas's standards. In an interview Vincent Tse gave the following example: If a factory had its employees working seventy hours a week and Adidas's standard is sixty hours a week, the local Adidas staff would work with the factory to develop a plan to implement Adidas's standard and would then follow up several months later to ensure those standards were being met (Tse, personal communication, October 6, 2008).

According to Anderson, he and his colleagues are concerned about some of the same issues as the anti-sweatshop activists. The main difference is that they differ in how they define the role of retailers in ensuring decent working conditions. He argued, "The companies will see their role defined by programs that they have developed. Sometimes you will see that the NGO expectation is far greater than the ability—the NGO would see it as the willingness, we would often see it as the ability—of the global company to respond to the things that they think global companies should do" (Anderson, personal communication, October 6, 2008). In his view activists assume that the retailers have a much greater ability to influence working conditions in their suppliers' factories than they do. He suggested that, compared to activists' assumptions and expectations, retailers have relatively limited power in enforcing labor standards and that this responsibility ultimately rests with governments.

This emphasis on whether retailers should be the enforcers of standards ignores the fact that many of the retailers' sourcing practices—such as low prices, unrealistic delivery times, and short-term contracts—exacerbate poor working conditions in the industry. Few retailers have made drastic changes to their sourcing practices in order to improve working conditions. However, some retailers have begun to make some small, but significant, changes as a result of anti-sweatshop activism. For example, since it first became a target of anti-sweatshop activism in the early 1990s, Nike has changed its approach to its suppliers (Nike 2006). A recent event highlights changes in how Nike responds to criticism in its suppliers' factories. In 2008 reporter Mike Duffy posed as a fashion buyer and toured the factory of Nike subcontractor Hytex in Malaysia. He filmed facilities where twenty-six men were forced to sleep in one room, and three hundred people had to share inadequate bathing and toilet facilities (Duffy 2008). The workers had come to Malaysia from Sri Lanka, Nepal, Bangladesh, Vietnam, and Indonesia, and they were required to pay fees equivalent to a year's salary in order to secure employment. They were then forced to hand over their passports and sign documents in a language they did not understand, committing them to lengthy contracts to repay their debts (Oxfam Australia 2008a; Read 2008). By all accounts these conditions constituted forms of forced labor and were in direct conflict with ILO labor standards and Nike's own code of conduct. Shortly after being notified of the findings, Nike issued a press release confirming the findings and laying out a remediation plan requiring Hytex to return workers' passports, move workers into alternative accommodation, and reimburse the employment fees (Nike 2008b). The conditions at Hytex were not unique. In fact, these conditions are not exceptional in the industry. What is different about this case is the quick response from Nike.

After almost fifteen years of anti-sweatshop activism targeting Nike, the company changed its strategy from one of outright denial of any involvement in the poor working conditions in its suppliers' factories to acceptance of the findings as well as acceptance of some responsibility to rectify the situation. Although Nike does not directly employ these workers (a distinction Nike is quick to make), Nike executives are aware of the power Nike holds over Hytex managers and employees. Another clear difference in Nike's response is that, following the exposure of Hytex, Nike did not sever its contract with the factory, which it had done in previous cases when confronted with media coverage of poor conditions in its factories.

In the Hytex case Nike committed to seeing changes made at the factory and not, in the words of activists, "cutting and running" once confronted with the scandal. This has been an important aspect of the second and third phases of anti-sweatshop advocacy pushing buyers like Nike to retain contracts and help ensure that conditions are remedied rather than terminating contracts, which further harms workers. The speed with which Nike responded in the Hytex case and its approach to governance of its supply chain are clearly the result of fifteen years of cumulative campaigning by anti-sweatshop activists.

Activists secured another notable victory in 2010 against Nike. The Just Pay It campaign began in January 2009 when Hugger and Vision Tex closed their plants in Honduras, leaving twelve hundred workers unemployed. The two Nike subcontractors closed without notice and refused to pay workers severance payments owed to them. Students in the United States protested, urging their universities to sever contracts with Nike for refusing to pay severance to the dismissed workers. The University of Wisconsin severed its contract with Nike over the issue, and Cornell University threatened to do the same. In July 2010, as a result of the pressure, Nike announced that it would pay US$1.54 million toward a workers' relief fund and provide vocational training to dismissed workers (Greenhouse 2010a).

Tools of influence

Information politics

Lacking material and economic power, TANs rely on information to persuade others to take action. The ways in which activists gather, manage, and disseminate that information can determine the extent to which a particular campaign succeeds in achieving its goals. Two types of information that anti-sweatshop activists commonly use are factory reports and worker testimonials. Studies of factory conditions often detail health, safety, overtime, and wage violations. NGOs frequently compile the reports in conjunction with local unions and can be part of informal assessments or formal monitoring processes.

Worker testimonials personalize the data on worker abuse by presenting human stories about poor working conditions. The stories have the potential to reorient relationships between consumers and producers from simply being connected (or disconnected) by the item of clothing to stressing their shared humanity across political and geographic space. Organizations often present worker testimonials on their websites and in other publications or in the form of speaking tours. These stories are aimed at educating the public and encouraging consumers to change their behavior.

Information generated or obtained by anti-sweatshop NGOs often goes through a process of translation. Sometimes the translation is from one language to another, while other times it is a translation into language that fits a particular political arena. As Jordan and Van Tuijl note, "Information by itself is not enough to pursue effective advocacy. Often the available information needs interpretation in accordance with the political arena in which it is being articulated" (2000, 2055). There is tremendous room for Northern-based activists to mistranslate garment workers' stories. Brooks offers accounts of Northern anti-sweatshop activists appropriating the stories of Southern garment workers (2007). This can happen when Northern activists seek to package workers' stories into familiar tropes for Northern audiences.

The anti-sweatshop network uses a variety of strategies to communicate with consumers, including print media, radio, protests (such as mock sweatshops in front of retail outlets, corporate headquarters, or university campuses), cross-cultural delegations and many others. Activists also seek to influence consumers using speaker tours where garment workers or former garment workers speak to student groups, religious organizations, or social clubs. The CCC, Maquila Solidarity Network, FairWear, and Global Exchange all sponsor these types of speaker tours. One of the goals of such tours is to humanize workers, who often appear anonymous and distant to consumers in the global North.

Many of the anti-sweatshop NGOs use web-based tools to mobilize consumers. This is part of the broader trend of activists using new media to coordinate social movements (Kahn and Kellner 2004; Van de Donk et al. 2004). Small organizations especially benefit from using information and communication technologies that allow them to access large groups of people at minimal cost. These communications aim to inspire action among consumers, such as writing letters, signing petitions, attending protests, or changing their own consumption habits. Although small anti-sweatshop NGOs are not distinct in this regard from larger NGOs or for-profit institutions, they do tend to rely on these technologies to a greater extent since they lack the resources for using other forms of media.

The anti-sweatshop NGOs maintain websites, blogs, and electronic alerts and regularly post material on social-networking websites. The use of such social-networking sites is relatively new for most NGOs. It represents a merging of life politics (Giddens 1991) with more formal political engagement that is common among young anti-sweatshop activists in the United

States and elsewhere who were introduced to the anti-sweatshop movement through university campus-based campaigns in the late 1990s and early 2000s. This convergence is part of what Bennett describes as lifestyle politics, which are the ways that people create social and political meaning around their values and the personal narratives that express them. As individuals express their identities through their consumption habits, their relationship to the state and global politics is shaped by an emerging identity of citizens as consumers of public as well as private goods. This identification with consumption among many citizen-consumers in Western democracies and with the sense of agency attached to consumption activities has contributed to the success of consumer-oriented campaigns (Bennett 2006). The anti-sweatshop network has been able to tap into lifestyle politics, particularly with many young consumers in the North, in a way that other social movements have not.

The strength of such consumer campaigns has been their ability to turn localized sites of consumption, politics, media, and education into venues to expose widespread corporate abuses (Bennett 2006). The power of electronic communication comes in taking localized actions—such as a sit-in at Purdue University in Indiana or a satire of a fashion show in Melbourne—and transforming that local event into a global one. The Internet provides a way to shift actions from the local to the global arena (or perhaps, more realistically, from one local place to others). The action itself becomes a small part of the *overall* act, which takes on symbolic importance for a wider audience and for the participants themselves.

The communication of many small, localized protests helps foster a sense of solidarity among autonomous nodes in the network. There are many benefits from a diffuse, decentralized network. However, as Bennett suggests, "The recent entry of large numbers of less commonly purposed, networked players increases the prospects for unstable coalitions, greater communication noise, lack of clarity about goals, and poor movement idea-framing" (2006, 29). This is important because the framing of ideas can determine the extent to which activists are successful in communicating their messages and persuading targeted actors to change.

The inability of NGOs in the network to control a central frame is, indeed, a challenge, yet they benefit tremendously from the flow of information on the Internet about sweatshops and corporate campaigns. This even includes information that the anti-sweatshop NGOs themselves do not control. One example is SimSweatshop, a sweatshop simulation video game. The anti-sweatshop network also benefits from "communication noise" from those hostile to their work. This includes a critique by prominent economist Jagdish Bhagwati deriding anti-sweatshop activists on BBC, as well as less well-known critics such as Students *for* Sweatshops, created by a student in Mississippi on MySpace in reaction to anti-sweatshop activists. Even such "noise" helps to generate discussion, keep the issue alive in an already crowded field of social and political issues in the media, and provide an opportunity for the anti-sweatshop network to gain exposure and share information.

At a time when many NGOs are becoming more centralized and professionalized in their communication strategies, the organizations in the anti-sweatshop network are bucking that trend. Instead, they are becoming more diffuse and decentralized, benefiting from a multiplicity of people and actions on the web that serve to further their work. They are building networks of autonomous nodes rather than tightly controlled, centralized structures. Sometimes their actions are coordinated, but more often they are not. These autonomous nodes in the transnational anti-sweatshop network are creating and disseminating information that can be used by multiple NGOs in consumer campaigns.

Collective voice and framing

Despite its diffuse nature, the anti-sweatshop network behaves as a political actor with its own voice, a voice beyond the culmination of individual actors in the network. This voice is not necessarily the collection of all the disparate voices but is, instead, the outcome of negotiation and interaction among members within the network (Keck and Sikkink 1998, 207). In the anti-sweatshop network, as in other advocacy networks, perspectives range from reformist to more radical. Reformists often gain a greater sense of legitimacy among targeted actors as the "respectable face of dissent" (*The Economist* 2000, 87) precisely because of the presence of activists with more challenging agendas.

Another way of thinking about a network's voice is through framing. Framing is a concept from social movement theory that is used to uncover how ideology operates within movements. It recognizes that movements are "signifying agents engaged in the production and maintenance of meaning" (Snow 2004, 384). Frames can be deliberate and obvious, but they can also be the underlying messages and constructions of place and identities associated with a social movement. Understanding framing helps to develop a deeper understanding of the actors involved in the anti-sweatshop network and the mechanisms they use to participate in transnational advocacy.

Activist organizations construct frames, but the media and targeted institutions also shape how the public perceives activists' frames. In other words, NGOs have agency in developing the frames, but they do not have complete control over them. Ross notes that the U.S. media employed three different frames in response to activism in the United States in the mid-1990s around the sweatshop issue. The "foreign and immigrant workers" frame highlighted the connections between immigrant labor and exploitative conditions in U.S. sweatshops. The "celebrity" frame connected high-profile individuals with sweatshops. He describes a third type of frame as "movement as stupid," whereby conservative pundits painted anti-sweatshop activists as misguided and senseless. Each of these relates to the ways in which the media characterized garment workers and advocates, and influenced the way the public interpreted activists' messages (2004b, 208).

Activists used several different frames throughout each of the phases of anti-sweatshop advocacy described earlier in this chapter. Since phase three has begun, the most prevalent frames are what I characterize as a corporate accountability frame and a global justice frame. The corporate accountability frame presents labor violations as anomalies that can be remedied through targeted programs, certification, and labeling. This frame suggests that monitoring and evaluation of factories will be able to identify and remedy the worst offenders of an otherwise workable system. This frame is aimed at consumers and gives the impression that if consumers adopt conscious shopping habits, the garment industry can become "sweat free." This frame leads to focusing on consumers' shopping habits and monitoring factories.

The global justice frame links critiques of the industry with broader critiques of neoliberal globalization. The global justice frame acknowledges the routinized aspects of worker exploitation in the garment industry, so that underpayment of wages, forced overtime, and sexual harassment in the industry are not simply viewed as deviations from an otherwise just system but are seen as endemic to it. This frame strongly joins sweatshops to other issues, so that the garment industry is seen as connected to structural adjustment policies, unfair trade rules, and neoliberal policies, which are seen as part and parcel of exploitation in the garment industry.

Underlying both frames is a growing focus on workers' rights as human rights. This was not always the case. Throughout the first two phases of anti-sweatshop advocacy activists tended to emphasize working conditions over workers' rights. Esbenshade suggests that "a focus on conditions rather than on the rights of the workers has put the anti-sweatshop movement in a vulnerable position. Multinationals appear to take the high road by adopting codes of conduct for their contracting facilities and monitoring them for compliance, without changing the basic operating principles of the system" (2004, 202). Recognizing this, many activists have begun to emphasize the need for enabling rights such as freedom of association so that garment workers can take a more active role in pressuring employers to improve working conditions (Connor and Dent 2006).

Labor analyst Katie Quan suggested in an interview that along with getting big companies to recognize and accept responsibility for working conditions in their supply chains, reframing labor rights as human rights has been a major accomplishment of the anti-sweatshop network (Quan, personal communication, December 12, 2008). This focus on rights has been due to a realization among activists of the inability to effect lasting change without achieving enabling rights. It is also part of a broader trend toward rights-based approaches, or what Nelson and Dorsey (2008) call "new rights advocacy," which includes the advancement of economic and social rights that have long been overshadowed by an emphasis on political rights.

Issue framing is an important activity for NGOs in order to make their voices heard because they often compete with frames developed by the media and targeted institutions. Frames are also integral to shaping internal operations of NGOs and the network. By participating in the network, NGOs are able to mobilize particular frames, depending on the issue and audience. They may employ multiple frames at any given point or draw from different frames at different times. For example, many of the anti-sweatshop NGOs simultaneously use the corporate accountability and the global justice frames. They develop critiques of the system and use language of global justice while simultaneously developing specific programs that can intervene in the system in small ways to address the most flagrant abuses.

How an organization chooses to frame the issues depends in part on its ideological origins. The organizations in this study have their origins in religious organizations and social movements focused on human rights, labor rights, feminism, and international development. Sluiter says of the origins of the Clean Clothes Campaign, "Although socialist, feminist and anti-imperialist theories resounded in the background, the aim of the campaign was thoroughly practical: to improve labour conditions in the garment industry" (2009, 16). These theoretical traditions are still evident in CCC materials that emphasize global justice. At the same time the organization has developed the tools and language associated with the corporate accountability frame to communicate with retailers.

Within the global justice frame there are two predominant, overlapping perspectives: those that emphasize feminism in their work and those that prioritize the labor movement. These are not mutually exclusive, and many activists and organizations engage in both, but there are differences in terms of origin, analysis, and strategies. These differences can be illustrated by how NGOs coming from each perspective use the term *sweatshop*. The word *sweatshop* has become a central feature of the NGOs with their roots in labor movements. On the contrary, many of the organizations focused on women do not use the word *sweatshop*. This may be due to the fear of stigmatizing the women who work in the factories, furthering a perception of the women not as agents of change but instead as helpless victims. Another reason may be that some feminist scholars and activists tend to be ambivalent about garment factories, not wanting to assign the label of sweatshop and thus branding them as dens of exploitation. Few people suggest that the current conditions are healthy for women, but many cite the ambiguous and contradictory effects, economically and socially, of garment work on women (Kabeer 2000; Pearson 1998). Debates over the usage of the term *sweatshop* point to deeper divisions among anti-sweatshop NGOs over the emphasis of advocacy campaigns and the framing of workers' issues.[6]

The anti-sweatshop network facilitates NGOs becoming transnational political actors by building bridges across different frames. Each organization has its own supporters who are then exposed to the anti-sweatshop issue through the lens of their chosen NGO. For example, the International Labor Rights Forum draws significant support from American lawyers, law students, and law professors because it includes legal analysis and lawsuits as part of its strategy. Many of the supporters of the Campaign for Labor Rights (CLR) were drawn to it based on its work with Central American refugees and its involvement in peace movements in the 1980s. CLR also has strong contacts with churches and religious organizations in the United States. FairWear in Australia also has links with churches. Each organization's support base has different points of leverage, such as students with university apparel, citizens with local governments (in regard to sweat-free ordinances) and religious organizations through shareholder activism. Although each organization specializes in a particular approach to issues and strategies, they have managed to broaden support for themselves and one another by linking with other organizations in the transnational anti-sweatshop network.

An organization's credibility can also be bolstered through its engagement with the anti-sweatshop network. This is especially important for small organizations. These NGOs can be viewed as part of a broader movement in which they are engaged, which can reinforce their message and can mobilize broader support, if needed. Acting in concert with others also helps to establish NGOs' credibility and validate their work among the general public. Anti-sweatshop NGOs broaden support for one another by citing and distributing reports, films, photographs, and other materials that corroborate their joint claims. They also co-sign petitions, publicize one another's events, and act as plaintiffs in lawsuits against retailers.

In spite of all of the benefits for small organizations of working within a broader network, transnational networks are not necessarily harmonious, democratic, or even effective (Kaldor 2003). Networks often include exchanges that are acrimonious and sometimes disillusioning for activists. Moreover, racial hierarchies, class inequalities, gender discrimination, and differential access to resources, while present in local or regional networks, are compounded on a transnational basis because of cultural differences and the unequal distribution of power and privilege (Cohen and Rai 2000). Advocacy NGOs based in the North often have a comparative advantage over their Southern partners in terms of access to resources and institutions. They also have additional challenges in terms of legitimacy and a lack of knowledge of local situations. Other conflicts within the network are based on divergent ideological perspectives or orientations of different actors. Conflict can also exist between institutionalized and more grassroots-oriented groups. A certain level of conflict is probably a sign of a healthy network, but continual conflict can drain resources and hamper advocacy efforts.

Conclusion

Labor activists have developed a networked form of advocacy to transverse political jurisdictions and apply pressure to retailers as well as pressure the manufacturers and subcontractors that directly employ garment workers. The result is a vast network of NGOs, unions, and parts of IGOs aimed at improving working conditions in the industry. These actors are political agents in their own right as well as part of a network that is itself a political actor in international politics.

The number of Northern-based NGOs involved in transnational anti-sweatshop advocacy has increased significantly over the past three decades. The majority of organizations in existence today were founded in the early 1990s. These organizations, advocating on behalf of garment workers through consumer campaigns aimed at changing the behavior of retailers and consumers, rely on other actors in the network for information, reinforcing claims, and broadening support. These include international and nationally based unions, parts of the ILO and other IGOs, and workers' organizations.

Because of the decentralized nature of the anti-sweatshop network, individual actors—particularly those with minimal resources—can benefit from exposure and interaction with others. This is especially important for small organizations that may be more reliant on the network for such support, and it allows these actors to collaborate and thereby amplify their effectiveness.

Anti-sweatshop advocacy has gone through several key phases. With each phase NGOs pressured targeted retailers to acknowledge their responsibility for working conditions in their supply chains and to make changes in their policies and their suppliers' practices to improve working conditions and respect workers' rights. During the first phase retailers refused to extend responsibility for working conditions through their supply chains. After years of campaigning activists secured commitments from major retailers to improve working conditions in their supply chains. These retailers have adopted codes of conduct, and some have implemented internal auditing programs and joined MSIs. While these represent a departure from retailers' previous positions, these measures have not resulted in changes for large numbers of workers. Instead, targeted retailers have absorbed and deflected criticism from anti-sweatshop activists. The question is whether activists will be able to counter such actions and use retailers' acknowledgment and extension of responsibility to effect further change in the industry in the next phase of anti-sweatshop advocacy.

One of the main ways that the anti-sweatshop network influence targeted actors is by using web-based tools accessible even to relatively powerless organizations that have access to computers and tools to develop websites. NGOs' use of communication technologies links them into broader networks and amplifies their voices well beyond what their small staffs and relatively meager budgets would otherwise allow. Although they are not unique among for-profit or nonprofit entities in their use of these technologies, NGOs in the anti-sweatshop network derive substantial benefits from their access to them, particularly through the communication of information that fosters an identity among consumers as active political citizens. This information is particularly important because it is through this information that NGOs can enact communicative power and persuasion.

Chapter 3

Places and practices
of four anti-sweatshop NGOs

The concept of a network risks flattening distinctions among the various nodes or component actors. Therefore, this chapter looks in more depth at four NGOs: United Students Against Sweatshops, STITCH, FairWear, and the Clean Clothes Campaign (CCC). These NGOs are all involved in anti-sweatshop activism but from different local and national contexts. They also differ in their ideological origins, organizational structures, and targets of advocacy. By tracing some important differences among the NGOs, this chapter demonstrates how the histories and contexts of specific organizations affect their ability to engage in transnational anti-sweatshop advocacy.

This chapter also describes how activists seek to transform their own specific locations in the global North into platforms from which to participate in transnational advocacy. The emphasis on place may seem counter-intuitive at a time when globalization is interpreted as de-territorializing aspects of capital. Although capital is able to move quickly from one country to another, it is still very much tied to specific national and local contexts. Activists, on occasion, have been able to use this to their advantage. Although multinational corporations have become more mobile in recent years, they must still be located in places, no matter how temporary, and they must sell their goods in places. Even if the Internet is their main storefront, customers exist in specific locations beyond virtual reality. Activists seek to transform consumers' sense of place so that those places of consumption become spaces for political action that can reach across national borders.

This chapter offers insights into how the NGOs engage in forms of transnational, yet grounded, civic politics aimed at improving working conditions in the garment industry. The first section of the chapter introduces what Tarrow (2005) refers to as rooted cosmopolitanism, galvanizing support domestically for international causes. The second section compares the NGOs' modes and targets of advocacy, including their organizational structures; how the NGOs define targeted actors' responsibilities for improving conditions in the industry; and the NGOs' relationships to their audiences. Next, for each NGO the chapter outlines the relevant background and organizational structure and discusses the role of place and identities in the NGOs' campaigns. The last section of the chapter discusses how the NGOs enact rooted cosmopolitanism in their particular environments and how this affects their engagement with transnational anti-sweatshop advocacy. The chapter concludes with thoughts on how these connections to place and identity shape the NGOs' participation in transnational politics.

Rooted cosmopolitanism

The anti-sweatshop NGOs included in this chapter are connected to particular places. Yet place means much more than physical locale. According to Rocheleau, "place is neither a two-dimensional space nor a container, but is rather a nexus of relations . . . anchored in a given space and time" (2005, 77). Places can be understood as physical or geographic spaces, but also as a nexus of relations that shape the organizations' ability to engage in TANs and campaigns.

There are several ways to understand the relationship between networks and places. Castells describes this relationship through spaces of flows and spaces of place. He suggests that "the geography of the new history will not be made, after all, of the separation between places and flows, but out of the interface between places and flows and between cultures and social interests, both in the space of flows and in the space of places" (2005, 370). This interface provides a way to think about the fluidity and motion of places that are otherwise thought of as static.

Tarrow (2005) offers another way of conceptualizing relationships to place. He suggests that rooted cosmopolitans "mobilize domestic and international resources and opportunities to advance claims on behalf of external actors, against external opponents, or in favor of goals they hold in common with transnational allies" (Tarrow 2005, 29). Tarrow makes a distinction between transnational activists and other rooted cosmopolitans, which could include business executives, lawyers, and international civil servants among others. Transnational activists, he suggests, are "rooted in specific national contexts" and engaged in a transnational form of contentious politics allowing them to take advantage of the "expanded nodes of opportunity of a complex international society" (Tarrow 2005, 29). Although Tarrow's main analytical concern is rootedness to a domestic political sphere, he cites Cohen (1992) first using the term to convey a "multiplicity of roots and branches and that rests on the legitimacy of plural loyalties, of standing in many circles, but with common ground" (in Tarrow 2005, 42). It is this multiplicity of roots and plurality of loyalties that is evident in the activity of the NGOs analyzed here.

While my conceptualization of rooted cosmopolitanism owes a significant debt to Tarrow, it differs in important ways. First, these anti-sweatshop NGOs have a rootedness that may come from a sense of loyalty, but it can also be used strategically to develop a sense of solidarity and access points of leverage unavailable to outsiders. Second, my use of *rooted cosmopolitanism* includes rootedness to identity as well as to place. The anti-sweatshop NGOs employ various identity constructions as part of their transnational advocacy, which are described later in the chapter. Last, I include rootedness to issues and ideological origins. As shown in the previous chapter, anti-sweatshop NGOs often have their origins in one issue area and create alliances across places, identity, and issue areas in order to pursue common goals. *Rooted cosmopolitanism,* in this sense, can be understood as a grounding in one issue area, such as labor or women's movements, with *cosmopolitanism* referring to reaching out to broader issue areas. The NGOs do not use the term *rooted cosmopolitanism* for themselves. It is employed here to examine the ways that the anti-sweatshop NGOs' embeddedness in local and domestic politics influence their engagement in transnational advocacy.

Modes and targets of advocacy

The NGOs in this study differ in some basic but important ways. Table 3–1 shows the NGOs' primary modes of advocacy, issue orientation, and targets of advocacy. The NGOs share the goals of improving working conditions in the industry and ensuring workers' rights, yet they employ different modes of advocacy. The CCC, FairWear, and USAS aim to achieve those goals primarily through consumer campaigns. STITCH also participates in consumer campaigns, but not as its primary mode of advocacy, and only when the goal of the campaign is to strengthen local labor movements.

The anti-sweatshop NGOs differ in their ideological origins, often with multiple roots to various issues and social movements. These issue orientations reflect the origins of each NGO. For example, FairWear grew out of joint action between the Textile, Clothing and Footwear Union of Australia (TCFUA) and the Uniting Church. A group of participants in the AFL-CIO's Union Summer program founded USAS. The historical roots of an organization and its orientation influence how it defines problems in the industry and how it tries to effect change.

The NGOs also focus their advocacy efforts on different targets. The CCC and FairWear target retailers directly, while USAS targets universities, which then pressure retailers. STITCH targets unions and other NGOs in order to strengthen the anti-sweatshop network from within. These differing modes, issue orientation, and targets of advocacy are shown in Table 3–1.

In addition to these differences in mode, issue orientation, and targets, the NGOs differ in several other key ways. These include organizational structures, the ways that the NGOs define targeted actors' responsibilities, and the NGOs' relationships to their audiences. These are discussed in more detail below.

Organizational structure, scaling up, and diffusion

An organization's structure reflects and shapes its organizational culture. This can be seen in the level of hierarchy in an organization, its mission and values, and how it sustains itself. It can also influence how staff and volunteers share information and how decisions are made. The organizational structures of the anti-sweatshop NGOs also help explain how these small organizations, individually and collectively, are able to expand their impact beyond their local political arena.

Uvin, Jain, and Brown (2000, 1417) make a distinction between older and newer paradigms for expanding activities beyond the local level—what they call scaling up. In the old paradigm scaling up took place through NGOs becoming larger, more professionalized, and institutionalized. In the new paradigm NGOs scale up through "multiplication and main-streaming through spinning off organizations, letting go of innovations, creating alternative knowledge, and influencing other social actors." Describing a related process, Tarrow makes a distinction between diffusion as a horizontal process that has an initiator and an adopter, and scale shifting that "involves the coordination of episodes of contention on the part of larger collectivities against broader targets, new actors, and institutions at new levels of interaction" (2005, 122). Both processes are evident in the actions of the anti-sweatshop NGOs, which use a variety of methods to expand the reach of their activities beyond localized actions.

Organization	Primary mode	Issue orientation	Target of advocacy
CCC	Consumer campaigns	Labor/women	Retailers Government procurement
FairWear	Consumer campaigns Labeling and certification	Labor/religious	Government regulation and procurement Retailers
STITCH	Cross-border solidarity Consumer campaigns	Women/labor	Unions NGOs Retailers/manufacturers
USAS	Consumer campaigns	Labor	Universities ⟶ Retailers

Table 3–1. Modes of transnational advocacy

In personal interviews staff at each of the case study NGOs talked about the constraints associated with operating on a limited budget, yet none of them mentioned the desire to expand by becoming larger. For example, FairWear campaigners noted the desire to remain decentralized, linking autonomous nodes without attempting to control or coordinate local campaigns (Lynch, personal communication, February 3, 2009). In the groups studied diffusion and scaling up occur within organizations as well as across organizations in the anti-sweatshop network.

Defining targeted actors' responsibilities

Anti-sweatshop NGOs aim to ensure workers' rights to collective bargaining and freedom of association. Kuper states: "In a world of severe deprivation, in which absolute poverty and violence blight the lives of billions of people, it is relatively uncontentious to insist that someone must do something. It is far more difficult, both conceptually and politically, to identify particular agents who are able and obliged—let alone willing—to relieve such suffering" (2005, x). The case study organizations have all adopted the language of rights; however, they differ in their approach to defining which actors are responsible for delivering on those rights.

One way of thinking about how anti-sweatshop NGOs define target actors' responsibilities in the garment industry is through what Young refers to as political responsibility. Young distinguishes political responsibility from liability models of responsibility that assign blame for injustices. She argues that political responsibility does not assume direct blame, but rather acknowledges the obligations from participating in social structures that contribute to social injustices. She uses political responsibility to justify actions taken by Western activists in the anti-sweatshop network. Young suggests that taking responsibility for sweatshop conditions in other parts of the world involves "recognizing a shared responsibility, persuading others that they share it as well, and organizing forms of collective action designed to change the incentive structures, alter the constraints, or shift the distribution of benefits in continuing to buy and sell goods manufactured by superexploited workers" (2004, 382–83).

Young notes that many political philosophers "reject the idea of such transnational responsibilities, believing that the requirement to rectify injustice toward others extends only to those who live within the same political jurisdiction and/or share a sense of common national membership" (2004, 371). In contrast, she argues that political responsibility is not limited to those who share political boundaries. In relation to the garment industry she argues that consumers are participating in the social structures that allow, and even facilitate, those conditions to exist by purchasing goods produced in sweatshops.

While each of the anti-sweatshop NGOs invokes workers' rights, they differ in their approach to "who bears counterpart obligations to deliver on those rights" (Kuper 2005, ix). Some of the claims are based on social connections, while others rely on economic, political, or moral arguments to assign responsibilities. These arguments, discussed later in this chapter in relation to the case studies, are designed to persuade consumers, retailers, manufacturers, and governments to take action to ameliorate the poor working conditions in the industry.

Relationships to audiences

The NGOs also differ in how they choose to mobilize different audiences. I use the term *audience* to refer to the people who these Northern-based NGOs aim to mobilize in one form or another in order to exert pressure on retailers, universities, or other targets. The NGOs request a variety of actions from their audiences, including signing petitions, sending letters or emails, and making phone calls to elected officials or corporate executives, attending events and protests, and providing tool kits to launch local campaigns to influence local governments. Some of the NGOs define their audiences narrowly, while others are more general in their appeals. The idea is that these audiences will then act as points of leverage in transnational advocacy campaigns. The extent to which those actions are aimed at specific groups reflects the type of leverage they have with targeted actors. It also reflects the extent to which their rootedness to specific places and groups of people can be expanded in support of a transnational cause.

The NGOs also vary in their demands. While they share common goals, some NGOs pressure retailers to take specific steps such as adopting a code of conduct or joining a multi-stakeholder initiative. Other NGOs are less specific in their demands, believing that the depth and complexity of labor abuses in the industry cannot be solved with retailers making piecemeal policy changes. NGOs' relationships to their audiences and NGOs' demands on targeted actors, are discussed with regard to the case studies later in the chapter.

The following section discusses how rooted cosmopolitanism relates to each NGO and the factors that influence its ability to engage in transnational advocacy. These include material aspects, such as organizational structure and physical space, as well as the ideational elements of how each organization defines targeted actors' responsibilities for improving conditions in the industry. These factors shape their participation in the anti-sweatshop network and their ability to advocate effectively for improvements in the industry. The section on each NGO contains two parts: background and organizational structure, and a discussion of place and identities in the NGO's campaigns. The purpose is to show how NGOs use their particular political positions and geographic locations in different ways to engage in transnational anti-sweatshop advocacy.

Case studies

USAS

Background and organizational structure

In 1997 a group of university students attending Union Summer, sponsored by the AFL-CIO, developed a project to focus on ensuring the ethical production of university-licensed apparel. The Union Summer initiative was part of a broader transformation of the AFL-CIO in a bid to expand the scope of the U.S. labor movement, as numbers of union members were at an all-time low (Ross 2004b, 195). By 1999 students on fifty campuses were involved, and USAS was born. By 2007, USAS had active chapters on over two hundred campuses throughout the United States.

For those outside the United States the system of university apparel may seem like an unusual target. Yet it makes up 1 percent of the massive US$2.5 billion apparel market. Universities license companies to use their logos on clothing. In turn, the company pays the university between 7.5 and 8 percent of the revenue (Ross 2004a, 289). This can mean significant funding for universities, particularly those with high-profile athletic teams that fuel demand for clothing bearing the university's name. Logos are also valuable symbols. For many students and alumni university logos represent a sense of solidarity, community, and school spirit. Logos connote a sense of belonging, linking students, staff, and alumni across time and space (Eitzen 2006, 34). By wearing clothing, scarves, and pins bearing the school emblem, students and fans identify with each other and also identify against supporters of the opposing team or university.

When USAS began campaigning in the late 1990s, it focused on getting retailers to disclose where their goods were produced. Activists argued that there was no way that codes of conduct could be monitored if factory locations were unknown. Targeted companies and universities claimed that factory locations were confidential, akin to trade secrets. Although most companies are still reluctant to identify where their clothing is made, factory disclosure has become more common in recent years among companies producing for the university apparel market. For example, a University of Michigan database includes a list of two thousand factories producing University of Michigan branded goods and apparel (Ross 2004a, 291). Due to pressure from students, universities and retailers have begun to make their supply chains more transparent.

At the same time that the students began their campaigns across university campuses, U.S. president Bill Clinton's administration convened a working group called the Apparel Industry Partnership. This group eventually became the Fair Labor Association (FLA). It included industry representatives as well as union and NGO representatives. Many of the unions involved at the beginning later rejected the legitimacy of the FLA. They argued that it gave too much sway to garment industry executives. They also claimed that the FLA ignored some of the key demands of activists, including provisions for a living wage, factory disclosure, and independent monitoring.

USAS continues to pressure universities to reject the FLA and to join the WRC. USAS helped found the WRC and holds five seats on its board of directors. Unlike the FLA, the WRC does not include industry representatives as members, and it calls for the inclusion of a living wage and independent monitoring in its code. As of April 2010, 186 colleges and universities were members of the WRC. Although many university administrators joined the WRC reluctantly, it has subsequently become an important forum in which activists can hold universities accountable for their licensing contracts. The fact that the WRC has endured despite competition from the more industry-friendly FLA is evidence of the power of student protests in maintaining pressure on university administrators.

USAS focuses its claims primarily on university administrators, urging them to use their leverage to change policies and practices of the sportswear companies that license university apparel. USAS has not sought a greater regulatory role for the state or pressed for greater involvement of IGOs in regulating industry. This emphasis on universities is a function of USAS's ideological origins and its organizational structure, rooted in university campuses.

The structure of USAS is worth noting because of its unique form and its emphasis on local autonomy, thereby ensuring the specificity of activists' rootedness in place. It consists of four paid staff members in Washington DC and two hundred affiliated groups on university campuses throughout the country. The organization is highly decentralized; local affiliates have significant autonomy. Regional coordinators work with campus representatives in their area, all of whom are volunteers. National and regional conferences are held throughout the year for activists to share ideas, develop strategies, and participate in leadership development and training.

The regional coordinators maintain blogs on the USAS website that include announcements of campaign victories, lists of upcoming events, and discussions about ways to improve or expand campaigns. For example, the Northeast regional blog includes a section on how to build successful coalitions, facilitate a workshop, raise funds, simulate a sweatshop, and use the media. Each of these is designed for students on other campuses to use in their own campaigns. In addition to these regional coordinators, which organize around geographic spaces, four identity-based caucuses organize around notions of historically disempowered identities. The four identity-based caucuses identified on the USAS website in 2007 are "womyn-genderqueer, queer, people of color, and working class." The identity-based blogs focus on building solidarity across racial, gender, and class lines and on ensuring that USAS is responding to the needs of students. The identity-based blogs include questions for campus organizers to use in their own groups in order to get participants talking about their life experiences and activism. Student activists share their thoughts, concerns, and ideas about their particular identity affiliation either as a member of the stated group or as an ally, and discuss the implications for their involvement in the labor movement.

This attention to the politics of difference is a central part of USAS's organizing and a key part of how USAS frames its work as part of the labor movement and as part of the broader global justice movement. USAS organizer Zack Knorr explained in an interview, "If we are going to be an organization that is fighting classism, that is fighting racism, that is fighting sexism, that is fighting heterosexism, then we need to make sure that our organization is structured in a way so that we do not perpetuate the same systems of oppression" (Knorr, personal communication, January 18, 2007). USAS invokes a global justice frame, positioning itself within broader struggles against oppression.

In order to ensure that it remains a student-run organization, USAS employees hold their position for only two years. This bucks the trend of many NGOs moving toward a more professionalized, permanent staff. When asked about the difficulties of constantly changing staff, Knorr responded, "While it is important that we keep an institutional memory, it is also important that we are dynamic enough to change with our student base" (Knorr, personal communication, January 18, 2007). The paid staff positions, along with the chapters on university campuses, act as a learning ground for future activists and NGO staff.

USAS organizers conceive of their work as leadership development; the rotation of staff is part of this development. USAS's goal of cultivating new leaders in the U.S. labor movement seems to be working. Many of the people under thirty years old who are employed in anti-sweatshop NGOs and unions in the United States were first involved with USAS on their university campus. For example, UNITE HERE, the WRC, and the International Labor Rights Forum (ILRF) all include former USAS activists on staff (Dirnbach, personal communication, January 12, 2007; Steffan, personal communication, January 19, 2007; Tocco, personal communication, January 19, 2007). Katie Quan credits USAS with bringing a new generation of activists into the labor movement in the United States (Quan, personal communication, December 12, 2008).

While distinctly oriented toward mobilizing North American students, USAS has begun to make connections with other university campus–based movements in recent years. This includes Students and Scholars Against Corporate Misbehaviour in Hong Kong and students at York University in England. In each of these locations students share aspects of USAS's organizing model but have adapted it to their local conditions.

Place and identity

In each campaign the students are grounded in the local context and use symbols of their university campuses. This includes the use of university mascots in campaign materials. For example, the University of Houston anti-sweatshop student group produced banners with the school's mascot, a cougar with a tear in its eye, sewing a tee-shirt. By using mascots, university logos, and familiar slogans or jokes, the students create a sense of belonging and solidarity with other students of that particular university. The students then seek to use that position to pressure university administrators to change university policy.

USAS's organizing efforts focus on the physical space of university campuses as well as the identities of organizers as students with a connection to their universities. This call for students to use their positions on university campuses to push for change in the industry was seen on the USAS's 2007 homepage. It proclaimed:

> We believe that university standards should be brought in line with those of its students, who demand that their school's logo is emblazoned on clothing made in decent working conditions. We have fought for these beliefs by demanding that our universities adopt

ethically and legally strong codes of conduct, full public disclosure of company information and truly independent verification systems to ensure that sweatshop conditions are not happening. Ultimately, we are using our power as students to affect the larger industry that thrives on sweatshops.

The ways that students' identities—and their connections to place—are used in campaigns is evident in how students frame their own actions on university campuses. For example, in 2008 students at the University of North Carolina (UNC) organized a sit-in to pressure university administrators to commit to better working conditions in the factories where UNC apparel was produced. The students occupied the university president's office for three weeks. According to the UNC Student Action with Workers website, the sit-in ended when the students were arrested. Other students at Appalachian State, Pennsylvania State, and the University of Montana were also arrested for staging sit-ins on their campuses.

One of the UNC students, Salma Mirza, said in a press release printed on the group's website, "Even though we have finals this week, we feel its important to hold UNC to its ideals and mission as the university of the people." In this statement Mirza uses the protesters' identities as UNC students to make demands on UNC administrators. The students used the language of accountability in their campaigns, drawing attention to the gap between the university's stated commitments and its practices. The students also juxtaposed the university's stated values with the university's role in supporting poor working conditions in the garment industry.

Many of the USAS chapters also aim to highlight the connections between garment workers in the global South and workers on North American university campuses. Numerous campus groups, including the students at UNC, are involved in campaigns to improve wages and conditions for janitorial and food-service employees on their campuses. The campaigns to support campus workers seek to establish codes of conduct that would ensure workers on university campuses could join unions and bargain collectively. These campaigns also aim to get universities to adopt living-wage policies, guaranteeing a wage higher than the legal minimum wage. These campaigns link local struggles on university campuses with transnational ones targeting the garment industry. With both types of campaigns students are using their strategic position within universities to pressure university administrators to adopt policies to benefit workers.

STITCH

Background and organizational structure

In 1998 a delegation of U.S. union women traveled to Guatemala. Their trip was organized by the U.S. Labor Education in the Americas Project (USLEAP), formerly the U.S. Guatemala Labor Education Project. One result of their journey was the creation of STITCH, which, according to its website in 2007, aims to

> exchange strategies on how to fight for economic justice in the workplace. .... STITCH equips women with the essential skills through trainings and educational tools, and in the process, builds lasting relationships with women across the two regions, further empowering women in the labor movement. STITCH also ensures women's voices are heard in global debates and discussions on issues that impact them: globalization, trade agreements, immigration policy, and global labor standards.

STITCH's activities are aimed at building solidarity among women workers in the United States and Central America. Programs include workshops and training courses for union women in Central America, the development of a leadership manual, education and awareness raising in the United States, and sending delegations of women from the United States to Central America and from Central America to the United States. Other projects, according to its website, include a project that documents how women workers have been affected by the global economy "to build solidarity and to ensure their voices are heard across borders."

Unlike USAS, STITCH does engage in some limited actions to influence the state. For example, STITCH joined unionists, farmers, and development organizations across Latin America and the United States in opposing the Dominican Republic–Central American Free Trade Agreement (DR-CAFTA). STITCH urged its supporters to contact their representatives in the U.S. Congress to vote against the bill. Despite their efforts Congress approved DR-CAFTA by a slight margin in 2005. STITCH's opposition to DR-CAFTA was based on its connections to women workers in both the United States and Central America and its basis in feminism, arguing that such an agreement would place additional pressure on women's reproductive and productive labor.

Over the years STITCH organizers came to realize that the North-South exchanges between North and Central American women were less productive than South-South exchanges among Central American women (Myers, personal communication, January 5, 2007). This is because the political environments in which unions operate are vastly different in the United States and Central America. Political and economic situations vary across (and within) Central American countries but were found to be similar enough for women to transfer practices and strategies across both national and sectoral borders. For example, STITCH organized a workshop for Honduran women in an established textile union to train women in Guatemala. STITCH also organized training for women across sectors. For example, women in the banana sector conducted workshops for women in the textile sector. This indicates STITCH's understanding of place as affecting the different identities of women workers across Central America and in the United States, and among women within different sectors of the labor movement. Differences among women are important, but STITCH organizers believe that the struggle of women workers can unite and strengthen their causes.

STITCH's work is facilitated by the organization's structure, which differs from the other case-study NGOs. It has two offices, one located in Washington DC and the other in Guatemala City. Maintaining these two offices facilitates communication among staff, volunteers, and workers in both countries. STITCH's Washington DC office is housed within St. Stephen and the Incarnation Episcopal Church, along with many other community organizations that provide services to the local low-income community. These NGOs provide a wide range of services, including a play group for homeless children and a community radio station, as well as financial and emotional support for low-income senior citizens. By adopting this physical office location within St. Stephen's church, STITCH enhances its connections with local communities while engaged in its own transnational and domestic advocacy on behalf of women workers.

Place and identity

Although many of the other NGOs demonstrate an awareness of the gendered aspects of the garment industry, STITCH embraces the most explicitly feminist perspective of the anti-sweatshop NGOs. STITCH organizers recognize that women in Central America and the United States face similar issues relating to dual roles of paid and unpaid work, sexism within workplaces, and sexism within the union movement. Beth Myers, executive director of STITCH, said in an interview that other anti-sweatshop campaigners often ignore this last point. STITCH's role is not only to challenge corporations and their mistreatment of women workers, she said, but also to challenge "our friends within the movements themselves" (Myers, personal communication, January 5, 2007). In addition to challenging those within the movement, STITCH aims to educate those in the broader development sector about the labor movement and the necessity of supporting workers' rights to organize. Myers considers STITCH's work to be at the intersection of three movements: the labor movement, the women's rights movements, and the international development NGOs, each of which tends to ignore the significance of the other two. For example, she suggests that there are some IGOs that are "vaguely supportive of labor rights" but unaware of the important role that labor unions can play. She views STITCH's role as educating each of these groups of allies and working as a bridge between them (Myers, personal communication, January 5, 2007). With its roots in feminism, STITCH brings feminist analysis and perspectives to each of these other areas.

STITCH's emphasis on supporting unions and of women's places within unions is based on its belief in the "transformative power of having a collective voice" (Myers, personal communication, January 5, 2007). Activists have long struggled with how to create such a collective identity and voice. Gender and development scholarship presents several ways of approaching the use of particular identities as the basis for, or obstacles to, achieving transnational solidarity. In the 1970s and 1980s, women's movements in the United States and Europe called for global sisterhood with a reliance on the category of woman as the basis for solidarity. Many feminists from the global South, as well as women of color in the North, found the notion of global sisterhood unconvincing because the movement consisted largely of white, middle-class women pursuing issues that were most relevant to them. Many of these issues differed significantly from those facing black women in the North and women in the global South (Mohanty 2003). Activists and scholars developed other strategies for dealing with the question of identities and transnational solidarity ranging from strategic essentialism (Udayagiri 1995) to identities based on common interests as opposed to common experiences (Mohanty 2003), to those based on intersectionality, which recognizes the relationship among different identities (Symington 2004). All of these are ways to reconcile the groundedness of identities without being reduced to them. This is a fundamental part of rooted cosmopolitanism whereby actors embrace particular identities or local contexts from which to engage in transnational advocacy.

STITCH engages in domestic campaigns in addition to its transnational campaigns. In particular, STITCH advocates on behalf of immigrant women workers in the United States. It recently published a report, "The Other Immigrants/Las Otras Inmigrantes," to educate activists about women workers from Central America working in the United States so that the U.S. labor movement could better meet the needs of these women (STITCH 2008). The report was also designed to contribute to more visibility and leadership roles for these women workers. The image on the cover of the report shows two women with an American flag held tightly around their shoulders alongside a photograph of another woman holding an American flag. The images evoke U.S. patriotism and a sense of belonging for women workers from Central America, who are often marginalized and treated as outsiders in the United States. By using national symbols like the flag on the cover and a watermark of the Statue of Liberty inside, the report positions women workers from Central America in the United States as rightful members of the American working class. It may also reveal an attempt to appeal to nationalistic sentiment among activists and organizers in the American labor movement and to hold the U.S. movement accountable to America's inclusive ideals.

FairWear

Background and organizational structure

Founded in 1996, FairWear grew out of a campaign launched by the TCFUA and the Uniting Church to address exploitation of home-based workers or outworkers, as they are known in Australia. FairWear aims to encourage retailers to register with Ethical Clothing Australia (described later in this section), educate consumers about ethical shopping, lobby the government to ratify relevant ILO conventions, and urge the Australian government to implement social clauses in trade agreements. In addition to pressuring retailers and educating consumers, FairWear emphasizes the responsibilities of the state as a protector of workers' rights.

FairWear's institutional history represents a unique alliance between religious organizations and the labor movement. In 1995 a committee of church and union representatives produced a report, "The Hidden Cost of Fashion" that documented abuse of homeworkers in Australia (TCFUA 1995). The report generated significant media attention on homeworkers and led to a 1996 Senate inquiry. Churches and community groups were able to mobilize a different group of supporters from their allies in the union. FairWear's roots in the Australian labor movement meant that it had to find ways to balance support for domestic workers with support for garment workers overseas.

One of the main goals of FairWear's domestic campaign is to encourage retailers to register with Ethical Clothing Australia. In 1997 union and industry representatives created the Homeworkers Code of Practice (which later became Ethical Clothing Australia in 2010). It was designed to enable greater transparency in the garment industry by demanding that signatories disclose their suppliers and provide evidence of legal requirements being met in terms of wages, superannuation, and hours worked. By pressuring retailers to register with Ethical Clothing Australia, labor advocates are able to formalize the sense of responsibility retailers have for working conditions in their supply chains and to hold companies to their stated commitments. After a company receives accreditation from Ethical Clothing Australia, it is permitted to sew the Ethical Clothing Australia label into its clothing (previously known as the No Sweat Shop label).

FairWear's Shop of Shame campaign illustrates the complementary roles of FairWear and the TCFUA in pressuring targeted businesses to change their policies and register with what was then called the Homeworkers Code of Practice. FairWear held protests and rallies in front of targeted businesses at the same time that the TCFUA filed lawsuits against companies that breached the Federal Clothing Trades Award Contract and Outwork clause. Combining legal action from the union with public protest coordinated by FairWear proved to be an effective strategy, according to the group's website, resulting in several companies signing the Homeworkers Code of Practice on the eve of scheduled rallies. In this case FairWear activists used retailers' shops to launch their campaigns. The placards and signs appropriated store logos, linking these symbols to the exploitation of homeworkers. The Homeworkers Code of Practice (now Ethical Clothing Australia) is more powerful than standard codes of conduct, which are often vague and non-binding. While still voluntary, accreditation with Ethical Clothing Australia allows the TCFUA to monitor compliance and has the threat of legal action if signatories do not meet award conditions.

FairWear campaigns use street performances, petitions, and mock fashion shows in addition to circulating emails and online petitions in order to educate consumers about the conditions under which garments are produced. FairWear also produces materials for students to pressure their schools to purchase garments made from manufacturers who have signed the code. Educational materials include the FairWear Action Kit and the documentary *Twenty Pieces: Outworkers Tell the Real Fashion Story* (Pederick and Pederick 1998). All of these are tools that FairWear activists use to educate the public and apply pressure to targeted retailers.

Since the mid-1990s FairWear has grown in terms of scope but has purposefully remained small and decentralized. It is made up of autonomous groups throughout Australia, mainly in Victoria, New South Wales, and South Australia. In each state FairWear includes participation from community organizations, churches, and unions. The FairWear website provides resources and encourages local groups to use the campaign materials to act in their own localized ways. Annie Delaney, former outwork project officer with the TCFUA and one of the founders of FairWear, spoke of the decentralized nature of FairWear:

> We do not wish to control the members of the campaign; they are free to act in whatever way they believe advances the rights of homebased workers. Provided that members are committed to the stated aims of the campaign, we welcome diversity. This is one of the strengths of the FairWear campaign. Unity comes from a commitment to home based workers and the pressing need to improve their conditions. (cited in Nash 2001, 95)

FairWear's organizational structure includes two offices run by paid staff, with decentralized coordination between the two. Volunteer-driven chapters exist in other states. FairWear staff includes two part-time employees in Victoria and one part-time employee in New South Wales. The structure of the organization, with low overhead costs, minimal institutionalization, and a high level of decentralization, is part of the strategic vision of FairWear.

Institutional linkages are crucial for the organization's success. The FairWear office in Victoria is located within the administrative offices of the Uniting Church, and the FairWear office in New South Wales shares an office with the NGO Asian Women at Work. The Victoria chapter also works closely with the TCFUA. NGO and union alliances provide coordinated actions and an avenue to reach out to workers. For example, a group of outworker advocates, organized through Asian Women at Work, advise FairWear staff in New South Wales, identify targeted retailers, and speak at public events (Lynch, personal communication, February 3, 2009). FairWear also works closely with Oxfam Australia, which generates research on sweatshops in Asia and conducts public-awareness campaigns on sweatshop issues.

Place and identity

In recent years FairWear expanded from primarily focusing on clothing produced within Australia by homeworkers to addressing exploitation in the industry by Australian companies sourcing overseas. Daisy Gardener, FairWear coordinator, explained its "growing commitment to making

Australian companies responsible for the international supply chain as well as their workers in Australia" (Gardener, personal communication, November 21, 2006). FairWear organizers noticed a growing public awareness of sweatshop conditions in Asia due to media coverage in the late 1990s and wanted to link issues facing homeworkers in Australia to workers in factories throughout the global South (Gardener, personal communication, November 21, 2006). FairWear seeks to harness existing awareness of sweatshop conditions and mobilize Australians to pressure Australian-owned companies on conditions in their factories and supply chains.

FairWear's approach to the construction of the places of factory and home differs from other campaigns that have attempted to move home-based production into factories, where labor conditions can more easily be regulated (Prugl 1999). Through its work with homeworkers, FairWear and the TCFUA have realized that many homeworkers, especially women with children, value being able to continue working in their homes (Spyrou, personal communication, November 20, 2006). Working in the home can provide a site of independence and flexibility, but it can also lead to feelings of intense isolation. The majority of outworkers in Australia are first-generation immigrants from Vietnam and China. In addition to providing English-language classes and leadership development, TCFUA and FairWear sponsor a Vietnamese-language community radio program for outworkers in order to raise awareness about their rights and provide links with other women working in their homes. FairWear's domestic advocacy is focused primarily on this transnational workforce, which has been shaped by flows of immigration, social exclusion of migrant communities, and the changing nature of the garment industry. It aims to link this domestic focus with its transnational campaigns aimed at benefiting garment workers outside Australia.

Clean Clothes Campaign

Background and organizational structure

The CCC is a prominent node in the anti-sweatshop network. According to its 2006 homepage, its aims are to "improve working conditions and to empower workers in the global garment industry, in order to end the oppression, exploitation and abuse of workers in this industry, most of whom are women." Its goals have remained consistent since Dutch activists interested in labor and feminist issues founded the CCC in the late 1980s. The early campaigns targeted Dutch retailers with factories in Asia.

The CCC operates through four main strategies: raising awareness, pressuring companies, bolstering solidarity, and using legal approaches. The CCC educates consumers about the global garment industry through public demonstrations, the media, and the CCC website. The emphasis on consumers is clear from the website, which states, "above all the CCC is a consumer campaign—its strength comes from consumer power." A 2008 report described the CCC as "a network operating in the spaces of consumption" (Merk 2008a, 15). CCC also employs a strategy that focuses on local governments as a site of consumer politics. For example, the CCC launched an initiative called Clean Clothes Communities, similar to SweatFree Communities in the United States. The program urges local governments to enact ordinances to ensure that their procurement policies require all goods and services purchased by the government to be produced under "sweat-free" conditions.

A key aspect of CCC's work is providing support to labor advocates in the global South. One mechanism that it uses to respond to Southern unions and NGOs is its urgent appeals process. The CCC receives requests from labor activists regarding a specific claim, verifies the claim, and then distributes it to its allies in the United States and Australia to disseminate among their own networks. CCC staff members acknowledge that addressing labor violations like those highlighted in its urgent appeals is not necessarily going to change systemic violations, but the appeals are important to the people involved, and it is important for this international coalition to respond to the direct needs and desires of Southern labor activists (Merk, personal communication, February 16, 2007). In other words, it is a way for the CCC agenda clearly to be informed by labor activists working directly with garment workers.

Although the CCC is mainly focused on European retailers, it is also a clearinghouse for the whole anti-sweatshop network. The CCC is one of the most densely connected NGOs in the network, linked to dozens of other actors in the network. Other anti-sweatshop organizations such as the Maquila Solidarity Network, FairWear, and Oxfam Australia regularly distribute CCC materials and support CCC's urgent appeals.

The initial group of activists has grown since the 1980s to include over two hundred NGOs and unions in fourteen countries. The international secretariat in Amsterdam coordinates the chapters, which are fairly autonomous. The fifteen chapters (North and South Belgium account for the additional chapter) are themselves coalitions of NGOs and unions.

This structure means that each chapter in the CCC network is itself a network and has distinct qualities based on local politics and the make-up of the activists involved. Esther de Haan, one of the founding members of the CCC, said of the organization's structure:

> We modelled the organisation on the anti-apartheid campaign that put pressure on Shell to withdraw from South Africa: a neat campaign with a broad support base, targeting one company, and with a coalition structure. While the participating groups formed a legal body, the campaign as such was collective property, open to everybody. (cited in Sluiter 2009, 18)

The CCC has grown substantially since then, but it maintains a similar model of decentralized coordination among distinct organizations that target the same companies.

Place and identity

The CCC demonstrates the most cosmopolitan views of the anti-sweatshop NGOs. Although each CCC chapter includes targeting companies based in that particular country, each chapter also engages in campaigns reaching across national borders. The CCC does not advocate buying Dutch-made goods or even buying European-made products. Its focus is on supporting workers in the global garment industry including, but not limited to, workers in Europe.[1] This commitment appears in the first point in the CCC's principles, stated on its website, which reads:

> All workers—regardless of sex, age, country of origin, legal status, employment status or location, or any other basis—have a right to good and safe working conditions, where they can exercise their fundamental rights to associate freely and bargain collectively, and earn a living wage, which allows them to live in dignity.

This same document lays out the responsibilities of workers, consumers, governments, and companies to improve the industry. First, it states that workers take the lead in their own organizing. Second, it says that the public can and should take action. It does not include specific actions other than clearly stating that the CCC does not support boycotts. Third, it states that national governments should enforce labor laws based on ILO standards. Fourth, it states that the sporting-goods industries have a responsibility to ensure good labor practices throughout the industry. It goes on to detail specific responsibilities for brand-name garment companies, including developing and implementing codes of conduct, joining multi-stakeholder initiatives, and signing collective framework agreements. Last, it states that trade unions and NGOs should cooperate locally, nationally, and internationally to "improve conditions in the garment and sports shoe industries and facilitate worker empowerment, without resorting to protectionism." This emphasis on collective responsibility and the call to avoid protectionism demonstrate the CCC's embodiment of cosmopolitan values.

The CCC's principal vehicle to communicate with its supporters, consumers, and the media is its website. In addition to reports exposing labor abuses in garment supply chains, the website includes photographs of workers' protests and activists leafleting outside retail shops throughout Europe. One image reproduced on a 2008 CCC web page is of a painting on the side of a building in Islington, England. The image, an emplaced critique by guerrilla artist Banksy, depicts two children, a boy and a girl, standing at attention before a flagpole, while a third child raises the flag. Rather than a national flag, however, as one would expect from the long-standing rituals of nationalistic piety, the children gaze up at a plastic Tesco bag flapping in the wind. By appropriating the public space of buildings and sidewalks, the art piece critiques both nationalistic rituals and the threat that TNCs pose by replacing those rituals of obedience and allegiance to a brand.

The photograph of Banksy's painting was both communicative and productive. It communicated how specific people and artists make statements in and from their particular communities—in this case, a street in Islington. But its reproduction on the web helped translate those place-based experiences to the CCC website visitors, whose own identities are shaped and influenced by their interaction with the art pieces and the CCC itself. The pieces are therefore both rooted in the time and place of their making but become concretely cosmopolitan in their open-ended transmission and reception.

The production of the image also illustrates the movement between multiple nodes in the anti-sweatshop network, connecting the artist with the photographer who then posted the image on Flickr, where CCC activists acquired the image and posted it on the CCC website. The CCC shared the image with an international audience, using it to illustrate its Better Bargain campaign, which aims to change the sourcing practices of large discount retailers. The original place of the artwork is a street in England, but then anti-sweatshop activists appropriated, shared, and distributed it to a wider audience, connecting the nodes in the anti-sweatshop network and ultimately multiplying and broadening its reach.

Discussion

The NGOs differ in their organizational structures, how they define targeted actors' responsibilities, and their relationships with their audiences. The anti-sweatshop NGOs' organizational structures mirror the dense, decentralized structure of the broader anti-sweatshop network. This is especially true of the CCC, FairWear, and USAS. These organizations rely on chapters as collections of autonomous nodes, loosely coordinated by a secretariat. STITCH's structure is slightly different; it is based on coordination between two small offices, without using chapters to replicate and diffuse its campaigns.

There are ideological and practical reasons for the anti-sweatshop NGOs' organizational structures mimicking the structure of the network. Many of the activists are committed to decentralized, non-hierarchical structures as part of an ideological commitment to power sharing and cooperative decision making. As Esther de Haan explained, she and other founding members of the CCC wanted to have the campaign open to everyone, using a coalition structure, with all parties targeting the same company (Sluiter 2009). Decentralized structures of autonomous nodes also suit the anti-sweatshop NGOs for practical reasons. With few resources the NGOs are unable to staff and coordinate large groups of people. Instead, they disseminate resources for others to apply in their local contexts. FairWear does this with the action kits and education materials on its website. USAS diffuses its campaigns by establishing chapters on university campuses, which are coordinated regionally, and by its identity-based caucuses. Students then use the symbols and language of their particular university to pressure university administrators to join the WRC. This structure gives anti-sweatshop activists significant flexibility; chapters can adapt strategies to their particular location.

The NGOs also vary in terms of which actors they target (such as retailers, universities, governments) and how they define targeted actors' responsibilities in the industry. STITCH views strengthening labor movements as the main site of struggle, as opposed to seeking greater responsibility from retailers or the state in securing workers' rights. Although FairWear works directly with garment workers at times, its advocacy strategies focus on the state—and to a lesser extent on retailers and manufacturers—as the guarantor of workers' rights. USAS and the CCC are more closely aligned in their focus on retailers, and they highlight the political responsibility of consumers and the leverage of consumers to pressure retailers to take responsibility for working conditions in their supply chains. However, USAS and CCC differ in their approaches. CCC focuses on a broad base of consumers throughout Europe, relying on name recognition of brands to mobilize supporters, while USAS appeals to a narrowly defined base of supporters. USAS approaches students because they occupy a unique position as consumers of logoed apparel and as consumers of university education. This extends political responsibility to students, who can then pressure universities and retailers that have a direct economic relationship to exploitative conditions in the garment industry. Students have a specific relationship to universities, which enter into licensing contracts with retailers. This relationship gives students leverage to apply pressure to university administrators.

STITCH also appeals to a narrower audience of women workers and those interested in empowering women in the labor movement. FairWear and the CCC cast a broader net, including anyone concerned with labor rights. Their audiences have some leverage as consumers and also as citizens of Australia and European countries, but for the most part these audiences do not have specific leverage like that of the university students targeting university administrators.

Activists sometimes make broad demands without a specific prescription. This is the case with the CCC's Better Bargain campaign. The aims of the campaign are to improve labor standards implementation, push for a living wage, improve purchasing practices, and support worker organizing (Hearson 2009). The campaign includes ways that companies can begin to achieve these goals broadly, without offering companies specific actions they can take to alleviate pressure from campaigners. In other cases activists demand that universities take a specific course of action, such as joining the WRC. FairWear asks retailers to register with Ethical Clothing Australia. There are costs and benefits to each approach. By making specific demands, universities and retailers are more likely to consent. However, in order to gain their engagement, activists' demands must often be scaled back, reflecting more modest goals.

Table 3–2 shows how the anti-sweatshop NGOs differ in their relationships to targeted actors and their audiences. It illustrates (1) how broadly or narrowly activists define their audiences; and (2) the extent to which activists make demands on targeted actors specifying clear actions (such as joining a multi-stakeholder initiative or adopting a code of conduct, implying that if that action is met, the campaign will cease). The extent to which an NGO defines its audience and articulates specific demands influences the organization's ability to utilize specific points of leverage.

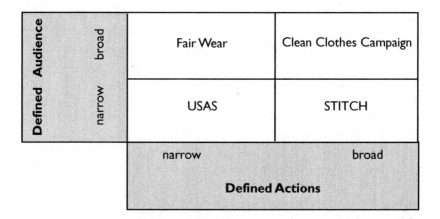

Defined Audience	broad	Fair Wear	Clean Clothes Campaign
	narrow	USAS	STITCH
		narrow	broad
		Defined Actions	

Table 3–2. Audience and actions

Rooted cosmopolitanism operates in slightly different ways within each of the NGOs as they seek to balance the organization's mission and commitment to transnational advocacy with the needs and desires of specific audiences. The two organizations with broadly defined audiences, FairWear and CCC, operate on similar models. The staffs of these organizations provide resources and information that others then tailor to their local context. The main difference is that the CCC is larger and more institutionalized than FairWear. This means that CCC's nationally based campaigns already have networks in place to activate campaigns. FairWear relies on a smaller, diffuse group of volunteers, mainly through its contacts with NGOs, students, churches, and unions. With each of these strategies, the NGOs construct campaign messages to mobilize particular audiences, with varying degrees of success.

Conclusion

This chapter expanded Tarrow's concept of rooted cosmopolitanism to include rootedness to place as a strategy, rootedness to identity, and rootedness to issues. An example of rootedness to a place as strategy was evident in the USAS campaign at the University of North Carolina, where students strategically used their affiliation with the university to pressure its university administrators to join the WRC. STITCH provides an example of rootedness to identity because women are encouraged to develop a sense of solidarity across national borders and across sectoral borders to find common ground as women workers and to use that identity as a source of strength to build local labor movements. Rootedness to issues was seen in FairWear's origins in the Australian labor movement and the ways that it has used this position to engage with domestic religious organizations and homeworker advocates worldwide. Each of the NGOs relied on networked allies to disseminate information and diffuse its campaigns. Their campaigns were strengthened by all the NGOs' participation in the broader network and its connections.

Anti-sweatshop NGOs embrace specific geographic and political locations from which they engage in transnational advocacy. The NGOs' ability to navigate the transnational political arena is determined as much by politics at the supra-national level as by local and national institutions and ideologies. USAS students use their position within university structures to pressure university administrators to join the WRC, thereby requiring licensees to take greater responsibility for labor violations in their supply chains. In a related but different organizing model, the CCC provides a framework for each chapter to use, to target the same companies from different countries and from different angles. FairWear uses a similar strategy to the CCC but on a much smaller scale. STITCH employs a different model altogether, seeking to build solidarity among workers based on shared identities and challenges as women workers. This chapter demonstrated some of the ways in which NGO activists in the anti-sweatshop network emphasize global connectedness but also recognize and reckon with the persistence of differences in place, in power, and in identity.

Chapter 4

Structures of governance and anti-sweatshop NGOs

Anti-sweatshop NGOs operate within the confines of social, economic, and political structures. At the same time, they contribute to the formation, maintenance, and mutation of the structures around them. The first part of the chapter compares the domestic structures in which each NGO operates and examines how these structures shape the NGOs' abilities to engage in transnational advocacy. The second section addresses international institutions and the constraints on NGO engagement with IGOs. These constraints led to NGO involvement in private MSIs, the subject of the third section. Anti-sweatshop NGOs sought out these alternative ways to regulate the industry because of state and IGO inaction and general lack of oversight of the garment industry. However, MSIs have proven to be weak substitutes for enforceable regulations. The chapter concludes with reflections on how all of these structures of governance facilitate and constrain transnational anti-sweatshop advocacy.

Domestic structures and anti-sweatshop NGOs

States interact with NGOs in various ways. Risse-Kappen (1995, 19) distinguishes between the state as an institutionalized structure of governance and the state as an actor. He explains that the state as a structure includes political institutions, legal procedures, and norms prescribing behavior. He contrasts this with governments and government actors interacting with other governments, making decisions, and negotiating treaties. Ahmed and Potter (2006) distinguish different aspects of relationships between NGOs and states. These include NGOs in states, NGOs as collaborators with states, NGOs as opponents of states, and NGOs as substitutes for states. These multiple relationships coexist since states rarely, if

87

ever, act as monolithic, self-interested agents. States have ambivalent relationships with NGOs, relying on the services they provide while attempting to contain their influence on political processes.

Several theories seek to explain the increase in the number of NGOs and the different characteristics of the nonprofit sector in various countries. In response to macro-economic theories that explain the increase in NGOs in terms of market or government failure, Anheier and Salamon developed the social origin theory, which emphasizes the extent to which nonprofit organizations are embedded in the "cultural, religious, political, and economic realities of different countries" (2006, 106). They suggest a division of nonprofit regime types that includes liberal, social democratic, corporatist, and statist, each characterized by a particular structure and composition of the nonprofit sector. Anheier and Salamon consider the United States, Australia, and the UK to fall into the liberal nonprofit regime, which is characterized by a relatively low level of welfare spending and a large nonprofit sector. Sweden, Norway, and Finland (and to a lesser extent, Italy) are part of the social democratic nonprofit regime, which is characterized by extensive state-sponsored and state-provided social services. The Netherlands, Germany, and Belgium fit a corporatist model, which Anheier and Salamon describe as exhibiting sizable government spending on social welfare as well as sizable nonprofit sectors. The last regime type is the statist model characterized by limited government spending on social welfare and a limited nonprofit sector. Anheier and Salamon suggest that this regime type is evident in Japan, Brazil, and much of the developing world. The regime types are determined by the relationship between the nonprofit sector and the state as well as the particular structure, financing, and composition of the nonprofit sector in each country.

The anti-sweatshop NGOs studied here fit within the broader trends in the nonprofit sectors in the United States, Australia, and the Netherlands, as characterized by Anheier and Salamon. FairWear, CCC, STITCH, and USAS have specific relationships to the states in which they are based. They engage with states in numerous ways—through states' roles as regulators, as funders, and as potential targets of advocacy campaigns.[1] These relationships and the multiple interactions between states and NGOs influence how NGOs operate, shape their positions as rooted cosmopolitans, and affect the positions from which they engage in transnational advocacy.

In the United States, Australia, and the Netherlands, NGOs must register with the state, which in turn certifies NGOs in one way or another as a nonprofit, nongovernmental organization. Once gaining certification, an organization must abide by particular restrictions on its activities and in return is provided with tax advantages, such as not being required to pay certain types of income and sales taxes. NGOs may also receive tax incentives to facilitate the receipt of private donations. In the United States this means that NGOs like USAS and STITCH are not required to pay sales taxes, but perhaps more important the donations they receive are tax deductible for donors, providing an incentive for individuals, businesses, and other civil society organizations such as churches and unions to donate funds. In each case the treatment of taxes for NGOs is closely linked to regulations governing the type and scope of the NGOs' activities. In the United States, NGOs are prohibited from certain political activities, under threat of the loss of certification and beneficial tax status. This restriction encourages NGOs to pursue less contentious action and can de-politicize their activities in the anti-sweatshop network. Such regulations also encourage NGOs to target private actors rather than government officials.

The case-study NGOs vary in their relationships to states as funding agents. For example, neither STITCH nor USAS receives direct government funding, while FairWear and CCC receive funds from government departments. This is consistent with broader trends in each country. The Australian and Dutch governments provide greater levels of support to NGOs, while U.S.-based organizations tend to rely more heavily on private donations. The source of NGO funding shapes the nature of an organization and its campaigns, since funding comes with explicit or implicit obligations to donor agencies. Through each of these interactions NGOs are persuaded to undertake certain activities and avoid other more overtly political actions.

NGOs in the Netherlands are less restricted than U.S.-based NGOs and Australian NGOs in terms of lobbying government officials. In the Netherlands, public-benefit organizations, a category that includes NGOs, are not restricted from lobbying or other political activity (Burger and Dekker 2001). Therefore, NGOs may be less likely to target the state in the Netherlands, not out of fear of losing their tax-exempt status (since NGOs are permitted to lobby), but by the strings attached to receiving government funding. In the United States and Australia, NGOs are expressly prohibited from engaging in overtly political actions. Both processes—states exercising control through legislation and through direct funding—persuade NGOs to undertake activities focused on reforming the private sector while avoiding more radical activities aimed at either the state or the private sector.

When anti-sweatshop activists do target the state, they do so in two distinct ways. The first approaches the state as regulator and policymaker. This type of advocacy views the state in its capacity to make policy and tries to influence policymakers' decisions. The second way that NGOs target the state is in the state's role as a consumer. This is a relatively new strategy in the anti-sweatshop network. Activists in the United States, Europe, and Australia have all launched appeals to Northern constituents as citizens to urge local and state municipalities to adopt sweat-free procurement policies with Sweatfree Communities in the United States, Clean Communities in Europe, and FairWear Councils in Australia. Each program aims to get local and state governments to exercise their purchasing power to improve working conditions in the garment industry. The programs put forward sweat-free ordinances that require governments to procure goods that have been certified as being produced under ethical conditions.

In this context activists appeal to governments as consumers rather than as potential regulators. Few of these municipalities have jurisdiction over multinational corporations or manufacturers, but developing anti-sweatshop ordinances harnesses money spent on government procurement and expresses a symbolic gesture to retailers and consumers alike. Activists argue that without such provisions, the public's tax dollars are used to support, and even subsidize, sweatshops. In essence these are consumer campaigns that, rather than focusing on individual or institutional consumers, treat the state and various levels of government as consumers.

This approach to governments is a function of broader trends toward the deregulation of industries where the state is seen as a facilitator of markets rather than as a regulator or enforcer of rights. In this sense such initiatives are consistent with the development of MSIs' and the private sector's voluntary self-regulation. The impact of these policies has yet to be seen in terms of dollars spent on goods produced in sweat-free conditions or the pressure they exert on suppliers. The main achievements may be in raising awareness, taking symbolic action, and contributing to a small but growing market for goods that can be certified as being produced under ethical conditions. These initiatives have the potential to further implement norms and standards set out in the ILO principles by bringing the discourse into common currency and applying it at a local level. The power of this kind of campaigning is in its local nature, allowing activists in the United States, Europe, and Australia to take local and accessible action with concrete outcomes.

A model focusing on states as consumers comes with several risks. One of these is that sweat-free procurement policies may help to solidify the role of governments in their consuming roles, neutralize dissent, and absolve states of their responsibilities as regulators. Another danger is that such practices can end up propping up protectionist measures (as some "buy local" campaigns can), even if it was not activists' original intention. For example, as part of a USAS campaign, students persuaded administrators of Occidental College that the main way to ensure goods were made under ethical conditions was to purchase them from a UNITE factory in Pennsylvania "on the grounds that the American union label provides the best available insurance that apparel is 'sweat-free'" (Kabeer 2002, 13).[2] In cases like these, purchasing goods from domestic suppliers certainly benefits union shops in Pennsylvania but leaves women workers in the global South no better off than before such campaigns.

Another strategy combines the roles of states as regulators and as consumers. The Decent Working Conditions and Fair Competition Act S.367 was introduced in the U.S. Congress in 2006 and 2007. The NLC helped draft the bill. Representative Michael Michaud sponsored the bill in the House with 174 co-sponsors (Govtrack.us 2008a). Senator Byron Dorgan sponsored the bill in the Senate with 25 co-sponsors (Govtrack.us 2008b). The proposed bill had two parts. It would have prohibited the sale of goods that were produced under sweatshop conditions either domestically or abroad. It would have also required the Federal Government to procure uniforms and other goods certified as sweat-free.[3] Each time the bill was introduced, it died in committee, and therefore was not put into law. Even though it was not enacted, the introduction of the bill shows lawmakers' awareness of working conditions in the garment industry.

The proposed legislation framed ethical sourcing as a fair business practice, positioning companies that produced goods under sweatshop conditions as engaged in unfair competition. The language surrounding the bill focused on unfair competition for American workers. One of the bill's sponsors, Representative Sherrod Brown said in a speech, "Sweatshop imports are economic suicide for our country. As we import sweatshop goods, we export American jobs, we weaken the bargaining position of U.S. workers fighting for wages with which they can actually support their families" (2006). The bill also contained a provision that the only parties that could bring a civil suit were investors and competitors. Although this would have limited the potential utility of the bill for activists, the bill's sponsors most likely included it to make the bill more likely to garner support from legislators who would otherwise dismiss it. Not even this provision was enough to get it put into law, and whether the sponsors of the bill will reintroduce it in future sessions is unclear.

Sweat-free ordinances and domestic legislation target different points of leverage in the complex system surrounding the garment industry. Sweat-free ordinances target local governments and are based on the ability of citizens to influence local officials. The Decent Working Conditions legislation focused on American lawmakers. If reintroduced and put into law, it would codify decent working conditions for factory workers overseas in U.S. legislation (albeit based on the language of workers in sweatshops unfairly competing with American workers). States can become targeted actors, but here they are targeted to act in a different capacity than Keck and Sikkink's (1998) boomerang pattern, in which Northern states apply pressure to other states where the violations occur. With the sweat-free ordinances, activists treat the state as a powerful consumer to be pressured to use its buying power to support ethically produced goods (and avoid using public funds to subsidize garments made under sweatshop conditions). The Decent Working Conditions legislation, on the other hand, targeted the state in its capacity as a regulator. If passed, it would have given activists the ability to take legal action against corporations in violation of the law. The following section compares domestic structures in the United States, Australia, and the Netherlands affecting the case-study NGOs. It includes their regulatory frameworks and the scope of the third-sector (nonprofit organizations) in each country, and how these factors influence transnational anti-sweatshop advocacy.

United States

The nonprofit sector in the United States is large, and its activities are fairly well documented. This is due to requirements from the Federal Government for organizations to register with the Internal Revenue Service (IRS) in order to receive tax-exempt status. For example, in 2004–5, 1.4 million nonprofit organizations were registered with the IRS. This included 850,000 public charities (in which NGOs are included), 104,000 private foundations, and 464,000 other nonprofit organizations such as chambers of commerce, fraternal organizations, and civic groups (Urban Institute 2007). The U.S. National Center for Charitable Statistics developed a National Taxonomy of Exempt Entities (NTEE) that is widely used in the United States to classify nonprofit organizations. In 2004, 5,694 organizations in the United States were classified as dealing with international and foreign affairs as their primary activity.

Very small organizations with annual budgets of less than US$500,000 make up the majority (72 percent) of all registered nonprofit organizations in the United States (Urban Institute 2007). Although this may seem like a large number, it does not actually capture the total number of small organizations. Many small organizations are not registered with the IRS as separate entities with their own 501(c)3 status (granted by the IRS to indicate that an organization is permitted to receive tax-deductible donations).

For example, in her study of small peace organizations with budgets under US$30,000, Colwell (1996) found that 70–90 percent were not counted in national statistics because they had not registered as separate organizations with the IRS. Many small organizations contract with larger organizations to operate as their fiscal sponsor, providing administrative support and financial management in exchange for a small fee. This is the case with USAS, which works with Alliance for Global Justice as its fiscal sponsor. STITCH, on the other hand, does have its own 501(c)3 status with the IRS. This means that STITCH would be included in the IRS figures previously discussed, while USAS would be left out.

U.S.-based NGOs' activities that might resemble lobbying are tightly regulated. The limitations on their political activities make interactions with policymakers and legislators a sensitive area for NGOs. Most organizations shy away from activities that could be considered lobbying out of fear of losing their tax-exempt status. Large organizations in the United States commonly split their organizations into separate entities to facilitate clear divisions between their lobbying activities, managed by a 501(c)4 organization, and their education activities, managed by the arm holding the 501(c)3 status. Organizations like Planned Parenthood are structured in this manner to facilitate lobbying while maintaining service and their education wings. Neither USAS nor STITCH is large enough to warrant the development of a separate organization dedicated to lobbying; therefore, these organizations limit their engagement with policymakers, due in part to the constraints they face in participating in overtly political activities.[4]

STITCH and USAS have very different funding structures. For example, STITCH relies primarily on individual donors. It receives approximately 55 percent of its funding from individuals, each of whom donates anything from one dollar to two thousand dollars. The organization solicits funds from its seven thousand to ten thousand members through direct mail and email. The remainder of its funding comes from foundations, delegations, and the sale of outreach materials. This structure—primarily drawing on individual donors—allows STITCH to draw upon a wide support base. However, raising funds from individuals can be laborious. Regardless, this structure suits the organization. In an interview Executive Director Beth Myers said that STITCH wants to grow organically and not "follow the funding" (Myers, personal communication, January 5, 2007). As a small organization, the search for funds is always a struggle, yet STITCH management has chosen to keep the organization small and autonomous rather than be subject to large government or foundation granting agencies.

Like STITCH, USAS operates on a limited budget, reporting expenditures of US$205,000 in 2006. Yet unlike STITCH, USAS does not raise much money from individual donors. Instead, it relies on unions and grants from private foundations. Along with several other anti-sweatshop NGOs, USAS received funding early on from the U.S. Department of Labor under the Clinton administration. Several other anti-sweatshop organizations in the United States still receive a mixture of public and private funds. For example, the State Department, USAID, and the Department of Labor have all provided funding for the ILRF. As an example of the sensitive political nature of such grants, in 2005 the Department of Labor blocked the release of a report that it had commissioned from the ILRF and rescinded a portion of its US$900,000 grant. At stake were findings in the report regarding labor conditions in Central America that could have potentially hindered support of the DR-CAFTA, supported by the Bush administration. The Department of Labor claimed that the report was biased and was critical of DR-CAFTA. The department eventually allowed the report to be published on the condition that it was not disclosed as a Department of Labor–funded project (Forero 2005; Margasak 2005).

These features of American political structures and context help explain USAS's and STITCH's orientation and modes of advocacy, including their size and reliance on private funding. Combined with the analysis of the political economy of the garment industry in Chapter 1, the domestic political structures described here also help to explain the NGOs' reluctance to target the state and their focus on influencing the private sector.

Australia

As of 1996, there were approximately 700,000 nonprofit or third-sector organizations in existence in Australia. Of these, 34,000 had paid staff, employing over 630,000 people, equivalent to 7.6 percent of the entire workforce (Lyons 1998, 17). In addition to NGOs, these figures include clubs and professional associations. It is difficult to ascertain the number of these organizations engaged in transnational advocacy in Australia. Nevertheless, according to its website, the Australian Council for International Development (ACFID) maintained in 2007 a list of 109 member organizations, all of which were involved in aid and development. While many of these may aim to change policies and practices, a good number is also oriented toward providing services rather than participating in advocacy activities.

Like the United States, Australia is part of what Anheier and Salamon (2006) consider a liberal nonprofit regime. The liberal model is characterized by a large nonprofit sector with a relatively low level of government welfare spending. Although both the United States and Australia exhibit a liberal nonprofit regime, they differ in their treatment of funding NGOs. In Australia donations to certified charities are tax deductible, providing an incentive for private philanthropy. However, the Australian Tax Office (ATO) maintains more restrictions on the types of NGOs that can receive designated gift recipient status than does the U.S. Internal Revenue Service, which allows a wider range of NGOs to receive tax-deductible gifts. Individual philanthropy is not as widespread in Australia as it is in the United States. This may be due to the greater percentage of religious participation in the United States and the history of tithing associated with the churches. It may also be due to the Australian government historically playing a larger role in providing social services than the United States, which means that the Australian government provides many services that are left to the nonprofit sector in the United States.

Like USAS, FairWear receives funding from civil society organizations, mainly the Uniting Church and the Australian Clothing, Textile, and Footwear Union. FairWear has also received funding from government departments such as the Federal Office for Women, which provided funding for leadership training for outworkers (Gardener, personal communication, November 21, 2006). FairWear has a more direct relationship with the government than do the other NGOs, because it seeks to influence Australian government policy in some of its campaigns. For example, FairWear organized a letter-writing campaign and a delegation of outworkers to meet with lawmakers in Victoria to encourage them to maintain protections for outworkers in industrial-relations legislation. In 2007 FairWear advocates were successful in securing protections for outworkers in Work Choices legislation. This was a clear success but a muted one because FairWear activists did not support the legislation overall. They were doing what they could to assist outworkers, given the constraints. This precarious position—fighting for small changes to a flawed policy—puts activists in an awkward position and further complicates their roles as simultaneous insiders and outsiders of the political structures they seek to change.

The Australian government permits NGOs in Australia to participate in political activities as long as the NGOs' political activities are consistent with the NGOs' primary charitable purpose. In recent years there have been several attempts to clamp down on NGO activities. In one such attempt the Howard government proposed a Charities Bill in 2003 that would have explicitly banned NGOs from advocacy-related activities. Because of significant opposition, the bill was never put into law. In another attempt Treasurer Peter Costello proposed restrictions on NGO activities limiting their political participation to that which could be deemed ancillary or incidental. Continuing this trend in 2005 a ruling by the ATO made it easier for the ATO to revoke the charitable status of an NGO if it was found to be "promoting a particular point of view." In one such case the ATO revoked the charitable status of AIDWATCH for openly criticizing the U.S.-Australia Free Trade Agreement and other government policies (AIDWATCH 2007). Such ambiguity in the law breeds confusion and reticence among NGOs that are fearful of jeopardizing their status with the government.

In addition to restrictions of NGO activities overall, FairWear faces restrictions specifically related to its focus on the garment industry. Uncertainties in Australia's regulatory environment have the potential to restrict FairWear's ability to engage in direct actions against garment retailers. For example, in August 2007, Treasurer Peter Costello proposed an amendment to the Trade Practices Act that would restrict community organizations' abilities to participate in "secondary boycotts." Even though it did not pass, the suggestion of such measures contributed to a climate of uncertainty among activists and community advocates about the potential legal ramifications of their activities.

A survey of 290 Australian NGOs found a similarly uneasy relationship between NGOs and the state. The report, prepared by the Australia Institute, found that many NGOs perceived significant barriers to engaging in dialogue with federal and state governments. The barriers cited included lack of funding, indifference from state officials, and an unresponsive media. Others cited self-censorship in their engagement with the state out of a fear of losing funding. As one respondent put it, "It does have a chilling effect . . . wondering whether critical comment may ultimately affect our funding security" (Maddison, Denniss, and Hamilton 2004, x). Many of the NGOs in the survey perceived that federal and state authorities silenced debate through denigration and public criticism, bullying, management of consultation processes, and diversionary tactics. In each case the legal standing of NGOs was not directly threatened, yet NGO activity was contained or diverted through less direct forms of control.

FairWear operates, in this context, in cooperation with certain government departments and in conflict with others. The domestic structures simultaneously provide opportunities through consultation and funding for NGOs while fostering a climate of uncertainty and informal mechanisms that constrain or divert NGO advocacy. Nevertheless, FairWear has a reasonably good relationship with the Labor government. For example, soon after the 2007 election, the Rudd government repealed the Work Choices legislation opposed by FairWear and other labor advocates. It also promised additional funding for the Homeworkers Code of Practice/ Ethical Clothing Australia. FairWear also provided input into a 2008 review of the textile, clothing, and footwear industry in Australia, although it is unclear at this point if the government will adopt the recommendations related to homeworkers. All of these factors contribute to FairWear's engagement with governments and the ways in which it assigns responsibilities for abuses in the industry, articulates demands, and communicates with its audience.

The Netherlands

The Dutch nonprofit sector is similar to other European countries in terms of structure but is larger than in most other European countries. As of 1995 the sector included expenditures of US$61 billion, making up 15.5 percent of the country's gross domestic product. Similar to other Western European countries, the nonprofit sector in the Netherlands is primarily funded by the state, with 60 percent coming from government sources, 38 percent from fees and only 3 percent from private philanthropy (Burger, Dekker, and Toepler 1999). The nonprofit sector in the Netherlands makes up 14 percent of total employment. This is significantly greater than the rest of Europe, the United States, and Australia. It also has one of the highest levels of volunteer participation (Burger and Dekker 2001).

Anheier and Salamon (2006) include the Netherlands in a corporatist nonprofit model characterized by a large nonprofit sector and sizable governmental welfare spending. The nonprofit sector in the Netherlands is characterized by "pillarization," or the segmentation of society along religious and political lines. Pillarization led to the creation of numerous publicly funded and privately operated schools, hospitals, and other service organizations. Some argue that the processes of "de-pillarization" and privatization are causing a significant change in the nonprofit sector as the lines among the government, nonprofit organizations, and private enterprises are beginning to blur (Burger and Dekker 2001). Increasing integration within Europe and a greater influence of EU–level policy will also continue to shape the Dutch nonprofit sector. Like the nonprofit sector in the United States and Australia, the Dutch nonprofit sector can be seen as both a force for social control and a base for social empowerment (Anheier and Salamon 2006). In other words, the nonprofit sector, and civil society more broadly, are spheres where elites can be challenged. The nonprofit sector is also a space where power relations are continually enacted and reproduced, particularly through the use of state funding of nonprofit activities.

The CCC is registered as a private foundation in the Netherlands. Consistent with the rest of the Dutch nonprofit sector, it receives funding from the state to carry out certain projects and services. The CCC secretariat receives most of its funding from the Dutch Ministry of Foreign Affairs and from the European Union, with some small amounts coming from private sources. Each chapter throughout Europe raises its own funds and relies on a variety of public and private sources. The Ministry of Foreign Affairs recently awarded the CCC a four-year contract for a program titled Local Action, Global Campaigning (CCC 2007a). The purpose of the program is to assist activists in encouraging local councils to adopt procurement policies that would require manufacturers to demonstrate that they adhere to certain standards or codes. The financial support of the Dutch government has contributed to the structure of the CCC and its mode of advocacy. Rather than pressure the government to take on greater regulatory functions, the CCC focuses on consumers and retailers and their responsibility to improve working conditions in the industry.

IGOs and anti-sweatshop NGOs

Although IGOs do not provide a comprehensive regulatory framework for the garment industry, numerous institutions, multilateral and bilateral agreements, and international norms have contributed to shaping the industry into its present form. Activists rely on norms, such as the core labor standards from the ILO, to draw attention to poor working conditions. Although the buyer-driven supply chains in the industry grant significant power to retailers, these organizations are subject to quota restrictions in bilateral agreements like the U.S.-China MOU and to provisions set by IGOs such as the WTO. In this way the international political arena places restrictions on trade, facilitates it in other ways, and contributes to the industry's overall structure.

NGOs have also used this structure to pressure retailers and to contribute to the development of norms of behavior. For example, due in part to NGO pressure, the United Nations established the Global Compact to encourage businesses to sign a voluntary code stating their adherence to principles around human rights, anti-corruption, labor, and the environment. Although NGOs play an increasingly important role in debates at the United Nations, none of the case-study organizations has consultative status with the United Nations. The barriers to meaningful engagement with IGOs are due in part to the structure of intergovernmental institutions based on nation-states. In most cases these organizations do not have the resources to lobby the United Nations or high-level government officials. Anti-sweatshop NGOs are also constrained due to the political imperatives of institutions such as the WTO, which emphasizes trade liberalization and a limited role for labor regulation.

Formal engagement between the labor movement and IGOs takes place primarily between unions, such as the ICFTU, and several agencies, including the ILO, IMF, and World Bank, as well as the Organisation for Economic Co-operation and Development (OECD) (O'Brien, Goetz, Scholte, and Williams 2000). Aside from the CCC, the rest of the case-study organizations have little direct engagement with the ILO or OECD. The other NGOs engage indirectly with the ILO through the use of its core labor standards. The NGOs also join other civil society organizations in critiquing trade agreements supported by the WTO and structural adjustment packages promoted by the IMF. However, these actions targeting IGOs tend to be a small part of their overall activities.

Of the UN agencies, the ILO is the one most closely concerned with issues relevant to the anti-sweatshop network. Yet, the ILO is constrained in its ability to influence the industry significantly. Benjamin suggests that "the alternative to the hodgepodge of codes and monitors would be national and international regulations that can be enforced with some kind of sanctioning power. But the only organization that sets labor standards, the International Labor Organization, has no teeth when it comes to enforcement" (2001, x). It is the only agency with a unique tripartite structure that allows workers to have direct input into decision making. However, this structure does not allow for significant NGO involvement. Each national delegation includes four members: two representatives of the state, one from business, and one from labor. Even with input from labor leaders, however, the ILO is unable to influence the industry significantly because it lacks enforcement capabilities.

The ILO's Fundamental Principles and Rights at Work, also known as the core labor standards, were outlined in Chapter 1. Elias critiques the "gender-blind, and neoliberal compatible, approach to the economic rights" (2007, 45) set out in the ILO's core labor standards. She argues that the standards emerged without sufficient attention to the specific problems women workers face in the global economy. She outlines several critiques of the core labor standards from a feminist perspective. These include that the core labor standards privilege (mostly male) formal employment and overlooks women's work as homeworkers and domestic workers, and their work in the informal sector. She also critiques the standards for their foundations in human rights discourse, which she claims rest on traditional Western notions of the public/private sphere. She views the commitments contained in the core labor standards to nondiscrimination and equality of opportunity as insufficient in addressing the particular needs of women workers. The emphasis on freedom of association and collective bargaining privileges formal employment and fails to recognize that "trade unions themselves often reflect a pervasive male bias in terms of both rates of unionisation and the upholding of gender discriminatory employment structures within the workplace" (2007, 52). She raises another concern about the roles that corporations have taken on in enforcing labor standards in supply chains through codes of conduct. She claims that the standards are designed to work within, and complement, a neoliberal development paradigm. Therefore, Elias argues that they do not necessarily meet the needs of women workers in either their formulation or their application. She suggests developing alternative feminist understandings of economic rights that would dissociate economic rights from public-sphere activity.

The ILO core labor standards are often incorporated into corporate codes of conduct, which activists use to draw attention to inconsistencies between the conditions in factories and the stated code. The case of the ILO Better Factories Cambodia (BFC) project, mentioned in Chapter 1, illustrates an alternative path to pressuring corporations directly through consumer campaigns, including a greater role for state and intergovernmental intervention. It also represents a deviation from the ILO's usual activities. The BFC project was the result of activist pressure applied during the drafting of a trade agreement between the United States and Cambodia. The purpose of BFC was to improve working conditions in the garment industry through training and independent monitoring in exchange for expanding Cambodia's quota to the United States by 14 percent under the MFA (Elliot and Freeman 2005, 88). Wells considered BFC to be the "best example of links between enhanced trade and improvements in labor standards in the global South" (2006, 361). The project provided assistance to factories to improve compliance and provided a tool to international buyers to use in their sourcing decisions. One of the main differences between the BFC and other projects was that it rewarded compliance with increased quotas rather than fining or punishing those found out of compliance. Although the project continues, rewarding compliance with increased quotas no longer exists because of the phaseout of the MFA in 2005.

IGOs make up one part of the structures of governance that encourage, discourage, and shape NGOs' political actions. None of the existing IGOs provides comprehensive governance of the industry. This lack of IGO oversight, combined with a lack of oversight from states, has left a regulatory vacuum, prompting activists and the corporations they target to develop private regulatory structures of governance.

Multi-stakeholder initiatives and anti-sweatshop NGOs

Neither national laws nor intergovernmental entities provide adequate mechanisms to ensure decent working conditions in the industry. Since the 1990s a relatively new form of governance emerged in the garment industry. MSIs are made up of private and nonprofit stakeholders, and set standards, monitor compliance with the standards, and establish certification programs as incentives for companies to meet the standards (O'Rourke 2006). These entities are distinct from state regulatory structures and rely on voluntary participation. MSIs are creating a relatively new form of governance of the garment industry that is taking place largely outside formal state or inter-state structures. MSIs often present NGOs with a way to participate in the governance of the industry, either through active participation on the MSI's governing board or in an advisory role. O'Rourke suggests that the rapid expansion of MSIs is in response to "recent trends in the weakening of national regulatory systems, the strengthening of multi-national corporations, increasing importance of brands, and growing demands from civil society actors for new mechanisms of corporate accountability" (2006, 899). Similar structures can be seen across a range of sectors including forestry, diamonds, and tourism.

MSIs related to the garment industry include the Fair Labor Association, Worker Rights Consortium, Worldwide Responsible Accredited Production (WRAP), Social Accountability International, Ethical Trading Initiative, and the Fair Wear Foundation (FWF) (see O'Rourke 2006). None of these MSIs includes direct participation by government officials, however both the Fair Labor Association and the Ethical Trading Initiative were supported by the Clinton and Blair administrations, respectively (Chang and Wong 2005). Retailers and NGOs have developed several new MSIs in the past few years. These include the MFA Forum, which prepared retailers and activists for the fall-out following the end of the MFA, and the Joint Initiative on Corporate Accountability and Workers' Rights (Jo-In), which coordinates several of the MSIs in order to reduce duplication of efforts.

The garment industry MSIs vary in terms of composition, participation, and certification mechanisms. Most MSIs in the garment industry are set up as independent nonprofit entities and solicit retailers and manu-facturers to participate by signing voluntary codes of conduct and agree-ing to periodic monitoring and verification. Labor advocates debate the legitimacy of various MSIs based on their membership and the extent to which industry executives control the agenda. Activists criticize some, like the Fair Labor Association and WRAP, for pandering to industry leaders.

As described in Chapter 2, many corporations shifted their responses to activists' campaigns during the second phase of anti-sweatshop advocacy, between 1999 and 2004. Previously, they had denied any responsibility for working conditions in supply chains. During the second phase many tar-geted retailers joined MSIs to counter the negative publicity from anti-sweatshop campaigns. Companies like Nike, Reebok, and Gap, which had been the prime targets of early campaigns, became some of the most ar-dent advocates of MSIs and participated in multiple programs and en-couraged their competitors to do the same.

When joining an MSI, retailers are often required to align their own codes of conduct to those endorsed by the MSI. Most retailers in the gar-ment industry adopted codes of conduct in the 1990s. The benefit of re-tailers aligning their codes to MSIs is that it can provide greater consis-tency across the industry. MSI codes are also usually based on the ILO's core labor standards. Even though the ILO does not take a direct role in any of the MSIs, it does provide a framework that can be used to develop uniform norms and standards.

The scope and level of commitment in MSIs and corporate codes vary widely. At a minimum the codes record the retailer's stated commitment to meeting national labor laws where clothing is produced. In other cases, as with Swedish retailer H&M, the code of conduct, available on its website, includes provisions banning the use of child labor, protecting workers' health and safety, and stipulating that workers have the right to join an associa-tion and bargain collectively. The H&M code also includes language com-mitting the company to take responsibility for working conditions in its supply chain: "Most importantly we have a responsibility toward all the thousands of people taking part in the production of our garments. We have to make sure that nobody whose work is contributing to our success is deprived of his or her human rights, or suffers mental or bodily harm." Activists debate the merits of various codes, some of which refer to adher-ing to minimum wages, while others include provisions for living wages. While the utility and effectiveness of corporate codes of conduct are de-batable, most activists agree that codes can be useful tools in training workers and negotiating with management (Kearney and Gearhart 2005). Activists can also use codes of conduct and membership in MSIs as tangible campaigning goals around which to organize, that is, activists can point out the inconsistencies between a company's code and working conditions where its goods are produced.

A principal lure for corporations to join MSIs is to avoid regulation by states. Elias (2007) notes that instead of acting as complementary mechanisms to binding regulations, codes have become a substitute for such regulations. By developing their own standards and participating in voluntary codes and monitoring programs, retailers decrease the likelihood of outside oversight. MSI membership also offers corporations a coordinated framework to address complaints about abuses in supply chains. Participation in these private, voluntary initiatives can be presented as a "win-win" solution for activists and retailers. By participating in an MSI, retailers can appear to be making a good-faith effort to consumers and activists to improve conditions in their supply chains. Retailers also benefit from consolidating monitoring activities with other retailers in the industry, which lowers the cost of monitoring suppliers. In this way MSIs fit into a neoliberal frame that resonates with businesses, emphasizing voluntary participation, self-regulation, and nonintervention by states.[5]

Activists contend that codes and MSIs may be useful tools, yet they are by no means ideal solutions to address widespread abuses in the industry. While many NGOs actively pressure retailers to join MSIs, others are skeptical about the nature of the codes and monitoring mechanisms. Although some note that MSIs have the potential to be more "flexible, efficient, democratic and effective than traditional labour regulation" (O'Rourke 2006, 899), others suggest that MSIs undermine broader labor movements based on solidarity among workers (Chang and Wong 2005). The extent to which MSI participation and the adoption of corporate codes of conduct are actually implemented, and translate into changes for workers, is debatable, but their presence alone does suggest that corporations are unable to ignore advocacy claims and that there is an increasing level of dialogue between corporations and NGOs. Indeed, the widespread existence of codes and the establishment of MSIs is the result of anti-sweatshop campaigns. Although MSIs have obvious limitations, there have also been some notable positive outcomes from MSIs. Retailers have disclosed factory locations, consented to having monitors inspect factories, publicized the findings, and agreed to remediation plans to address the most egregious abuses—especially those related to child labor, forced overtime, and physical abuse.

NGO engagement with MSIs

Most activists welcome the increase in retailers' participation in MSIs in the absence of an adequate alternative, but their growing presence does present activists with a dilemma. While pressuring retailers to join MSIs and take greater responsibility for working conditions in supply chains, the participation of retailers in MSIs may actually reinforce retailers' dominance in the industry (in relation to manufacturers, unions, and government). A system in which mostly Northern-based TNCs are positioned as the watch-dogs of manufacturers in the global South only reinforces existing power dynamics. This is done without actually changing retailers' own practices, such as paying more for goods produced under ethical conditions, establishing long-term relationships to avoid abuses associated with piece-rate work, or stipulating more realistic turnaround times to limit forced overtime.

The case-study organizations approach this dilemma in different ways. The types of engagement can be summarized as active engagement (FairWear, USAS), participation (CCC), and disengagement (STITCH). FairWear and USAS actively engage with MSIs. FairWear and USAS both hold seats on the boards of MSIs and advocate directly for targeted companies or universities to join particular initiatives: Ethical Clothing Australia in the case of FairWear, and the WRC for USAS. FairWear's engagement with Ethical Clothing Australia reflects its roots in the Australian labor movement. USAS's engagement with the WRC is deeply connected to its roots in the student movement; student activists pressure universities to join the WRC as an alternative to the more industry-friendly FLA.

The CCC participates in the Fair Wear Foundation (FWF), an MSI. In fact, FWF's code of conduct is based on the CCC's model code, CCC activists were involved in the establishment of the FWF, and a member of the CCC sits on its board. Nevertheless, the CCC's activities are not directly tied to increasing the membership of the FWF. This differentiates its type of engagement from FairWear and USAS's active engagement with MSIs. The CCC also participates in Jo-In.

Unlike the other NGOs, STITCH does not advocate for MSI membership or expansion. STITCH argues that the emphasis on external monitors is misplaced and that external monitors should be used to support workers' attempts to organize and act as their own monitors. STITCH Executive Director Beth Myers said in an interview that developing an elaborate system of third-party monitoring diverts attention from the work of supporting workers to become monitors on the shop floor by strengthening unions (Myers, personal communication, January 5, 2007). Each of these represents different ways that NGOs interact with MSIs and the extent to which anti-sweatshop activists view MSIs as a viable tool to improve working conditions in the industry.

Implications for governance of the industry

MSIs implicitly expand notions of governance beyond states and IGOs, and link economic networks and interests in the garment industry with a system of non-state regulation. Stienstra argues that "when we consider global governance as the process of constructing and maintaining common norms and standards, our focus necessarily is no longer state centered. We recognize that states work together and with NGOs to develop and maintain these norms. But they also have dynamic relationships with other forces in the world order, including transnational capital and global finance" (1999, 268).

The reliance on MSIs to regulate the industry is troubling for two reasons. The first relates to the outcome of MSIs in terms of the norms they generate. Activists question whether norms generated through MSIs' codes of conduct are adequate to protect workers. MSI codes differ on wage levels as well as health and safety standards. For example, differences between the codes of the WRC and the FLA are discussed in Chapter 7. This comparison shows the different standards that different MSIs apply to wages, overtime, and safety standards, and the impact this could have on workers.

The second concern relates to the implications of private regulatory initiatives becoming the sites of constructing and maintaining those norms and standards. Lipschutz (2005) considers MSIs to be part of a broader trend of private, transnational regulation that involves the use of market-based mechanisms to alter behavior, which he refers to as a new international division of regulatory labor. He notes that one problem with this approach, particularly in the garment industry, is that even when changes are made in a specific sector, there may not be much, if any, spillover to other industries. Lipschutz argues that even if MSIs contribute to behavioral changes on the part of individual corporations, they do little to alter the broader structures that "states have put in place to attract capital and reduce social costs, both of which lead to the demand and need for social regulation in the first place" (2005, 178). In this way, he suggests, MSIs take place within a structure of politics and economics that supports neoliberal institutions and practices. Placing regulatory functions with such bodies supports the same system and power structures that anti-sweatshop activists seek to change.

Lipschutz and other critics of MSIs also point out that the focus on private regulatory structures distracts workers and activists from seeking more robust national or international governmental regulation of the market. He states:

> The arguments and justifications for regulation—and to whom they are made and why—must come about through politics, which must take place not within or through the market but in the *public* sphere. It is the *ethical* basis of the state's exercise of its power—especially the structural power to constrain the market that must be changed, and not simply the moral behaviours of individual corporations. (Lipschutz 2005, 243)

By focusing on the politics of consumption and the regulatory systems in the private sphere, activists neglect politics in the public sphere and the state shifts its role to regulate the market to a secondary and inadequate private, voluntary system.

One of the main functions of MSIs is to monitor adherence to the stated code of conduct. In her study on sweatshop monitoring, Esbenshade found that

> private monitoring to date has been more successful at improving conditions (such as availability of potable water, hygiene of bathrooms, levels of harassment, correct payment of minimum wage, and reduction in forced overtime) than at guaranteeing respect for workers' basic rights to organize. Thus, workers have not achieved an avenue to defend their own interests on a day-to-day basis or raise wages beyond the legal minimum, which is below subsistence level in most countries. (Esbenshade 2004, 165)

Esbenshade makes a distinction between private monitoring and independent monitoring. Most MSIs rely on private monitoring, which is controlled by retailers. In contrast, what she refers to as independent monitoring (meaning independent from the corporations they seek to regulate) is conducted by local nonprofit organizations or third parties such as the WRC (itself an MSI, but one that does not include retailers as members). Esbenshade favors the approach of the WRC, not as an alternative form of private monitoring but, as she sees it, a radical departure from private monitoring because it focuses on workers' *rights* as opposed to *conditions* and is triggered by workers instead of by manufacturers (2004,

165). Esbenshade concludes that codes have the potential to be a useful tool for change, but that existing MSIs would need to be reformed by including more emphasis on freedom of association and collective bargaining, as does the WRC code. Without these provisions, private monitoring negates the role of unions and undermines the potential for government enforcement.

While supporting independent monitoring, Esbenshade shares Lipschutz's concerns about the broader implications of a system that relies on voluntary regulation outside of the state (Esbenshade 2004; Lipschutz with Rowe 2005). Esbenshade suggests that "private regulation has reinforced the power imbalance engendered by global capitalism to some degree by turning enforcement over to the private sector rather than demanding that government fulfill its mandate or bolstering the power of workers to negotiate for themselves" (2004, 203). MSIs are more receptive to NGO anti-sweatshop campaigns than states and IGOs, yet such structures are unable to secure lasting improvements for garment workers.

MSIs give campaigners a point of reference and a set of standards to which they can hold corporations accountable. However, activists become constrained by the corporate accountability frame underpinning most MSIs, which highlights the actions of individual corporate actors rather than broader systemic structures. MSIs can obscure broader claims of systemic exploitation in the industry by presenting individual cases as atypical of the industry and retailers' involvement in MSIs as a voluntary act of charity rather than a point of obligation and responsibility. Therefore, while creating alternative transnational structures of governance, MSIs also reinforce corporate power in the industry in ways that are amenable to recent and problematic neoliberal transformations.

Conclusion

NGOs simultaneously interact with multiple, multilayered structures of governance. All the structures of governance discussed in this chapter shape NGO strategies, their organizational structures, and ultimately the extent to which their campaigns can succeed. Building on the previous chapter—on how the NGOs enact rooted cosmopolitanism—this chapter compared their relationships to structures of governance and the ways these relationships shape the NGOs' abilities to engage in transnational anti-sweatshop advocacy.

In all three countries the NGOs are shaped by domestic structures, including structures of funding that influence NGO activities, and by political environments that limit the role of the nation-state in regulating transnational capital. Anti-sweatshop NGOs are also encouraged to engage with the state, or discouraged from engaging with the state, through tax regulations and differing levels of access to government officials. While the case-study NGOs are consistent with trends identified by Anheier and Salamon in each country, in terms of their relationship to the state (and particularly in relation to funding), the case-study NGOs highlight differences between the United States and Australian nonprofit sectors in terms of funding. USAS and STITCH do not receive much, if any, government funding. In contrast, FairWear has been instrumental in galvanizing government funding for Ethical Clothing Australia, the MSI it supports. The CCC is consistent with the corporatist model, receiving a significant portion of its funding from the state. Whether based on funding or restrictive legislation, these interactions with the state contribute to an environment where NGO influence is limited when targeting the state other than in the state's capacity as a consumer.

Strengthening regulatory functions at the national level takes political will that currently does not exist. These regulations would require the support of retailers, who would most likely reject such measures unless regulations imposed industry-wide changes that would apply to their competitors. Adoption of such measures would require changes in corporate culture as well as consumer expectations, since one of two things would have to happen: consumer prices of garments would increase to reflect fair wages and better standards in the industry, or retailers would have to accept smaller profit margins and/or curb marketing and advertising budgets. Retailers are likely to resist both, and states are unable and unwilling to compel them to do so without massive support for such measures.

Challenges within the domestic state structures led anti-sweatshop activists to seek alternative paths for improving working conditions in the industry. In some cases this has meant seeking change through IGOs; in others it has resulted in voluntary initiatives within the private sector. Although NGOs engage with political authorities at each layer of the structures, advocates have concentrated their interventions in those areas where they can exercise political action.

When retailers acknowledge their responsibilities for working conditions in supply chains and join MSIs, it is a clear victory for anti-sweatshop activists. Yet, these private, voluntary initiatives have not replaced the need for enforceable regulations of transnational capital. Many private MSIs include the very same retailers they are designed to monitor. This has resulted in reinforcing and possibly expanding the influence that retailers have over suppliers in developing countries. This is not the outcome that activists had hoped for. It presents a dilemma for activists over how to increase the level of responsibilities of retailers without legitimizing or augmenting their already dominant position. Activists continue to debate the merits of the various monitoring systems as they face new opportunities and new constraints in structures of governance at home and abroad.

Chapter 5

Consumer campaigns and the use of civic politics

Anti-sweatshop NGOs express a mode of civic politics aimed at changing behavior of retailers and consumers in the global North because of the particular structure of the global garment industry and because they have found a point of leverage with retailers that are heavily reliant on branding. The campaigns analyzed in this chapter illustrate both the potential and the limitations of civic politics in general, and consumer campaigns in particular. In the garment industry, transnational retailers wield extraordinary power over subcontractors and workers, and governments are unwilling to implement existing labor laws. The power of retailers in the industry contributes to the harsh working conditions in the industry through fierce price competition, downward pressure on wages, and unrealistic turnaround times resulting in forced overtime, but it also poses an opportunity for activists. Since retailers are heavily reliant on branding and subcontractors are not, activists can specifically target retailers by associating their brands with unethical production.

This chapter examines the NGOs' uses of civic politics and their ability to access points of leverage in consumer campaigns. The first section situates anti-sweatshop advocacy within campaigns that aim to mobilize consumers' political action. The second section reviews Keck and Sikkink's (1998) boomerang pattern of transnational advocacy. The third section analyzes four campaigns with different boomerang patterns, demonstrating the range of political tools and actors at work in anti-sweatshop advocacy. The last section of the chapter compares the patterns of advocacy in terms of points of leverage, movement across political arenas, and the role of states and IGOs in advocacy campaigns. Each of these characteristics influences the extent to which campaigns can succeed in achieving their goals.

Consumer campaigns

Activists have used boycotts in a variety of social movements ranging from the civil rights movement in the United States to struggles for independence in India. In each case activists put economic pressure on businesses to encourage them to take a desired action. In contemporary anti-sweatshop campaigns activists rarely employ the boycott as a strategy, but neither do they want to support the purchase of goods made under sweatshop conditions. Activists want to attract the attention of targeted companies without adversely affecting workers. What this means is that few companies have been severely affected, financially, by these campaigns. Instead, the potential damage comes from the negative image associated with their brand (and potential damage to future sales). The power of NGOs aimed at influencing corporate behavior comes from their ability to persuade consumers to demand ethically made products rather than their ability to inflict significant financial damage on targeted actors directly.

Contemporary campaigns treat consumption as a political act in an era when corporations are highly dependent on brand images. Anti-sweatshop NGOs appeal to Northern constituents through their consumption habits, mobilizing a form of political consumerism (Micheletti, Follesdal, and Stolle 2006b) that relies on the marketplace as a site of political engagement. These NGOs are able to access Northern consumers and governments in a way that is often unavailable to their Southern allies. Micheletti and Stolle (2008) distinguish among negative, positive, and discursive political consumerism. For example, boycotts are forms of negative political consumerism. "Buycotts" are the promotion of fair trade or ethical goods through labeling and certification programs. This is a form of positive political consumerism. Unlike positive and negative political consumerism, discursive political consumerism is focused on communicative efforts aimed at businesses, political institutions, and the public rather than on monetary transactions.

Chang and Wong (2005) refer to the style of campaign focused on brands as the Action-Alert-Branding-Targeting-Campaign (AABTC). They recognize that these campaigns may be effective in some cases, such as those aimed at reinstating dismissed workers and recognizing new unions. However, they argue that these campaigns are limited because of the ways that they obscure class-based politics. They suggest that AABTC tactics ultimately undermine the potential for a broader labor movement aimed at developing an alternative development model. Chang and Wong claim that the individualist approach of AABTCs focused on specific companies and factories allows companies to make minor changes without altering the broader social structures that facilitate and reinforce capital accumulation.

Brooks (2007) also critiques consumer campaigns but from a different angle. She critiques the assumption that consumers have agency as political actors simply through their consumption habits. She refers to this as a double granting of agency and suggests that campaigns focusing on consumers reinforce the very same categories of gender, class, and citizenship that the production side of the industry relies on.[1] Young (2006) is far less critical of anti-sweatshop campaigns, and although she does not offer any specific suggestions as to how consumers should act, she believes that consumers should take whatever action is necessary in order to fulfill their obligations of justice to remedy the exploitation in the industry.

When used alongside other strategies, consumer campaigns can be useful tools for garment workers and advocates of labor rights. These campaigns allow Northern-based activists to use their particular positions in strategic ways as rooted cosmopolitans to pressure retailers and consumers to change their policies and practices.

Boomerang patterns of transnational advocacy

Keck and Sikkink illustrate a pattern of transnational advocacy using the boomerang pattern depicted in Figure 5–1. In a boomerang pattern, when domestic NGOs face blockages with their own states, they seek out international allies who then pressure their own states, or in some cases IGOs, to apply pressure to the first state. This pattern helps explain how less powerful actors are able to create influence by developing alliances with those who have access to pressure points unavailable to domestic NGOs. Keck and Sikkink provide examples from the women's movement, environmental movements, and human rights movements. In these cases domestic NGOs used different variations of the boomerang pattern to bypass blockages with their own states by creating linkages with international allies, which then pressured states and IGOs.

Keck and Sikkink's model requires a state to exert pressure. While useful for many situations, this model requires modification to fit the garment industry. Like many other sectors, the garment industry is not governed by any unified international regulatory framework. Instead, governance takes place through a patchwork of national labor laws and private governance structures that rely on voluntary participation, as described in the previous chapter. This raises several questions: what shape is the boomerang pattern

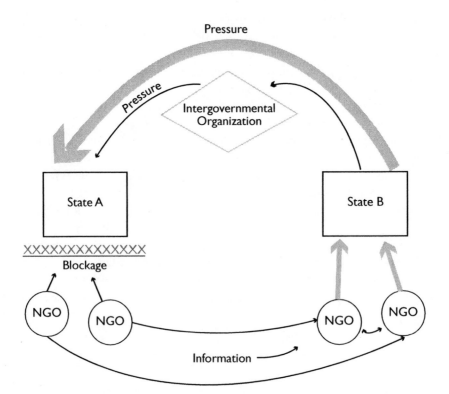

Figure 5–1. Boomerang pattern of transnational advocacy (see Keck and Sikkink 1998, 13). State A blocks redress to organizations within it; they activate network, whose members pressure their own states and (if relevant) a third-party organization, which in turn pressure State A.

when states and IGOs lack political power or will? How does the pattern appear when governance takes place outside of state control? What form does it take when the targets of advocacy are transnational corporations operating across national borders? What pressure points are available to NGOs and other non-state actors in this context? Finally, what has worked, what has not, and why?

Exerting influence on retailers with well-known brands has become a central part of anti-sweatshop campaigning and provides activists with important points of leverage. Klein refers to campaigns targeting retailers as brand boomerangs, where Northern activists exert pressure on multinational corporations to address abusive labor conditions in sweatshops. When asked why campaigns target corporations as opposed to states, one labor activist told her, "because we have more influence on a brand name than we do with our own governments" (Klein 2000, 380). In addition to targeting retailers, the anti-sweatshop NGOs intervene at multiple points within the garment industry system. As rooted cosmopolitans the NGOs' relationships to places, identities, and ideologies shape the ways in which they seek to intervene in the system. In each case their roots shape their ability to access strategic points of leverage and create influence. Campaigns have different boomerang trajectories based on relationships between Southern and Northern activists and the various forms of politics and points of leverage available in each case.[2] Several campaigns are described below.

Clean Clothes Campaign

On September 26, 2007, a judge in Bangalore, India, issued arrest warrants against members of the Amsterdam-based CCC. They were charged with cyber crime and criminal defamation for publishing information on the Internet about abusive practices in garment factories owned by Fibre & Fabric International (FFI) (Ghiase 2007). Within days, the news appeared on dozens of activist websites and blogs calling on supporters to contact FFI and G-Star, a well-known retailer in Europe with contracts with FFI. Human rights organizations such as Amnesty International joined the call, denouncing the lawsuit against the activists as a breach of international human rights law.

The struggle began in August 2006 when the Garment and Textile Workers' Union (GATWU) and three Bangalore-based NGOs conducted an investigation into workers' claims of unpaid overtime, unsafe working conditions, and physical and verbal harassment (CCC 2007b). The results of the investigation were forwarded to the CCC. The CCC subsequently published the results of the investigation on its website and distributed the results to FFI's customers, which included the Dutch retailer G-Star and U.S.-based retailers Tommy Hilfiger, Ann Taylor, Gap, and Guess.

Retailers' responses varied widely. G-Star initially denied any wrongdoing but then reluctantly entered into dialogue with CCC. Ann Taylor conducted its own investigation, which substantiated the activists' findings, and later withdrew its contracts with FFI. Several retailers, such as Mexx, joined MSIs. Others took some action through their existing affiliation with MSIs. For example, Gap encouraged FFI to enter into dialogue with local stakeholders and agreed to a joint response to the issue through the Ethical Trading Initiative. Although retailers' involvement in MSIs like FWF and the Ethical Trading Initiative did not result in any decisive action in relation to FFI, it did represent the companies' acknowledgment of a shared responsibility for the conditions under which their clothing is made.

FFI responded to the pressure from activists, and questions from retailers, by filing for an injunction prohibiting the CCC from distributing information about working conditions in the FFI factory. Ignoring the injunction, the CCC encouraged thousands of European consumers to send letters and emails to the multinational retailers that subcontracted their manufacturing to FFI. CCC activists encouraged their supporters to demand that FFI lift the gag order against the activists.

CCC also contacted the National Point of Reference of the OECD, alleging that G-Star had been in violation of the stated principles of the OECD by disregarding international law and national Indian labor law and by violating workers' human rights. The National Point of Reference of the OECD responded by saying that it would investigate the matter. Ironically, while all of this was going on, FFI was being considered by an MSI, Social Auditing International (SAI), to become SA 8000 certified, which means that a factory meets certain labor standards. Although SAI was reluctant at first to listen to workers' complaints, it eventually suspended the certification process until further notice (CCC 2008c).

The FFI lawsuit filed in June 2007 named several defendants, including the CCC secretariat, the India Committee of the Netherlands, the CCC Task Force of India, Women Garment Workers' Front (Munnade), Civil Initiatives for Development and Peace, and the New Trade Union Initiative. Among the defendants were two Internet service providers who had hosted the CCC website. The complaint claimed that the CCC, along with the Bangalore-based NGOs, had defamed FFI by spreading false information about the company, causing it financial harm. It also claimed that the CCC was involved in a form of cyber crime for publishing material about FFI on its website and encouraging people to write letters to FFI management through the Internet. The complaint claimed that this was in direct violation of the injunction, which prohibited activists from publishing the findings of their investigations of FFI factories. The prosecution claimed that CCC disregarded the court injunction since the activists continued to publish materials about the case on the CCC website.

CCC allies participated in the campaign by encouraging their own supporters to take action. For example, Oxfam Nike Watch sent a message to two thousand members in its network in support of the CCC activists in the FFI case. Court documents in the FFI case claim that the ability of the Internet to reach vast audiences allows organizations like CCC to engage in "virtually limitless international defamation" (Ghiase 2007, 22). FFI claimed that the CCC and the other defendants were not only guilty of cyber crime, but that they had insulted the court and, furthermore, insulted the nation of India. FFI's claims sought to discredit the activists, accusing them of protectionism and claiming that the activists had masqueraded as advocates of social justice but were actually maligning Indian-made goods and the country as a whole.

The FFI case illustrates NGOs' abilities to bring international attention to local labor disputes, mobilize consumer pressure on multinational retailers, appeal to IGOs, and develop institutional relationships among Southern and Northern NGOs and unions. The case also provides an example of the ways that activists, suppliers, and retailers struggle over who bears responsibility to improve conditions in the industry. The campaign initially focused on workers' freedom of association in Bangalore, but, following the lawsuit, focus quickly shifted onto Northern activists' freedom of expression. In other words, the method of communication—publishing material on the Internet—became as contested as the information about forced overtime and physical abuses in FFI factories. This secondary aspect of the campaign, which dealt with the activists' ability to publish material on the Internet, garnered significant media attention and catapulted it from the realm of Internet activism to the political arena of diplomatic negotiations.

The Indian minister of trade, Kamal Nath, brought up the case against the activists during the Dutch queen's visit to India. Shortly after, former Dutch prime minister Ruud Lubbers brokered an agreement that included the dismissal of all charges against the Indian and Dutch activists, the appointment of an ombudsman to deal with future complaints, provisions to allow FFI workers to join a union of their choice, and the end of the activists' campaign against FFI and G-Star. The resolution addressed the dual facets of the campaign: the workers' rights to organize, and the activists' rights to publish allegations of labor abuses on the Internet. This lawsuit and the subsequent mobilization of supporters around the world highlighted the multiple forms of politics in transnational campaigns. In this case activists pressured retailers in addition to making appeals to government officials. Figure 5–2 illustrates the boomerang pattern in the FFI case, incorporating advocacy on behalf of workers at the FFI factory, and later advocacy aimed at encouraging FFI to drop the case against Dutch and Indian NGOs. After the charges against the activists were dropped, and workers were given the means to lodge grievances with their employer, the CCC concluded its campaign against FFI.

The CCC has also been involved in campaigns that are part of a longer, cumulative process of industry-wide change. One such campaign was Play

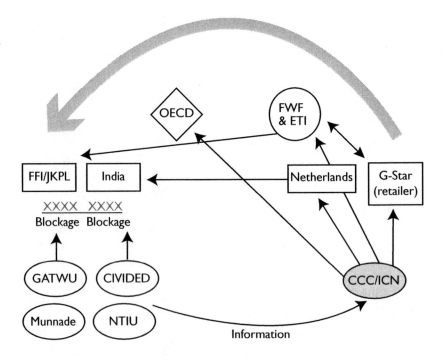

Figure 5–2. Boomerang pattern in the Fibre & Fabric International campaign

Fair at the Olympics, in which the CCC was a key player. The Play Fair at the Olympics campaign included five hundred demonstrations, protests, and picket lines in more than thirty-five countries coinciding with the Olympic Games in Athens in 2004.[3] For example, activists and athletes carried an alternative torch through major garment-producing centers in India (Murthy 2004). All of the activities around the world focused on raising public awareness and applying pressure to the sportswear industry. The campaign focused on the International Olympic Committee and seven companies: Asics, Fila, Kappa, Lotto, Mizuno, Puma, and Umbro. Until the campaign began, the seven highlighted companies had escaped the level of scrutiny that the top retailers had faced (Merk 2005, 6). By focusing on these companies, along with earlier actions aimed at Nike, Reebok, and Adidas, Play Fair at the Olympics aimed to create industry-wide change. This industry-wide approach is particularly appropriate because many of the same factories produce goods for multiple retailers.

In addition to the petitions, street protests, and other direct actions, the campaign engaged with the companies through letters and meetings.

Campaign organizers issued a report and a follow-up letter and convened a sectoral meeting at the ILO. The report, "Play Fair at the Olympics," contained research from six countries, highlighting the results of 186 interviews with workers and 10 representatives of sportswear companies (Oxfam 2004a). The report documented extensive violations in factories that produced goods for each of the targeted companies. Activists used the report to document and substantiate claims of abuse in the industry. The companies' responses to the campaign varied.[4] Some acknowledged the need to develop an industry-wide approach to labor abuses through the World Federation of the Sporting Goods Industry (WFSGI), although neither the WFSGI nor the International Olympic Committee was particularly responsive to Play Fair organizers' demands. Representatives of the WFSGI met with Play Fair organizers; however, the WFSGI was unwilling and unable to coordinate a sector-wide approach to labor abuses in the industry (Miller 2005).

In both the FFI and Play Fair campaigns, CCC used what Keck and Sikkink (1998) call information politics to produce and disseminate alternative information to the public about the practices of targeted actors. Campaign organizers used information politics strategically to produce and disseminate critical information about sportswear manufacturers' labor practices. This information proved to be essential to both campaigns because it meant that claims of abuse and maltreatment could be substantiated by hundreds of interviews with workers and by falsified time sheets. This information proved to be so threatening that its release led FFI to seek the injunction prohibiting activists from distributing the information on its website.

In the Play Fair campaign this information was then used at an emotive and symbolic level. Activists highlighted the hypocrisy of sportswear companies' claims to express global goodwill while exploiting workers who make clothing for the Olympics. By exposing this contrast activists were able to build upon the symbolic value of the Olympics. Other campaigns may not have such a clear association with symbolic politics, but activists can publicize the links between high-profile brands and sweatshop conditions. This was the tactic used in the FFI case. Activists in that case were able to influence European retailers but were not as successful in translating that pressure on retailers into changes for workers until the focus of the campaign became activists' freedom of speech, at which point Indian and Dutch officials got involved.

The Play Fair campaign effectively used material leverage by focusing on the corporations' vulnerabilities—namely, their public image and branding—and linked this to their sponsorship contracts. Sponsorships for the

2004 Olympics were valued at US$648 million (Oxfam 2004a, 33). Corporations rely on the positive image and subsequent earnings that sponsorships are designed to bring about. Play Fair organizers chose the seven companies because of their level of brand recognition rather than focusing on suppliers that were unfamiliar to consumers. The only problem with this strategy is that it can result in activists' targeting the retailers with the most familiar brands rather than focusing on the most flagrant abusers. In the FFI case activists used both material and moral leverage. CCC exerted moral leverage on the European retailers that, in turn, exercised material leverage on FFI by threatening to suspend their contracts with the supplier.

Some of the organizers of Play Fair, such as the CCC and Oxfam, have had success with accountability politics with other campaigns. For example, once corporations join the FWF or FLA (almost always as a concession following pressure from NGOs and consumers), they are monitored for compliance to the MSI's code of conduct. The problem, of course, is that this deters corporations from agreeing to make any changes because they know that they will be judged according to higher standards once they enter into dialogue with activists. Campaign organizers may be able to take advantage of the cyclical nature of the Olympics and other sporting events, such as the World Cup, exercising accountability politics with these same corporations and reporting on targeted companies' progress or lack of it (Merk, personal communication, July 8, 2005).

Play Fair campaign organizers used information about working conditions and brand sponsorships to highlight the inconsistencies between targeted companies' stated principles and working conditions in the companies' supply chains. Although many companies have adopted the language of corporate social responsibility—mainly because of previous pressure from activists or the threat of a targeted campaign—these policies often lack any meaningful implementation. Such corporate social responsibility policies give activists greater traction in mobilizing shame and exercising accountability politics. Activists can point out that companies are falling short of their stated commitments (as opposed to failing to measure up to externally imposed standards). Activists did this in the Play Fair campaign by publicizing the contrast between the rhetoric in the companies' codes of conduct and the abusive labor practices in their supply chains.

United Students Against Sweatshops

USAS focuses on the purchasing power of American university students at a time of significant politicization in many young peoples' lives. Its aims are to raise awareness about working conditions in the garment industry and link consumers, and the products they purchase, to the conditions under which those products are made. While many NGOs exert pressure on retailers, USAS has used leverage with third parties to exert financial pressure on retailers, in addition to applying pressure directly to retailers. USAS mobilizes students to exert material leverage on retailers directly and through their universities. Universities are often reluctant to exercise this leverage, but students have been vigilant in their protests and have succeeded in getting over 150 universities to join the WRC. The reason that universities are so resistant to exerting pressure on licensees is that the universities face significant financial consequences when adding terms to licensing contracts. For example, Nike CEO Phil Knight withdrew a pledge of US$30 million to the University of Oregon after university administrators joined the WRC (as a result of student protests). A statement from Nike said, "The University of Oregon, despite its unique relationship with Nike and Phil, is free to align itself with the Worker Rights Consortium. However, it does not mean that we are required to support those efforts with which we have fundamental disagreements" (Greenhouse 2000). Such action was clearly intended as a message to other universities attempting to change the terms of licensing contracts. In order to maintain Knight's support, the University of Oregon renounced its membership in the WRC. Subsequently, in 2007, Phil and Penny Knight donated US$100 million to the University of Oregon to build a new basketball arena and to create the Oregon Athletic Legacy Fund. This case clearly shows the power of retailers in relation to licensing agreements. It also highlights the power of wealthy individuals in the industry, who wield tremendous power, to either bestow or withhold sizable contributions to universities.

It is widely acknowledged among activists in the anti-sweatshop network that the existing system of corporate codes of conduct, exposure of abuses, and piecemeal monitoring has not had the desired effect of widespread improvement of working conditions in the industry. A cycle emerged where workers spoke out, negative attention was generated in the international press linking retailers to the abuse, and the retailers withdrew their orders and moved on to the next factory, where the process started over again.

In response to this problematic cycle, USAS and the WRC developed the Designated Suppliers Program (DSP) in consultation with Southern unions and NGOs. As part of the DSP, licensees (such as Nike and Reebok, which license university logos) would be required to source the majority of their products from factories that have been approved by the WRC as meeting various labor standards. On behalf of the universities that join the

DSP, the WRC would be responsible for monitoring and verifying factories. The program states that "licensees are required to pay a price to suppliers commensurate with the actual cost of producing under applicable labor standards, including payment of a living wage; they are required to maintain long-term relationships with suppliers; and they are required to ensure that each supplier factory participating in the program receives sufficient orders so that the majority of the factory's production is for the collegiate market" (DSP Working Group 2006). In 2007 the WRC sought a favorable Business Review Letter for the DSP from the Antitrust Division of the U.S. Department of Justice in order to prevent future anti-trust litigation. Once it became clear that the Department of Justice would not issue such a letter, the WRC withdrew its request and waited to resubmit it once the Obama administration took office. As of May 2011 the DSP remains on hold as activists wait to receive the necessary letter of endorsement from the Department of Justice in order to prevent anti-trust allegations.

Even though the DSP has not yet been implemented, students have exerted more pressure on universities to join the DSP. The idea is that once the Department of Justice issues a favorable Business Review Letter for the DSP, the WRC will be ready to implement it. In an effort to get their universities to adopt the DSP, students on dozens of campuses organized rallies, petitions, speaking events, street theater, mock sweatshops, office stormings, and sit-ins. Photographs and video of the events were then circulated on the Internet and posted on websites such as YouTube in order to link university apparel with sweatshop labor and to share tactics with other anti-sweatshop activists. As of May 2011 the students had succeeded in getting forty universities to sign on to the DSP.

The inability of activists to intervene in the relationship between retailers and suppliers has proven to be a substantial obstacle in the past. If implemented, the DSP would signify activists' growing influence in the industry. According to the WRC's Nancy Steffan, one of the most important outcomes of the DSP might be to create model factories in order to demonstrate that it is, in fact, possible that the apparel industry can still be profitable while respecting workers' rights to unionize, paying living wages, and ensuring a modicum of job security (Steffan, personal communication, January 19, 2007).

In the meantime, USAS concluded a major campaign focused on Russell Athletic. The campaign is illustrated in Figure 5–3. In direct conflict with Russell Athletic's own code of conduct regarding the rights of freedom of association and collective bargaining, the company intimidated, harassed, and fired workers trying to establish an independent union. A report by the WRC in 2007 found that Russell Athletic illegally fired 145 workers in retaliation for union activity. In January 2009 Russell Athletic closed its Jerzees de Honduras factory, placing twelve hundred people out of work. An announcement by the WRC stated:

> If allowed to stand, the closure would not only unlawfully deprive workers of their livelihoods; it would also send an unmistakable message to workers in Honduras and elsewhere in Central America that there is no practical point in standing up for their rights under domestic or international law and university codes of conduct and that any effort to do so will result in the loss of one's job. (WRC 2009b)

USAS pressured universities to sever their contracts with Russell Athletic over the closures, as shown in Figure 5–3. One of its organizing strategies included a speaker tour of North American campuses for Moises Elias Montoya Alvarado and Norma Estela Mejia Castellanos, the president and vice president of the SITRAJERZEESH union, the workers' union at Jerzees de Honduras. Their tour, and the subsequent student activism surrounding it, led twelve universities to terminate their contracts with Russell Athletic. USAS reached out to student networks in Canada and the UK, which were also successful in getting universities to cut contracts with Russell Athletic. Activists used social-media sites such as Facebook and Twitter to communicate with one another, coordinate their efforts, and apply pressure to Russell Athletic. USAS also helped get sixty-five members of Congress to sign a letter to the CEO of Russell Athletic.[5] The transnational student campaign was successful. By early October 2009, one hundred universities had severed contracts with Russell Athletic. The goal of the campaign against Russell was to get the company to reopen the factory and reinstate dismissed workers (USAS 2009a). The campaign resulted in significant negative publicity for Russell Athletic. Some estimates put the financial loss to Russell Athletic at tens of millions of dollars due to the severed university contracts.[6] These tactics proved to be effective in pressuring Russell Athletic to change its course of action.

On November 18, 2009, Russell Athletic, SITRAJERZEESH, and the General Confederation of Workers announced an agreement that established a new, unionized factory, Jerzees Nueva Dia (New Day), extended employment to the twelve hundred dismissed workers, and committed to respecting and recognizing workers' rights to freedom of association in all of Russell Athletic's plants in Honduras. A headline in the *New York Times* read, "Labor Fight Ends in Win for Students" (Greenhouse 2009). USAS activists celebrated the news, claiming a victory for the lengthy campaign on dozens of campuses. The announcement read:

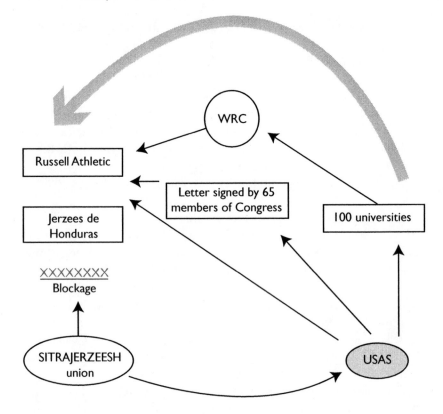

Figure 5–3. Boomerang pattern in Russell Athletic campaign

This is one of the most significant youth-led campaign victories in recent times and one of the most significant campaign victories of the global justice movement. No one has ever forced a multinational corporation to reopen a facility it shut down in the global race to the bottom. This victory has also proven that together, we can successfully fight back when those in power take advantage of the economic crisis to attack working people. We should take strength and inspiration from the example of the workers of Jerzees de Honduras. We can fight back—and WIN—against policies that benefit a privileged few and hurt our communities. (USAS 2009b)

In an email to supporters Scott Nova, executive director of the WRC, said that the agreement will bring Russell Athletic into full compliance with the WRC standards and "represents one of the most significant advances for fundamental workplace rights in the twenty-year history of codes of conduct in the apparel industry." He added that such an agreement was unprecedented in the history of the garment industry in Honduras and in Central America, "It is hard to overstate the significance of this break-through" (Nova 2009).[7]

The Jerzees de Honduras case was unusual in that USAS advocated for universities to sever their contracts with Russell Athletic, essentially calling for a boycott. A boycott was possible because the factory had already been shut down. Unlike boycotts as a form of negative political consumerism, the DSP (if implemented) would represent a positive form of political consumerism, rewarding companies (with university contracts) that source from factories that meet certain labor standards. Both forms of political consumerism seek to engage consumers as political agents, encouraging retailers to use their purchasing power and related leverage with universities and sportswear companies to improve working conditions in the industry.

The campaign against Russell Athletic was successful because of the cumulative actions of anti-sweatshop advocates over the preceding fifteen years. Many earlier campaigns were successful in the short term but were not sustained in the long term because corporations could easily "cut and run" from unionized factories. These campaigns helped lay the foundation for the success of the campaign against Russell Athletic. Previous campaigns helped build a network of student activists that could be mobilized when called upon. USAS had also helped establish the WRC, which meant that there was an institution in place that could mediate between the universities and Russell Athletic. This case represents a departure from previous campaigns in that it was an unmitigated success for anti-sweatshop advocates and workers. It also represents a continuation of campaigns in earlier phases of anti-sweatshop advocacy. USAS activists are hoping to capitalize on this victory and their victory in the Just Pay It campaign against Nike to gain momentum for future campaigns.

FairWear

FairWear exerts pressure on Australian companies to abide by fair labor standards in their supply chains. FairWear's role is to provide information about garment workers in Australia and abroad and encourage consumers to organize locally in place-based actions as well as to participate in online activism. FairWear's domestic campaigns focus on getting companies to join Ethical Clothing Australia. Once a company becomes accredited, it is able to sew the Ethical Clothing Australia label into products that meet the code.[8]

A FairWear chapter in Newcastle decided to focus on companies that produce surf apparel. The New South Wales government funded the initiative as part of its Behind the Label Strategy. This strategy resulted in the formation of the Ethical Clothing Trades Council, which included the Textile, Clothing and Footwear Union, the Australia Industry Group, the Australian Retailers Association (ARA), and Australian Business Limited. The council launched the Ethical Clothing Trades Extended Responsibility Scheme in July 2005. It required manufacturers to disclose their supply chains and notify all suppliers of regulations governing the employment of outworkers.

Even though the ARA was part of the Ethical Clothing Trades Council, the ARA worked to undermine the scheme. The ARA negotiated with the New South Wales Office of Industrial Relations to provide an exemption for retailers that committed to the ARA's voluntary code of practice. According to the ARA homepage in 2006, "The ARA is calling for all clothing retailers to sign up to the voluntary National Retailers Ethical Clothing Code of Practice which is far less time consuming to comply with than the mandatory scheme but at the same time helps stamp out the exploitation of outworkers." The ARA was successful, with 70 percent of Australian retailers signing up to the less stringent ARA code. This case highlights the role of government in the anti-sweatshop network in facilitating the development of industry codes and certification. It also illustrates the challenging environment in which anti-sweatshop activists operate and the power of industry bodies to undermine their efforts.

FairWear's international advocacy is aimed at pressuring Australian-owned companies to improve working conditions in the factories where their products are made. FairWear also shares information and publishes reports from international allies. For example, it posted calls to action on its website requesting that its supporters write letters in support of the CCC activists who were accused of cyber crime in the FFI case. FairWear is also closely linked with an international network dedicated to the needs of homeworkers around the world. This network is crucial in gathering information about people who are often hidden from the formal garment sector. FairWear aims to make homeworkers more visible to the Australian public, encouraging Australians to exert their influence as citizens to seek greater legal protections for homeworkers. It also appeals to its supporters as consumers, urging them to exercise political consumerism by publicly shaming companies and encouraging the patronage of companies that have accreditation from Ethical Clothing Australia.

Legal protections for outworkers enshrined in the Federal and State Awards give FairWear a point of leverage that is largely unavailable to the NGOs in the United States. The Awards stipulate terms of conditions such as wages, overtime, and benefits in the industry. In the United States, homeworkers do not have the same legal protections they do under Australian law.

FairWear does not have the same leverage points as USAS does with students. This is partly due to the absence of a collegiate-logo market in Australia akin to the U.S. system. However, the Australian education system provides opportunities for organizing at the secondary school level, where students are required to purchase school uniforms. Using materials by FairWear, high school students in Victoria urged their school administrators to source school uniforms from suppliers that were accredited by Ethical Clothing Australia. This campaign has succeeded in several schools but has not yet become widespread.

FairWear has participated in several transnational campaigns and is in the process of defining its role in the transnational anti-sweatshop network. One such case is described below and illustrated in Figure 5–4. In 2007 workers at the Vaqueros Navarra factory in Tehuacan, Mexico, voted for the independent September 19 union to represent them. Factory owners responded harshly. Hundreds of workers were harassed and fired for their involvement in the union and for their attempts to organize. Workers appealed to the state, but the State of Puebla refused to formally recognize the union.

The Maquila Solidarity Network (MSN) and other labor rights NGOs in North America began a campaign to pressure the companies sourcing from Grupo Navarra, owners of the Vaqueros factory. Activists urged the retailers to contact management to halt the harassment and firings of union organizers. Several retailers, including American Eagle Outfitters, Gap, and Warnaco, sent letters to Grupo Navarra asking it to respect workers' freedom of association. FairWear also urged its supporters to contact retailers and asked them to pressure Grupo Navarra to "stop the firings and harassment, reinstate all dismissed workers, and support a free and fair union representation vote without further delay" (FairWear 2007b). In addition to pressuring retailers, the MSN also urged supporters to contact the State of Puebla and ask that it recognize the union and address the unauthorized dismissals.

Despite this pressure—or possibly because of it—Grupo Navarra closed the Vaqueros Navarra factory in 2008, moving production to its other

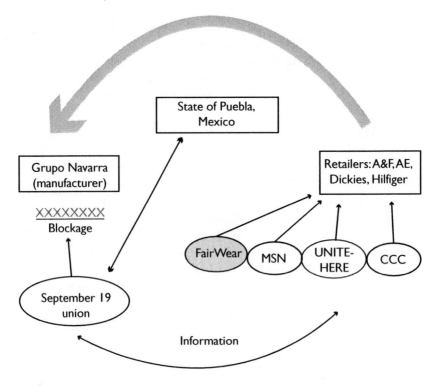

Figure 5–4. Boomerang pattern in Grupo Navarra campaign

factories, where no unions were present. In response, workers marched through the streets of Tehuacan to protest the closure and their employer's unwillingness to pay legally required severance pay. Workers blocked traffic and continued their protest in front of a factory owned by the president of the local *maquiladora* association (MSN 2008). Once again international pressure mounted, urging retailers to reopen the factory or at a minimum to ensure that workers received severance pay and any other legal entitlements. Workers and activists were unable to get the factory reopened or to obtain compensation for displaced workers. This case illustrates the significant challenges activists face in securing commitments from retailers even when workers are organized locally, applying direct pressure to manufacturers, alongside international anti-sweatshop campaigns applying pressure to retailers. These two aspects of the campaign (shown in Figure 5–4), in two different political arenas, were not enough to dissuade manufacturers from moving production to a lower-cost location with a non-unionized workforce.

STITCH

STITCH differs in its approach from the other organizations due to its grounding in feminism and in the types of politics it utilizes. USAS and CCC target well-known retailers and use the visibility of the retailers' brand images as a source of strength in their campaigns. Although this has been a point of leverage for these campaigns, it suggests a limitation as well, since Northern NGO–led campaigns are limited to focusing on labor conditions for workers producing branded products for export to Western consumers (Elliot and Freeman 2005). Many of the women whom STITCH works with in Central America do not have that same access to Northern consumers because they do not produce well-known, branded items.

For this reason STITCH has taken a different approach from the three other organizations. Instead of relying on linkages with Northern consumers, STITCH prioritizes the strengthening of local unions in Central America. Its model—of building connections between Northern and Southern union women, and among Southern union women—is aimed at encouraging women to learn from one another to take on leadership roles within existing union structures or to create unions where they do not already exist.

STITCH hosts workshops and training sessions for union women in Central America, brings delegations of women from the United States to Central America and vice versa, and is in the process of developing a leadership manual. STITCH tries to influence the consumer campaigns of other anti-sweatshop organizations by providing information and educating its allies about the ways that gender and gender identities frame women's experiences working in the industry. This includes the reasons that women were hired, the types of work they are assigned, their experiences of sexual harassment and forced pregnancy tests, and their reluctance or inability to join existing unions.

STITCH's strategies rely less on applying leverage to targeted actors and more on building solidarity among women workers. Yet in some cases, such as the campaign targeting Yoo Yang depicted in Figure 5–5, STITCH engaged in both advocacy and worker exchanges. Workers at Yoo Yang factories located in the EPZ Continental Park in Honduras first attempted to form a union in 1999. They sought to get their union, Union of Workers of the Maquila and Similar Industries Honduras (SITRAIMASH), formally recognized by the Labor Ministry in Honduras. In response to attempts to form a union, Yoo Yang management fired workers known for their union activities. Following extensive protests, the workers were reinstated. Meanwhile the Ministry of Labor stalled the application to grant

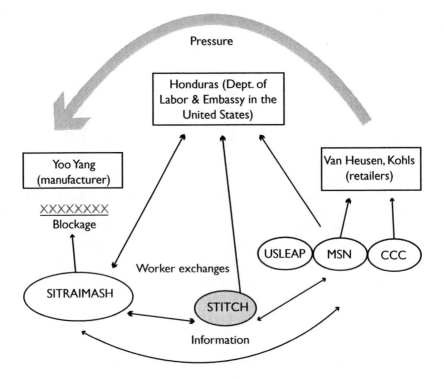

Figure 5–5. Boomerang pattern of Yoo Yang campaign

legal recognition to the union, despite a membership of 450 of the 600 employees.

Through its website STITCH encouraged its supporters to contact the Labor Ministry in Honduras and the Honduran Embassy in the United States. Other Northern-based NGOs involved in this campaign included USLEAP (the organization that STITCH grew out of), MSN, and the CCC. These organizations posted appeals on their websites in support of the Yoo Yang workers. In addition to encouraging supporters to approach the Labor Ministry and Embassy, NGOs put pressure on Yoo Yang buyers, including Phillips-Van Heusen. However, activists did this cautiously. One announcement implored activists not to leaflet retailers since they had not yet been instructed by workers do so (CCC 2000).

Workers held demonstrations inside and outside the factory, tied ribbons to their machines, and made numerous attempts to negotiate with management. They also collected signatures that were then sent to Phillips-Van Heusen. After forty-nine days of workers' actions and the intervention of Phillips-Van Heusen, workers who had been dismissed finally received 100 percent of the severance pay due to them (CCC 2000). This positive outcome for the Yoo Yang workers resulted from the combined pressure brought by workers and their allies in the anti-sweatshop network.

One union member, Marlena, said: "They had planned to fire all of us [union members] . . . I imagine to destroy the union. But there was . . . international pressure. . . . [The manager] said that he didn't want these problems" (CCC 2000). Although the government continued to refuse to recognize SITRAIMASH, it did grant approval for the establishment of the Yoo Yang Enterprise Trade Union (STEYY). Workers previously associated with SITRAIMASH were allowed to join STEYY or the Trade Union of Workers of Kimi Enterprise of Honduras, S.A. These were both factory-level unions, as opposed to SITRAIMASH, which would have been an industry-level union (ITGLWF 2000). This was less than the workers had wanted but was still considered a positive outcome. After eight months of negotiations STEYY signed a collective agreement with Yoo Yang.

Through its worker exchange program, STITCH provided funding for Yoo Yang worker Jesus Banegas to travel to El Salvador in 2002 to meet with workers seeking to develop a union at the Tainan *maquila*. One of the workers said of the exchange, "Hearing about how they won their contract has helped us understand better how we can achieve ours—and proves to us that it is possible" (STITCH 2002). This type of worker exchange is designed to strengthen workers' capacity to organize at the factory level by facilitating sharing information and strategies among workers.

Comparative analysis of boomerang patterns

These campaigns illustrate the complexity involved in building relationships, creating linkages, and maintaining pressure on targeted actors, all of which are necessary in transnational anti-sweatshop campaigns. The campaigns varied in their levels of success. The campaign against FFI was successful in securing some protections for workers, but only after the European CCC activists became the focus of the campaign. USAS students were successful in getting one hundred universities to sever their contracts with Russell Athletic, thereby causing it significant losses. This proved to be enough pressure to get Russell Athletic to reopen the factory and reinstate workers. In the Yoo Yang case, STITCH was also successful, but not to the extent that workers and activists had hoped. Although the campaign was successful in getting the STEYY union recognized, workers were unable to obtain legal recognition for an industry-wide union, which would have given workers more bargaining power with manufacturers. Despite the sizable mobilization among workers and consumers, the Grupo Navarra campaign was unsuccessful. The factory was not reopened with union recognition. The structural forces in the industry opposing this outcome were too great. The incentives for retailers to move their orders to lower-cost facilities outweighed the negative publicity and financial costs incurred from the campaign. In each campaign the anti-sweatshop network's involvement was only one variable among many that contributed to the relative success of the campaign. Other variables included the local labor context, domestic political environment, quota restrictions driving sourcing practices, the position of manufacturers within the industry, their abilities to move production to other facilities, and the costs and benefits of doing so.

While the obstacles associated with the structure of the industry were clear, the outcomes were not inevitable. They were the result of actions taken by purposeful actors. The anti-sweatshop NGOs were only some among many actors involved. The following section compares the points of leverage, movement across political arenas, and roles of states and IGOs in the various campaigns.

Points of leverage

Constructivist literature suggests that the power of NGOs is in the ideational realm, where NGOs marshal information to persuade more powerful actors to change their practices. With each of the anti-sweatshop campaigns NGOs used information to counter claims by retailers and to garner support for their cause. However, information and persuasive arguments were not enough to make retailers and manufacturers improve working conditions in the industry. The anti-sweatshop NGOs relied on strategic points of leverage to exert material pressure on targeted actors in addition to other forms of ideational power.

Each organization focused its intervention on a slightly different point in the garment industry. The difficulty they all faced was in acting without powerful allies. For this reason the NGOs relied on the leverage they had with third parties to exert pressure on retailers and manufacturers. This is why the boomerangs involved so many players and such lengthy paths between activists and manufacturers. For example, the USAS students applied direct pressure to Russell Athletic. They also used combinations of civil disobedience and formal channels to gain direct access to university administrators, who then exercised material leverage with Russell Athletic.

USAS aimed its actions at particular points in the industry, complementing the workers' actions at different points in the system.

While USAS focused on university contracts with retailers, the CCC campaign against Fibre & Fabric International applied pressure directly to G-Star and later to the Dutch government. STITCH encouraged its supporters to contact the Honduran Department of Labor and the Honduran Embassy in the United States in support of the Yoo Yang campaign. It also organized a worker exchange between SITRAIMASH workers and workers in El Salvador attempting to exercise their rights to form an association. FairWear lent support to the Grupo Navarra campaign by encouraging its supporters in Australia to contact retailers such as Abercrombie & Fitch, American Eagle, Dickies, and Tommy Hilfiger. The significance of these various points of leverage is in how such points worked in conjunction with other actors in the anti-sweatshop network and whether, together, they were able to create sufficient influence to achieve the desired result. While all these forms of politics were useful, none were sufficient on their own.

Based on these campaigns, the more direct the link between activists and points of leverage, the greater degree of success. For example, the USAS campaign against Russell Athletic succeeded in getting universities to sever their contracts because students on each campus focused on their own university. Even though these were local, decentralized actions, they were coordinated and had a unified goal, creating a transnational campaign. Activists provided university administrators with a focused, tangible course of action (to cut their contracts with Russell Athletic) to dissipate protest. What is noteworthy about this case is the willingness of universities to acknowledge some responsibility for working conditions in their contracting relationships. This recognition and action on the part of universities would not have happened without USAS and the students' rootedness to their particular universities, and their ability to use that position to apply pressure to university administrators.

Movement across political arenas

The boomerangs also show the importance of campaigns simultaneously operating in multiple political arenas. In the Fibre & Fabric case the fear of future material loss from activists' negative publicity led FFI to file a lawsuit against CCC activists. By filing the lawsuit against the CCC, FFI actually helped move the case from one political arena to another. This campaign received more attention than the other campaigns, including extensive media coverage and an outpouring of support from other labor and human rights activists. Within days of the arrest warrants being issued, in September 2007, numerous websites and blogs urged supporters to take action by contacting FFI and retailers in Europe and the United States that sourced garments from FFI. Dozens of NGOs, including FairWear, posted the CCC's urgent appeal regarding the FFI case on their websites, urging their own supporters to write letters and sign petitions. The case was finally resolved when it received international media attention and was elevated to a diplomatic issue during the Dutch queen's visit to India. This level of attention would not have been possible, however, without the participation of international NGOs and the media they generated. Without the shift in political arenas it is unlikely that the case would have received the necessary attention to negotiate a deal among all of the relevant parties.

Although the Grupo Navarra campaign shares some similarities with the other campaigns, it differs in some key ways. Like the other boomerangs, the campaign involved workers reaching out to international allies to pressure their employer. Despite a traditional focus on homeworkers in Australia, FairWear joined anti-sweatshop organizers in Canada, the United States, and Europe to encourage Australians to contact retailers sourcing from Grupo Navarra. By participating in campaigns like the Grupo Navarra case, FairWear linked its domestic advocacy of homeworkers with its advocacy for garment workers overseas. For its part in the campaign, FairWear extended the Grupo Navarra campaign to the domestic political arena in Australia, linking its supporters to consumers and workers in the United States, Canada, Europe, and Mexico.

Roles of states and IGOs

The campaigns show the range of actions taking place in different arenas, involving local labor movements, retailers, manufacturers, IGOs, and states. Anner (2001) notes that Keck and Sikkink's boomerang model prioritizes the relationship between domestic NGOs and states, paying less attention to the relationships between international organizations and international institutions. He points out that O'Brien et al. (2000) provide an alternative approach that emphasizes the relationship between global social movements and multilateral economic institutions. The main difference with the anti-sweatshop network is its use of boomerang patterns that rely less on state power and activists' abilities to influence states, and more on influencing companies, since activists see more opportunities to exert influence on the private sector.

However, IGOs are still important actors in the global garment industry. The CCC appealed to the OECD's Contact Point in the Netherlands
on the basis of G-Star's violation of OECD guidelines. Although the Dutch
Contact Point accepted the complaint, no firm action was taken. Even
though the ILO was not directly involved in negotiating or brokering an
agreement, the ILO provided the basis for international norms and standards. Whether explicitly stated or not, ILO standards served as a common point of reference in each of the campaigns. For example, activists
highlighted that the FFI violated ILO standards on collective bargaining
and freedom of association. The campaigns involved IGOs to a greater or
lesser degree, but they all incorporated aspects of both civic politics and
politics aimed at influencing the state. However, the cases involved states
in a way different from Keck and Sikkink's boomerang pattern. In the Yoo
Yang case activists demanded that the Honduran government recognize
the union, with little success. Similarly, the Grupo Navarra campaign targeted the Mexican State of Puebla to earn formal union recognition to no
avail. Neither American nor Australian activists targeted their own governments in this campaign. USAS was able to get members of Congress to
sign a letter to Russell Athletic that helped bolster their case. The Dutch
government refused to get involved in the FFI case until the Indian trade
minister addressed the topic during the queen's visit. The ways in which
states were involved in each case depended on the national context in which
the NGOs operated, the receptivity of the state to intervene, and activists'
engagement with civic politics.

Conclusion

The campaigns demonstrate how activists exercised forms of world civic
politics informed by their specific rootedness to place, ideology, and identities. Each NGO participated in various campaigns based on the structures
available to it. Most organizations focused their attention on consumer
campaigns to influence powerful retailers. They did this due to the structure of the industry, which concentrates power among retailers and lacks a
comprehensive intergovernmental regulatory framework. With limited resources and few powerful institutional allies, anti-sweatshop NGOs developed ways to intervene in the complex system surrounding the garment
industry by using strategic points of leverage.

These various boomerang patterns illustrate the complexity of contemporary transnational advocacy. The boomerang patterns of the anti-
sweatshop campaigns differ from Keck and Sikkink's boomerang pattern.

In these anti-sweatshop campaigns states were sometimes involved, but not always, and rarely as the primary target. Instead, the most effective campaigns combined civic politics with politics aimed at government institutions, addressing violations of workers' rights from multiple angles.

Emerging from each of these boomerang patterns is the collective and cumulative nature of anti-sweatshop advocacy. The case-study NGOs played small parts in larger processes, demonstrating the importance of the broader anti-sweatshop network and the reliance on that network for information and support, and pressuring targeted actors simultaneously. While each of the NGOs chose to focus on specific actors and intervene at specific points, they used resonant frames that helped multiply the impact of each organization's actions.

Chapter 6

NGO accountability
and political responsibility

The anti-sweatshop NGOs act as vehicles for concerned individuals to exercise their power as consumers and citizens. They pressure retailers to take greater responsibility for working conditions in the industry. They also bear their own responsibility to donors, allies, supporters, and the garment workers they aim to support. Although some organizations may have clear responsibilities to specific groups of people, they must also develop mechanisms to ensure that they fulfill additional, more diffuse, responsibilities to act in a manner consistent with the values they espouse.

As NGOs gain greater visibility in global political arenas, they are coming under increasing pressure to defend their legitimacy as political actors (Bendell 2006). Some critics on the political left contend that NGOs are becoming more corporate in design, gaining insider status, and reinforcing the current structure of global capital by making small, cosmetic changes to the status quo and that this functions to divert resources and attention from more radical grassroots mobilization (Escobar 1995; Incite! Women of Color against Violence 2007). Critics of NGOs also come from a conservative, anti-NGO movement, which claims that transnational NGOs are undemocratic and unaccountable (Bob 2004). They argue that transnational NGOs undermine the free market, circumvent national democratic processes, and threaten the sovereignty of nation-states (see, for example, Manheim 2003, xvi; Johns 2003). Simultaneously NGOs themselves have created self-regulatory initiatives—including One World Trust's Global Accountability Project, Humanitarian Accountability Partnership International, and CIVICUS's Legitimacy, Transparency and Accountability Programme—in order to develop greater accountability within the NGO sector. NGOs created these initiatives on accountability as a response to the criticism from the anti-NGO lobby and to preempt additional restraints on the sector (Lloyd 2005). This focus on NGO accountability is due to the growing number of NGOs in international political arenas and the awareness that NGOs' abilities to make effective claims is tied to their perceived legitimacy.

Approaches to NGO accountability

Accountability is often thought of in one of three ways: (1) financial accountability to donors, (2) accountability to members, or (3) accountability to beneficiaries for NGOs that serve distinct groups of people. One approach that seeks to address all three types of accountability is a stakeholder approach. Lloyd describes a stakeholder approach that "transfers the right to accountability from exclusively those that have authority over an organisation to anyone that has been affected by the organisation's policies" (2005, 3). This is an improvement on previous conceptions, which focused solely on financial accountability. However, by adopting a term associated with business, a stakeholder approach risks de-politicizing the issues and stripping accountability of the uneven power dynamics inherent in such relationships. It can also risk marginalizing workers, because garment workers are considered to be just one of many stakeholders. After all, workers' voices should be more important than other stakeholders in anti-sweatshop advocacy campaigns, since they are the most vulnerable actors in the industry. The point is not that other entities (allied organizations, donors, and staff) are unimportant or irrelevant, but that the concerns of garment workers should take precedence.

NGOs are often not representative of their constituents, nor do they aim to be. This is one of the ways that advocacy NGOs differ from membership-based NGOs or unions, which often aim to be representative of their constituents. Representativeness is just one path to accountability and not usually the most relevant one for transnational advocacy NGOs. As Edwards argues, "NGOs do not have to be representative to be legitimate, but they do have to be accountable for their actions, whatever they are, if their claims to legitimacy are to be sustained" (2006, ix). For anti-sweatshop NGOs to establish their legitimacy as transnational political actors, they must demonstrate responsibility to garment workers.

Political responsibility of NGOs

Jordan and Van Tuijl explain that "political responsibility is a commitment to embrace not only goals in a campaign but to conduct the campaign with democratic principles foremost in the process." They continue: "Within transnational advocacy networks there are no formal mechanisms to enforce obligations. Thus, to discuss accountability within these networks would be to suggest something that is not yet existent" (Jordan and Van Tuijl 2000, 2053). Jordan and Van Tuijl suggest several factors that contribute to the level of political responsibility achieved within transnational networks. One factor is the extent to which NGOs within the network focus their attention on different yet complementary political arenas. Another factor is the ability of each actor in the network to articulate its goals and strategies. Other factors include the ways in which the network raises and allocates financial resources, manages flows of information within the network, and the frequency and format of information within the network. These factors relate to the inner workings of a TAN and the need for advocates to operate their campaigns in a manner consistent with their values.

Young proposes a different model of responsibility that further broadens an understanding of NGOs' responsibilities. Her social connection model of responsibility is "based on social connection as an interpretation of obligations of justice arising from structural social processes," which do not necessarily align with political jurisdictions. Structural social processes, in this case the process of the production and wearing of clothing, connect people who do not reside within one nation-state. Although Young applies the term to the rights and duties of Western consumers and retailers, that same concept can be applied to the NGOs themselves in order to examine their connections to garment workers, and their political responsibilities to workers (2006, 102).

Young argues that consumers have a duty to take action to improve conditions in the industry by virtue of their participation in the social and economic systems that perpetuate exploitation. Her model situates Northern activists in a broader context of global justice, bringing analysis of power back into notions of accountability. This is something that most existing work on NGO accountability fails to do. Acknowledging activists' and consumers' positions within a broader economic and political context is fundamental to developing a comprehensive view of their political responsibilities. In fact, paying attention to these complex relationships acknowledges the subject position of each actor without allowing that position to be overly deterministic of its actions.

The source of strategic engagement for Northern-based activists in advocacy networks is their particular identities and connections to place as rooted cosmopolitans. The same aspects of their identities that can contribute to a sense of paternalism—citizenship, location, and access—also make them valuable allies in transnational networks. The key is to figure out how to manage those relationships, and instead of ignoring the particular position of Northern activists, acknowledging the power dynamics and strategic locations of each party.

Jordan and Van Tuijl's notion of political responsibility establishes the necessity for TANs to embrace democratic principles. Young's social-connection model brings an analysis of power into accountability, with political responsibility extended through the social and economic processes of the production and purchase of clothing. Drawing on these two bodies of work, I view NGOs' political responsibilities as broader and more demanding than traditional notions of accountability. A new conceptualization of anti-sweatshop NGOs' political responsibility begins to address the multiple layers of responsibility NGOs have to garments workers and their allies to conduct campaigns in a manner that is consistent with their values.

The fusing of goals and practice is at the heart of many activist campaigns to improve conditions in the garment industry, as it is in many campaigns in the broader global justice movement (Croeser 2006). Slogans like "Another world is possible" and "This is what democracy looks like," along with consensus-based decision making, seek to convey the importance of demonstrating an organization's values through its daily practice. Groups like the Zapatista indigenous movement in Mexico utilize a collective decision-making process that can be slow and arduous for those more accustomed to short-term, quick decisions. But for the indigenous people involved in the movement, the process itself is an act of resistance to neoliberalism and their actions are a demonstration of an alternative to the demands of the state and private enterprise. For anti-sweatshop activists, their relationship to workers and how they are either respected or remain anonymous and silent illustrates their capacity and potential for change.

While there are variations among organizations, the anti-sweatshop NGOs share certain values. These values include (1) commitment to acting in solidarity with garment workers, (2) embracing democratic processes and decision making, and (3) respecting difference and diversity (that is, being against sexism and racism). The following section develops ideas of NGOs' political responsibilities and how they can embody those values in the way they conduct their affairs.

Working toward greater political responsibility

A fundamental element of political responsibility in the anti-sweatshop network is aligning values with the ways that campaigns are conducted. Political responsibility should not be seen as an end result, with a clear assessment of whether it has been achieved or not. Instead, it is a dynamic process that is foundational to the work itself. Several ways in which advocacy NGOs move toward achieving greater political responsibility are included in Table 6–1.

One way that NGOs move toward greater levels of political responsibility is by increasing garment workers' and Southern labor advocates' participation in decision-making processes. Some NGOs do this by hiring former garment workers as staff or board members. For example, Chie Abad worked in a garment factory in Saipan before becoming a sweatshop policy analyst with Global Exchange in San Francisco (Abad, personal communication, December 12, 2008). Another way to increase participation is to link services with advocacy. Some organizations in the anti-sweatshop network, such as Oxfam Australia, already do this by linking labor rights advocacy with services provided through their development projects.

Value	Actions
Acting in solidarity with garment workers ⟶	Engaging garment workers in decision-making: • as analysts and advisory members; • by linking services with advocacy; or • through communication and by incorporating information from workers into campaigns.
Embracing democratic processes ⟶	• Implementing horizontal organizational structures and collaborative decision making. • Committing to greater transparency to disclose funding and ideological origins.
Respecting difference and diversity ⟶	Practicing respectful and accurate representations of Southern workers in discourse and images to avoid class, race, and gender stereotypes.

Table 6–1. Demonstration of political responsibility: Linking values and actions

Combining services with advocacy allows organizations to have ongoing consultations with workers and others affected by the NGOs' advocacy campaigns. Small advocacy organizations, unable to provide extensive services, develop other ways to communicate with those they aim to benefit. Although electronic communications such as email, web-based phone calls, and mobile phones have made some of these communications easier, they still rely on a network of people and the ability to make the necessary translations across languages, communication styles, and political arenas. NGOs' participation in the broader anti-sweatshop network can facilitate these exchanges, allowing NGOs to combine resources and ensure greater communication.

Information alone, however, does not necessarily lead to better outcomes. This depends on the extent to which information from workers is incorporated into consumer campaigns. Feedback loops refer to the extent to which people have input into a process as well as the NGOs' willingness to take action by either incorporating that information or changing course. Feedback loops can be part of a constant, informal process or may include more formal processes of complaints and redress. In either case, Northern-based anti-sweatshop NGOs use this information to adapt as the political and economic environment changes and the needs and desires of their Southern allies change as well.

Another way to work toward achieving political responsibility is to commit to greater transparency. Within the literature on accountability, transparency is usually defined as the extent to which an organization makes its financial records open to donors or the public. This is certainly an important aspect of transparency, but what I am referring to here is transparency as it relates to anti-sweatshop activists and their relationship to garment workers. Transparency in this case means making documents available to garment workers in accessible forms, in multiple languages if needed, and clearly disclosing an organization's funders and the organization's ideological origins and values.

Small organizations often do not have the same level of formality and "bureaucratization" of their processes as larger organizations. This can allow them to remain flexible and respond quickly to changing circumstances. It can also lead to a confusing and exclusionary process for those interested in participating more fully with the organization. Some NGOs seeking to achieve greater political responsibility formalize processes of engagement to improve transparency and develop greater consistency between their mission and actions. Formalizing processes and disclosing how decisions are made allow an organization to demonstrate its commitment to political responsibility.

Barriers to achieving political responsibility

There are several barriers for small organizations to exercise fully their political responsibilities. The first is a lack of resources. The small anti-sweatshop NGOs are under tremendous pressure to stretch existing resources as far as possible. In particular, they are discouraged (by funders and the public) from spending any resources on what could be considered administrative costs that would appear to detract from program work. For example, STITCH spends twice as much on printing as it might, because it uses union print shops instead of non-unionized ones. STITCH director Beth Myers said STITCH chose to do this in order to maintain consistency between the organization's stated values of paying a living wage and its day-to-day practices. However, this commitment comes at a financial cost that some funders may not readily support.

A second barrier is allocating the time needed to develop relationships and establish lines of communication. Small NGOs consumed with meeting immediate needs may choose to forego long-term activities that could cultivate and sustain political responsibility. A focus on immediate needs is often built into funding structures, with few grants supporting the long-term planning and relationship building necessary to sustain political responsibility. A third barrier is distance from those they seek to benefit. Northern-based anti-sweatshop NGOs are located close to the consumers and retailers they target. Distance from centers of garment production can greatly limit personal contact with garment workers themselves. This can mean that there is a risk of Northern-based advocates misrepresenting garment workers' needs and interests.

In addition to barriers due to distance and lack of resources and time, some directors of small NGOs may resist formalizing processes and creating what they see as unnecessary bureaucracy. After all, flexibility is one of the key strengths of small organizations. Flexibility allows organizations to respond quickly to changing situations, relying on personal connections and relationships of trust. These same factors mean that it is important for NGOs to formalize some of their processes so that the organization gains an institutional memory. This can avoid the so-called founders' syndrome of some small NGOs that limits their ability to function beyond the relationships established by the founding members of the organization.

Perhaps the most significant barrier is the structural weaknesses of NGOs, in general, and small NGOs, in particular. Their relative lack of power in the global political arena means that they are unable to advocate adequately on behalf on workers. Small NGOs' participation in the anti-sweatshop network can increase their political responsibility by providing links between workers and advocates as NGOs share information, multiplying their efforts. This reliance on other organizations in the network to act as mediators with workers can also diminish accountability if the staff of one NGO assumes that other organizations have taken adequate steps to develop relationships with garment workers and obtain accurate and credible information about workers' needs and desires.

Overcoming these barriers can contribute to NGOs' achievement of greater political responsibility. For NGOs engaged in issue-oriented transnational advocacy, political responsibility is an ongoing process rather than a clear measurement of their success or failure. Eade suggests that one way to measure an advocacy NGO's success would be "the extent to which NGOs (North and South) had opened doors for those who were denied access to the institutions that shaped their lives, helped them to organize their own advocacy agendas—and then stepped aside" (2002a, xv). These are laudable goals, yet they do not recognize the strategic place of Northern activists, not as benevolent missionaries, but rather in their strategic position as rooted cosmopolitans with access to markets and states, as consumers and citizens that can be of value to their Southern counterparts. This is not to romanticize or idealize the privileged position of Northern advocates, but rather to acknowledge their specific location in the global economy and in global civil society. With this position and their access to Northern consumers and limited access to Northern governments, these NGOs have multiple responsibilities to those around them.

Relationships and representations of garment workers

The ways that anti-sweatshop NGOs represent workers in their campaigns, both discursively and through images, are indicators of the extent to which an organization embodies its stated values. This aspect of political responsibility is often overlooked in the existing literature, yet it is a fundamental part of anti-sweatshop NGOs' establishment of themselves as legitimate political actors.

Struggles to create meaning through text and images are part of the anti-sweatshop network's framing process. Although framing can be a deliberate activity, some of it is a product of activists' political positions in the global economy and involves their unconscious reproductions of that position. Images that appear in anti-sweatshop materials often contain photographs of unnamed workers with downcast eyes sitting behind rows of sewing machines accompanied by a caption about the squalor and filth of the conditions in which people live and work. Framing the complex issues facing garment workers in this way is designed to garner international media attention and mobilize supporters in the global North to take action.

An example of this comes from the U.S.-based National Labor Committee. The NLC has been a vocal part of the anti-sweatshop network and a particularly important actor in the early name-and-shame campaigns. The NLC website contains an article entitled "Toys of Misery Made in Abusive Chinese Sweatshops: May Also Be Carrying Bed Bugs." The report describes conditions in two toy factories in China, where workers complained of low pay, forced overtime, poor health, and low safety standards. The NLC emphasizes in particular the workers' complaint about bed bugs in their dorm rooms. The NLC report then quotes a professor of entomology who suggests that bed bugs could travel in the cardboard used to package toys that are sent to the United States, potentially infecting consumers. While the NLC's goals are to improve conditions for these Chinese workers, language about bed bugs finding their way into American consumers' homes conjures up images of contagion. This type of reporting rests upon the assumption that the worse the image, the more emotive, the more media attention it will garner.[1] This may be true, but using such language and images does a disservice to those it intends to help because it contributes to portrayals of workers as helpless victims and denies their sense of agency.

Northern-based activists often focus on a particular type of identity formation of garment workers as voiceless, agentless victims. Since consumer campaigns rely on stirring consumers' emotions, images are often chosen for their emotive value. Kabeer cites a report by a member of UNITE that constructs garment workers in Bangladesh as abused, victimized, and passive, ignoring women's agency and the ways that they engage with the garment industry, which is a site of hardship and exploitation but also a place for new opportunities for economic independence and autonomy (2002).

The representation of women workers in advocacy campaigns is particularly important given the history of marginalization that women in the global South have faced in both labor and feminist movements (see Mohanty 2003). Brooks found that Northern-based anti-sweatshop campaigns aimed at improving working conditions in Bangladesh, El Salvador, and Honduras drew upon and reproduced imperial and colonial relations, even though this was in contrast to the organizers' stated goals. She contends that categories of gender, race, nation, and class are central to the production side of the garment industry. Furthermore, she argues that American and European activists are also guilty of reproducing these categories and using women garment workers, through their testimonies and their bodies, in order to contest globalization in a manner that is convenient for Northern activists (Brooks 2007).

These portrayals of garment workers are particularly problematic when coupled with women workers being largely absent in the planning and decision-making processes about anti-sweatshop campaigns and how workers are represented. Problems arise when Northern activists incorporate workers in consumer campaigns in ways that suit their own needs but do not necessarily meet workers' needs and interests. The risk of instrumentalization is acute in the anti-sweatshop network because at times it is less connected to individual constituents than are many service-based NGOs; instead, it is focused on the garment industry for its symbolic position in the global economy. The fact that women workers in the garment industry are often seen as emblematic of the new global division of labor is not necessarily disempowering, but it can lead to workers being used for their symbolic value to campaigns rather than being engaged as active agents of change.

The NGOs analyzed in this study struggle with how to present workers in respectful ways while still acknowledging how strategically important sensational images and stories can be to the media, consumers, and retailers. None of the case-study NGOs has a static relationship with garment workers. They all have shifted over time in how they engage with workers and the ways that they represent workers in organizational publications. This shift appears to have corresponded with broader shifts within development and labor movements. Within international development the shift toward rights-based discourse and the mainstreaming of gender (both of which have been informed by anti-colonial and feminist critiques of development) have contributed to a growing awareness among activists of the need for an accurate portrayal of women in the global South.[2]

Case studies

The anti-sweatshop NGOs seek to fulfill their political responsibilities to garment workers and their allies in different ways. This section emphasizes (1) NGOs' values, structure, and engagement with garment workers, and (2) representations of garment workers in campaign materials. It focuses on how the NGOs demonstrate political responsibility by linking their values and actions.

Clean Clothes Campaign

Values, structure, and engagement with garment workers

The CCC states its commitment to incorporate its mission into its organizational structure, thereby enacting its values of collaborative decision-making and egalitarianism. According to its 2006 *Annual Report,* "CCC is internally in line with the values it externally promotes: grass-roots democratic organizing, participatory methods of research, workplace assessments, direct involvement of workers themselves in all processes established to promote their rights." Its organizational structure is non-hierarchical, and all employees receive the same pay regardless of age, seniority, or tasks.

The CCC has achieved a significant level of political responsibility through engaging with Southern workers and labor activists, having advisory boards, responding to requests using its urgent appeals system, and representing workers in images and text beyond stereotypical versions of garment workers as agentless victims. The CCC secretariat elicits input from garment workers through field visits, regional meetings, and regular contact with representatives of unions and worker organizations. One of the ways that the CCC responds to its Southern allies is through its urgent appeals system. In 2006 the CCC took up thirty-four appeals, 67 percent of which were received from unions and the rest from NGOs working directly with workers (CCC 2007a). The appeals submitted concerned workers' rights violations in Cambodia, the Philippines, Thailand, India, Turkey, China, Bangladesh, Mexico, Indonesia, and Malaysia. When the CCC receives an appeal, the staff verifies it, determines whether the CCC is able to act on the appeal based on a set of criteria, then distributes it to the CCC network of over two hundred unions and NGOs, encouraging its supporters to take the necessary action, usually writing letters to European retailers and sometimes staging protests (Ascoly and Eyskoot, personal communication, February 7, 2007).[3]

Since the appeals originate with Southern unions and NGOs, the relationship is fairly straightforward. However, input from workers is more complicated for global campaigns. In an interview, CCC campaign coordinator Jeroen Merk said that with global campaigns the challenge is to ensure that Southern workers and organizations are integrated into the campaign beyond a superficial level, to ensure that they are involved in the design and preparation of the campaign (Merk, personal communication, February 16, 2007). He pointed to the advisory committee set up for the

Play Fair at the Olympics campaign as a way to increase participation of relevant partnered organizations.

Communicating with allies in garment-producing countries and also across Europe involves many challenges, including language barriers. CCC organizer Nina Ascoly said in an interview that there is often one person in each office in a non-English-speaking country who has to deal with international communication, and that person is often overwhelmed with work (Ascoly, personal communication, February 7, 2007). Therefore CCC secretariat staff try to streamline communication so that their Southern partners do not receive the same requests from each of the CCC chapters. Beyond obvious complications due to language and translation, CCC organizer Jeroen Merk mentioned the importance of timing requests for input from Southern allies and the importance of designing the planning process of campaigns to avoid reinforcing patterns of exclusion (Merk, personal communication, February 16, 2007).

The CCC organized an international meeting in 2006 to discuss codes of conduct and their implementation in response to questions from Southern allies about the growing discourse around codes of conduct. Ascoly said that she saw the role of the CCC in that case as providing a clearinghouse for information, gathering research, and bringing people together to get information to sort out the confusion surrounding multiple—and often competing—codes of conduct (Ascoly, personal communication, February 7, 2007). In the same year the secretariat coordinated a meeting in Delhi that included fifty-five participants from fifteen countries and nine campaigners from Europe (CCC 2007a).

The Asian Transnational Corporation Monitoring Network contends that even though the CCC—and particularly the Play Fair at the Olympics campaign—improved the level of participation from Southern activists and unionists in comparison to other anti-sweatshop campaigns, it still prioritized consumer leverage over worker solidarity. It argued that regardless of the level of consultation, consumer campaigns prioritize the role of consumers and European TNCs at the expense of building workers' movements. In other words, Northern campaigns that seek workers' input or Southern NGO input still rely on a framework that positions Northern NGOs as the decision makers and drivers of change (ATNC 2006).

Representations of garment workers

While many Northern activists' websites are dominated by pictures of garment workers with their heads down sitting behind sewing machines, most of the images on the CCC website are of activists and workers engaged in protest activities. For example, one photo on the CCC website shows workers protesting the closure of the A-One factory in Dhaka. The photo includes a group of women marching in the street with their fists raised in the air. In 2005, A-One workers were unfairly dismissed for their attempts to join a union. The case was settled two years later when Tessival, the factory's remaining buyer, offered former A-One workers a severance payment of 5,000 Taka (US$76) each. The workers had originally demanded reinstatement at the factory, so the settlement was far less than workers had hoped to achieve. The CCC expressed its disappointed that none of the buyers was willing to support freedom of association in the Dhaka EPZ. Nonetheless, it recognized Tessival's "willingness to pay severance as a first step in the direction of taking responsibility for social compliance in its supply chain" (CCC 2008f).

Images on the CCC website include those of garment workers sewing, marching in the streets, standing on picket lines, and mourning the loss of murdered colleagues. These are interspersed with photographs of activists throughout Europe engaged in protest activities. In one of its publications, *Made by Women*, the CCC includes profiles of Northern and Southern activists along with articles about working conditions, campaign activities, and the garment industry (CCC 2005a). It is unique for an NGO publication to weave in stories of European activists with photographs of individual (and named) garment worker-activists. The publication conveys various aspects of women's activities and their agency as workers, mothers, friends, and activists. Nina Ascoly, one of the authors of the publication, said that one of the goals of the publication was to "put a face on the issue and to show the diversity of the movement, not just in terms of ethnic diversity, geographical diversity, but also in terms of age" and the various ways that women have chosen to engage in the issues (Ascoly, personal communication, July 3, 2006). The CCC developed *Made by Women* after a meeting in Barcelona in 2001 where participants expressed the need for gender to be more explicit in the CCC's work. The CCC continues to develop ways to motivate European consumers and retailers to change their behavior without resorting to sensational images with media appeal.

FairWear

Values, structure, and engagement with garment workers

FairWear is highly decentralized, with each chapter operating somewhat autonomously from the others. Each chapter has a different relationship to its constituents, based upon structure, institutional affiliation, and location. As a result, it is difficult to designate its modes of accountability. FairWear staff interacts with homeworkers by providing training, supporting a radio program, and offering consultations. Amity Lynch, coordinator of the FairWear campaign in New South Wales, said in an interview that she is guided in her work by an active group of outworker advocates (Lynch, personal communication, February 3, 2009). First organized through Asian Women at Work, FairWear is advised by the outworker advocates to identify retailers to target, speak at schools and rallies, and make presentations to government officials. The FairWear chapter in New South Wales is located within a suburb where many outworkers live and work, and it is housed within the offices of Asian Women at Work.

In Victoria, FairWear has taken on a very different relationship and employed different strategies and organizing tactics from other chapters because of its outgrowth from the union and links with social justice religious groups. It is located within the offices of the Uniting Church in downtown Melbourne. Owing to its roots in labor and social justice struggles, the Victoria chapter is more activist oriented than the other chapters. The chapters in other states are less formal and do not maintain designated office space.

FairWear has achieved certain levels of political responsibility to outworkers in Australia by providing leadership training and English classes and through its outworker advocates group. Of the case-study organizations, FairWear is most clearly linked with a specific constituency: homeworkers. However, this is so only for its domestic campaigns aimed at homeworkers in Australia. Even though vast geographical distances do not separate advocates and garment workers in FairWear's domestic campaigns, many barriers to managing its responsibilities effectively still exist. Barriers include differences in language and culture, difficulties building trust, and time constraints, since many homeworkers work long hours in addition to their family obligations.

FairWear's interactions with homeworkers are largely mediated through the TCFUA and Asian Women at Work. The union provides English classes for garment workers. The participants gain language skills that are crucial for wider communication and movement building. Equally important, the classes provide an opportunity for workers' mutual support and community formation. Furthermore, the classes enable workers to communicate their concerns to union staff (Spyrou, personal communication, November 20, 2006). Helena Spyrou, one of the teachers of such classes in Victoria, said in an interview that in addition to teaching English, she identified herself as a facilitator, providing a healthy environment where the participants guide discussion (in addition to covering the required materials). She said, "Once you've got a group that has bonded, they can

take on a life of their own. You can become redundant, which isn't necessarily a bad thing" (Spyrou, personal communication, November 20, 2006).
FairWear also conducts leadership training. One of the benefits of the training is that organizers continue to learn from the women about the material
conditions of their work. Daisy Gardener, FairWear coordinator, said in
an interview that in addition to learning about the material aspects of
workers' lives during the training, workers also shared their dreams and
aspirations with activists and one another (Gardener, personal communication, November 21, 2006).

The implementation and enforcement of the Ethical Clothing Australia
code, described in Chapter 3, rely on outworkers to report infringements.
In order to do this they have to be aware of the code and the provisions it
entails. They also have to be confident that they will not be adversely affected by reporting infringements to the union. The union usually obtains
this information from outworkers through outreach, English classes, and
phone calls. Although the union keeps the identity of the outworker confidential, there is still an understandable level of apprehension among
outworkers about reporting breaches to the code (Spyrou, personal communication, November 20, 2006).

Early on, FairWear encountered a great deal of interest from consumers, students, and its members in addressing issues facing garment workers
outside Australia (Gardener, personal communication, November 21,
2006). The public may have found it more palatable to address injustice
abroad rather than fully acknowledge the intersections of racism and class
in Australian society. Homeworkers in Australia are mostly concentrated
in Sydney and Melbourne, yet they occupy a liminal political and economic space in society. Initially, FairWear organizers resisted an international focus because they felt it would detract from their focus on
homeworkers in Australia. Nevertheless, FairWear organizers have begun
to connect issues in the domestic sphere to the global garment industry
(Gardener, personal communication, November 21, 2006).

Representations of garment workers

The FairWear website contains three garment-worker testimonials.
Through these testimonials workers tell stories of work and family. The
website also contains photographs of homeworkers, including one of a
woman working at a sewing machine while a child sits behind her reading
a book. This image reminds the viewer of the dual role of homeworkers as
garment workers and also often as mothers. The location of their work is
also their home, and the traditional boundaries separating formal work

from the private sphere are absent. Photographs of activists, including out-worker activists, also appear on the website. For example, one photo shows FairWear activists visiting a local politician during a campaign to get legis-lation to protect outworkers in Victoria.

Activists struggle with the challenge of wanting to shed light on the exploitation that homeworkers face, while at the same time being aware that homeworkers may want to remain anonymous for fear of backlash from employers (Spyrou, personal communication, November 20, 2006). Through a leadership workshop in 2006 several homeworkers wrote a let-ter to the editor that was published nationwide in the *Australian Financial Review*. The women in the leadership workshop did not feel comfortable having their names associated with the letter, so they did not sign it. Yet, once they received a response from another reader blaming them for en-couraging businesses to move overseas (by demanding fair pay), the wom-en responded by writing another letter to the newspaper. This time the letter was signed by one of the workers, Diep Tran. She felt confident attaching her name to the letter since she was approaching the end of her career and was not as worried about losing work due to her activism (Gar-dener, personal communication, November 21, 2006).

The second letter was also published in the *Australian Financial Review* and is included, in part, below:

> As a Vietnamese outworker and mother of two, who did homework for 10 years in Australia, I enjoyed being able to spend time with my kids at home. After taking the kids to school I would work from 9am to 3pm and then after picking them up again I would work from 6pm to 2am to finish orders. I suffer chronic neck and back pain because of these long hours and was often alone, so I couldn't social-ize and learn English. I was happy and proud of my work, but I knew that I wasn't getting enough pay for the amount of work. When I got injured while working, the companies would never give me compen-sation and I would lose work. Many outworkers I know are too scared to speak up about bad pay and conditions, but we want to be paid the legal minimum wage like factory workers. . . . It is time that com-panies treated outworkers fairly and supported Australia. Retailers and customers need to listen to outworkers and think about buying from ethical companies who have the NoSweatShop Label. (Tran 2006)

Her letter paints a complex picture of the lives and experiences of outworkers in Australia. In contrast to the representation of homeworkers as highly exploited and passive victims, which sometimes accompany consumer campaigns, Tran's letter expresses her position as a working mother who is proud of her accomplishments while demanding greater rights and protections for her work.

FairWear has not yet developed systems to ensure accountability to workers in its transnational campaigns, relying instead on allied organizations in the anti-sweatshop network, such as Oxfam Australia and the CCC. As FairWear has just two paid staff members, it is unrealistic to expect this small organization to develop its own direct relationships with workers in dozens of countries around the world. However, in the absence of cultivating its own systems of accountability with garment workers overseas, it relies on networked partner organizations. This highlights one of the many challenges for small NGOs with limited resources to exercise political responsibility to those they aim to benefit.

United Students Against Sweatshops

Values, structure, and engagement with garment workers

USAS operates under a broad set of Principles of Unity, which outline the values that the organization espouses and the philosophy behind the students' focus on global sweatshops as one of the most blatant examples of global economic exploitation, and as a metaphor for all struggles against "systematic problems of the global economy."

This organization relies on its own programs as well as its organizational affiliations to gather information from workers. USAS works closely with the WRC, which has consultants in Indonesia, El Salvador, Kenya, Thailand, and Cambodia, in addition to its Washington DC office. It also coordinates actions with the Solidarity Center, which sponsors programs in sixty countries through a network of twenty-nine field offices worldwide (Solidarity Center 2009). These relationships help facilitate USAS's interactions with garment workers in the global South.

USAS communicates with garment workers mainly through established relationships with Southern NGOs and unions. USAS has built up relationships with some unions over the years, with regular correspondence by email and telephone (Knorr, personal communication, January 18, 2007). Another way that USAS communicates with Southern allies and gathers information is through its summer internship program. Each year, twelve to fifteen interns spend ten weeks with a union or NGO learning about the structure of the industry and the local conditions. Zach Knorr, USAS coordinator of international campaigns, said in an interview that the students are trained by the partner organizations about factory organizing in that particular context (Knorr, personal communication, January 18, 2007). The students then bring back that information and awareness, which is integrated into USAS's campaigns. For example, students returning from these internships used their new insights, developed in dialogue with Southern organizers, to formulate the Designated Suppliers Program. Internships provide the foundation for lasting relationships that involve sharing information and strategy and for ongoing institutional communication (Knorr, personal communication, January 18, 2007). Knorr made it clear that a process of constant communication is important to ensure that USAS's activities are in line with the needs and desires of its Southern allies. This level of communication is also important because the environment is constantly changing.

USAS positions students as its primary constituents. For example, even the Principles of Unity are directed at being respectful and inclusive of the wider student population—and the diversity of that population—as opposed to developing ways to become more accountable to garment workers. Knorr said that the identity caucuses (womyn-genderqueer, queer, working class, and people of color) were important to ensure that USAS did not replicate the same systems of oppression that they intended to fight against. This emphasis on equity and valuing difference among students is important, yet it should not be seen as a proxy for accountability to garment workers. Having American college students of color in leadership positions, for example, does not mean that the organization is any more or less accountable to garment workers who produce goods for the U.S. collegiate market. Nevertheless, USAS has made significant attempts to highlight the links among different forms of oppression and struggles across political boundaries. An example of this is linking anti-sweatshop campaigns with its campaigns in support of low-wage workers on university campuses, described in Chapter 3.

USAS is focused on leadership development in order to reproduce and sustain itself. The four paid staff members are organized horizontally rather than hierarchically. They hold their position for a two-year term, at which time new student activists take their place. USAS provides training and workshops, regional conferences, and an internship program. The constant emphasis on leadership development is due in part to the fact that, as a student organization, their leaders on university campuses are leaders for usually only a year and a half (Knorr, personal communication, January 18, 2007). Knorr acknowledged that the only way to stay strong and continue to grow is constantly to train new people to take the place of those who graduate and move on. He understands USAS's role as trying to get young people active in, and excited about, the labor movement. "That, for us, in many ways, is a goal, that we help to get young people excited about the labor movement and that we help them find a place within it, and hopefully, be an agent of change in the labor movement as well" (Knorr, personal communication, January 18, 2007). One of the ways that USAS does this is by getting students to analyze relations of power and identify how to access key leverage points in order to challenge systems of power. USAS uses personal and institutional networks to assist students interested in finding out about paid and volunteer job opportunities in the labor movement.

Representations of garment workers

USAS organizers have made a conscious effort to change the way that they represent garment workers in their campaigns. According to USAS activist Molly McGrath, "We have put more analysis into the way we are representing these relationships, and have tried to change the rhetoric to show sweatshop workers with more agency and power" (Featherstone 2002, 72). Another USAS organizer, Evelyn Zepeda, said in an interview with Kitty Krupat that USAS has made attempts to distance itself from paternalistic attitudes of some anti-sweatshop NGOs in the United States, including the National Labor Committee (2002, 121). USAS documents, such as intern reports, frame workers in multiple roles as workers, activists, and allies. The USAS website does not include any images of garment workers. Most of the images focus on students and student protests on university campuses.

As a student-run organization USAS exercises considerable political responsibility to university students in its organizational structure, decision-making process, and efforts at fostering leadership development of diverse students. This is important as a student-run organization, but it may result in prioritizing students' interests above those of garment workers and in assuming that adequate representation of students is an adequate substitute for greater accountability mechanisms to those who are most affected by their campaigns—workers. USAS has been less active in establishing and demonstrating political responsibility to garment workers, choosing to rely on the WRC as the primary vehicle through which to engage with garment workers and seek input into campaigns, along with its own internship program. USAS's website does not replicate harmful images or language of garment workers; neither does it create space for garment workers to express themselves or be visible as active agents of change.

STITCH

Values, structure, and engagement with garment workers

STITCH is the only organization included here that prioritizes women workers in their roles as decision makers and labor organizers. This is part of its mission and is evident in its priorities, activities, and images of women workers. Featherstone (2002) credits STITCH and other feminist organizations with starting to bring a feminist, anti-colonial analysis to the North American labor movement. According to the STITCH website (in 2007), the organization

> strives to be accountable to a diverse group of women, in both Central America and the United States, which is reflected in our own leadership and staff. Our programs are developed in collaboration with the women they aim to support. As women leaders and activists in the United States and Central America, we face many of the same challenges, and what we have in common is greater than our differences. By connecting the struggles of diverse women across the United States and Central America, we believe that all of our organizations become stronger and women leaders grow and learn from each other.

The challenge is how to put these values into practice. This is particularly difficult for a small organization with limited resources. STITCH organizes delegations of union women from the United States to Guatemala twice a year. The delegations are designed to develop links among the women, gather information, and share experiences and strategies. The women from the United States also attend Spanish-language classes while in Central America in order to develop their own skills, learn about the language and culture, and be better able to communicate with the women in Central America and with Spanish speakers in their own communities in the United States.

In the past STITCH's documentation project focused on the stories of Central American women and resulted in two publications on the impact of free trade upon women in Central America and workers' testimonials from the *maquila* and banana sectors. Recently, STITCH expanded its work in the United States to document immigrant women's experiences in the United States through interviews with individual women about their immigration and work experiences. STITCH also held focus groups with immigrants' rights groups, workers' groups, unions, and groups of women. According to Beth Myers, executive director, the project design started with the women themselves in order to find out what they actually needed and wanted from the labor movement, as a whole, and STITCH, in particular (Myers, personal communication, January 5, 2007). The purpose of the project was to find out how labor unions in the United States can better serve immigrant women workers. Another goal of the project was to figure out how to encourage more immigrant women to get involved in the U.S. labor movement. The project resulted in the publications of "The Other Immigrants/Los Otros Inmigrantes: Women Workers in the U.S. Labor Movement" (STITCH 2008).

STITCH developed a training curriculum for union women using a participatory process. Myers described the process in an interview. Miriam Cardona, a native Guatemalan consultant with a background in popular-education techniques, was hired to develop the curriculum. Cardona later joined the STITCH staff in its Guatemala City office. The curriculum development process included a focus group of fourteen women from unions throughout Central America. This group got together for a workshop in popular-education methodology. It chose four main topics, each consisting of three chapters, for the curriculum. STITCH staff members drafted the training materials and then gathered the focus group together to perform the training. Then they critiqued the process, and STITCH made changes based on their recommendations. Next, STITCH staff members accompanied one of the focus group members to conduct the training with rank and file women in the factories or fields where women work. They took the feedback from the training and put it back into the chapter before considering it complete. This sort of model, says Myers, "has come about from recognizing the political context in which we work and also recognizing that there are different training styles that work there [Central America] that aren't necessarily from here [United States]" (Myers, personal communication, January 5, 2007). Although this process has proven to be effective with the women STITCH is trying to reach, North American funders have not always been as supportive of the process, viewing it as unnecessarily long and laborious (Myers, personal communication, January 5, 2007). Such a process is not conducive to the shorter time frames that most funders work with, but it does work toward fulfilling the organization's political responsibilities to operate in a way that is consistent with its values.

According to Kidder, many women's organizations engaged in labor issues address the non-financial issues women face, such as additional pressures from family and society, in addition to the financial ones, whereas more traditional union-led efforts tend to focus exclusively on financial matters within the workplace (2002). Some of this may have been strategic on the part of anti-sweatshop organizers. After all, it is easier to pressure companies to obey overtime legislation than it is to change society's perceptions about the value of women's paid and unpaid labor. Yet, both remain necessary. To have gender as an added category in a footnote of a report is not the goal. Rather, the goal is to incorporate the needs, desires, and demands of all workers into advocacy campaigns.

Representations of garment workers

The STITCH website includes a gallery of photographs titled *Mujeres en Accion/ Women in Action*. The images show groups of women preparing skits, signing petitions, sharing a meal, working, and protesting. The *Mujeres en Accion* images depict the day-to-day work of women engaged in discussions and workshops. These are not the sorts of images that will garner much media attention because they lack the sensationalism of victimized workers. They also lack the excitement of images of workers marching in the streets with their fists in the air. The images portray workers engaged in the slow day-to-day work involved in building labor movements in Central America.

Maintaining a STITCH office in Guatemala clearly facilitates exchange and feedback from Central American union women to women in STITCH's office in Washington DC. Communication with garment workers is made easier by having staff members located in somewhat closer geographical proximity to the workers they aim to support. STITCH enacts a high level of political responsibility by engaging workers in decision making, designing projects, and revising project design based on workers' input. STITCH does not use highly emotive images or language about workers, instead opting for pictures or text of women at work, gathering in meetings, or organizing protests. STITCH is able to do this, in part, because the organization does not rely on generating media attention to mobilize U.S. consumers and supporters.

Conclusion

As NGOs become increasingly important actors in international politics, they have come under growing pressure to demonstrate their accountability to those they aim to benefit. However, traditional ways of conceptualizing accountability are inappropriate to the particular context of NGOs engaged in transnational anti-sweatshop advocacy. Jordan and Van Tuijl's work on political responsibility in TANs, which emphasizes that actors within networks must conduct campaigns according to democratic principles, is useful for analyzing anti-sweatshop NGOs. Young's social-connection model of responsibility highlights dimensions of power in advocacy relationships, the relative positions of anti-sweatshop activists in the global economy, and the responsibilities associated with those positions. Both imply fusing goals and practice. Organizations can enhance their level of political responsibility to garment workers by embodying their values in their day-to-day activities.

Anti-sweatshop NGOs focused on American, European, and Australian consumers and retailers face many challenges in fulfilling their political responsibilities to workers in the global garment industry. These challenges include geographic distance, cultural differences, and language barriers. Political responsibility is a process. It is something to work toward, rather than something easily assessed as having been achieved or not. There are several ways that these NGOs can increase their political responsibility to workers, including engaging garment workers in decision making, adopting horizontal organizational structures, committing to greater transparency, and incorporating respectful and accurate representations of workers. The extent to which NGOs put these into practice reflects their level of political responsibility to garment workers.

It is perhaps obvious, but worth pointing out, that more contact between workers and activists contributes to garment workers being more involved in decision making and designing campaigns. This can be seen in STITCH's workshops and delegations among union women and in the CCC's advisory committees and urgent appeals system. Organizations that lack the resources to cultivate direct systems of accountability with garment workers must rely on partner organizations for contacts and information. Although FairWear has developed a system of political responsibility through its outworker advocates group for its domestic campaigns, it has not been able to develop such systems for its transnational campaigns. Relying on allied organizations requires a great deal of trust in, and coordination with, partner organizations, and it speaks to the importance of the broader anti-sweatshop network for these small NGOs.

Small organizations often face considerable challenges in committing to greater transparency. Organizations often disclose little beyond what is legally required by governments or demanded by funding agents. Increasing transparency of NGO operations, ideologies, and budgets to allied organizations and workers is equally important. Such disclosure would begin to create more open and responsive organizations. It would also increase anti-sweatshop NGOs' levels of accountability to garment workers.

In addition to engaging garment workers in decision making and committing to greater transparency, anti-sweatshop NGOs can increase political responsibility to garment workers by representing garment workers respectfully and accurately in campaign materials. The way in which anti-sweatshop advocates depict garment workers in campaign materials shapes the way that consumers view workers. These depictions can either help empower and support workers in their struggles or reinforce racial and gender stereotypes. The CCC and FairWear include images of women in various stages of work and protest on their websites. USAS does not have images of workers on its website, focusing instead on the protest movements of the university students involved in its campaigns. STITCH portrays women in their organizing roles in its workshops and delegations. These depictions (or absences) can reinforce images of women workers as passive victims or portray women as active agents of change. The latter portrayal is likely to garner less media attention. However, by depicting women workers respectfully and with dignity, an organization, through such portrayals, shows a greater level of political responsibility to the workers it aims to serve.

In my interviews, staff members at each of the NGOs acknowledged the challenges of developing and maintaining systems of accountability in complex environments, but they also pointed to ways that the organizations were seeking to develop greater responsibility to garment workers. For example, the CCC's urgent appeals system is designed to be responsive to requests made directly from workers, unions, and NGOs. Several of the organizations have made explicit changes in their discourse around garment workers. For example, in its 2001 Principles of Unity, USAS made a commitment toward greater diversity and representation of students within its organization. At the same time, USAS activists made a conscious effort to move away from the paternalistic language and images of workers as helpless victims and toward more respectful representations (Krupat 2002). These represent ways that NGOs' relationships to garment workers change over time, and how they are seeking to be more accountable to workers, despite the challenges in doing so.

Chapter 7

Effectiveness
of anti-sweatshop advocacy

There are several compelling reasons to assess critically the effectiveness of NGOs in their advocacy roles. The main reason is to be able to demonstrate that an organization is acting in good faith on behalf of those it aims to benefit—and is actually making a difference to their lives. This is a particular challenge to Northern-based anti-sweatshop NGOs that are located far from garment workers and sites of production. Another reason is because effectiveness is connected to the perceived legitimacy of NGOs as global political actors. Without being able to demonstrate their ability to effect change, NGOs are less likely to attract an audience and garner the support they need to participate in an influential advocacy network.

This chapter assesses the effectiveness of anti-sweatshop advocacy from three different angles. The first section focuses on the effectiveness of the anti-sweatshop network as a whole. It develops criteria to assess effectiveness using a modified version of Keck and Sikkink's (1998) stages of influence of TANs and applies those stages to the anti-sweatshop network. The second section focuses on the four case-study NGOs and their differing strategies to improve working conditions in the industry. The last section highlights two anti-sweatshop campaigns and the challenges activists face in achieving, and maintaining, policy and behavioral changes in the industry.

Approaching effectiveness in this way—by examining the network, the individual NGOs, and campaigns—provides insight into the actors involved in anti-sweatshop advocacy and the complex environment in which they seek to improve working conditions. This approach accounts for the interconnectedness of the actions of individual NGOs and the anti-sweatshop network. Approaching effectiveness in this manner also illustrates change over time and the instability of the gains that activists have made against the backdrop of powerful structural forces in the global garment industry.

Effectiveness of the anti-sweatshop network

Keck and Sikkink suggest that TANs can be effective in various stages: (1) by framing debates and getting issues on the agenda; (2) by encouraging discursive commitments from states and other policy actors; (3) by causing procedural change at the international and domestic level; (4) by influencing policy, and (5) by influencing behavioral changes in target actors (1998, 201).

Since anti-sweatshop advocates focus much of their attention on retailers rather than on states, their patterns of advocacy differ from Keck and Sikkink's TANs. This was illustrated in the various boomerang patterns in Chapter 5. For the anti-sweatshop network the first stage of influence is raising awareness of sweatshop issues among consumers and getting retailers and universities to participate in debates on their roles in the global garment industry. The second stage of influence is achieving discursive commitments from retailers and universities regarding their responsibilities for ensuring adequate working conditions in the industry. The third stage of influence is getting retailers and universities to change their policies pertaining to the garment industry. It is useful to think of two parts to the third stage—achieving policy changes in the primary target (retailers and universities), and the extent to which changes in the primary target have led to policy changes in the secondary target (manufacturers). The fourth stage is influencing behavioral change of manufacturers to implement adequate labor standards and directly improve working conditions in the industry.

Before assessing the extent to which the anti-sweatshop network has achieved its goals, it is necessary to reiterate anti-sweatshop advocates' goals. While each organization has its own emphasis, together the actors in the network hope to improve working conditions in the industry and secure workers' rights. A more specific articulation of these goals can be seen in the WRC's model code of conduct. The WRC standards, mentioned in Chapter 1, are based on the ILO Fundamental Principles and Rights at Work. The WRC code is summarized below, noting how it differs from more industry-oriented codes.

- The WRC code makes a provision for workers to be paid a living wage (as opposed to a minimum wage). A living wage is intended to provide for a family's basic needs including housing, energy, nutrition, clothing, healthcare, education, potable water, childcare, transportation, and savings.

- The WRC code states that overtime must be voluntary and that employees shall receive one and a half times their regular pay for hours worked over forty-eight hours in a week.
- In addition to requiring that women receive remuneration and treatment equal to that of male employees, the WRC code includes a special provision for women's rights, including banning the practice of forced pregnancy tests and dismissal of pregnant workers.
- The WRC code includes a ban on child labor, as do most other codes, but also urges that action be taken to alleviate the negative impact on children released from employment as a consequence of implementing the ban.
- The WRC code states that workers have the right to collective bargaining and freedom of association. It also includes a statement that workers should have the ability to join the union of their choice, that they should have access to that union, and that employers and retailers should recognize the union that employees choose.

The WRC standards are goals that activists strive for in the industry. It should not be assumed that if anti-sweatshop advocates have not achieved these standards, they have unconditionally failed or that they have been acting in bad faith. Achieving those standards is dependent on getting industry actors far more powerful than themselves to alter their policies and practices in ways that are likely to decrease retailers' and manufacturers' profit margins. Therefore, the WRC often struggles to achieve the implementation of standards well below the goals outlined in the code. Nancy Steffan, assistant director of policy and communications of the WRC, said in an interview that the WRC most often works on cases where workers are owed back wages, have been unfairly dismissed, or are verbally or physically abused. She said, "All factories are violating pretty much all of the code provisions. It is the nature of the industry" (Steffan, personal communication, January 19, 2007). For this reason the WRC focuses its investigations on the violations that workers in a specific factory identify as their most pressing problems rather than on more routinized problems such as wages that meet legal standards but are inadequate for workers to meet their basic needs. Therefore, the WRC standards should be seen as goals that the anti-sweatshop activists are striving toward, but should not be seen as a baseline standard from which individual factories deviate. This shows the significant challenges activists confront in achieving each stage of influence in light of powerful structures in the industry resistant to such changes.

Assessing effectiveness of anti-sweatshop advocacy requires stepping back from individual NGOs to broaden the focus on the cumulative and collective actions of the anti-sweatshop network. The next section addresses each of the stages of influence of the anti-sweatshop network. This is followed by a discussion of the case-study NGOs and a review of two campaigns in order to consider the challenges activists face in translating effective campaigns into lasting change for workers.

Stage 1: Raising awareness and agenda setting

One of the goals of consumer campaigns in the United States, Europe, and Australia is to garner media attention in these countries and to raise awareness among consumers of the inadequate working conditions in the garment industry. Connor charted the level of media attention focused on working conditions in the sportswear industry from 1990 to 2007. He found that the number of news articles peaked in 2000–2001 with over nineteen hundred articles. By 2006 coverage of sweatshop issues had decreased to 550 during the first nine months of the year. Whether or not this news coverage is in response to press releases by anti-sweatshop NGOs, admissions by corporations, or the result of independent journalism, the effect was to increase awareness about working conditions in the garment industry (2007, 125). Although there was a decrease in media coverage from 2000 to 2006, a certain level of media attention remained.

This type of media attention, or what Bob (2005) refers to as diffuse consciousness-raising, helps to place issues about workplace labor standards on consumers' and retailers' agendas. Agenda setting is one of the most important tasks that NGOs can perform in political arenas. As described in Chapter 2, much of the contemporary anti-sweatshop activism in the United States began with the media attention surrounding Kathie Lee Gifford and other celebrities in the mid-1990s. As a result of this media attention, anti-sweatshop advocates were able to get sweatshops on the Clinton administration's agenda. Government officials then convened a meeting of industry executives, NGOs, and unions, which became the Apparel Industry Partnership, later the Fair Labor Association. In other words, debate on the issues led to the formation of a multi-stakeholder initiative.

Since the mid-1990s the anti-sweatshop network has made noticeable gains in terms of public awareness among Northern consumers about working conditions in the garment industry. Its efforts have been joined by many others aimed at increasing consumers' awareness and willingness to pay more for goods produced under ethical conditions. Elliot and Freeman summarized the findings of three polls in the United States aimed at finding out whether consumers would pay more for a garment made under better conditions. In all three surveys, the majority of consumers (76–81 percent, depending on the price increase) responded that they would be willing to pay a slightly higher price if they knew that the product was made under good working conditions (2005).

These studies are not direct indicators of the influence of the anti-sweatshop network. However, the anti-sweatshop NGOs have been part of broader movements to increase awareness about ethical consumption, and these studies point to a broad awareness among consumers about the conditions under which goods are produced. Global Market Insite conducted a survey of fifteen thousand online consumers in sixteen countries in 2005. Consumers reported that they were willing to pay more for goods that were organic, environmentally friendly, or fair trade. This included 47 percent in the UK, 42 percent in the United States, 91 percent in China, and 71 percent in India (GMI 2005). Consumers reported different factors for determining if a company was socially responsible. Respondents in Australia, India, Canada, Germany, China, and Japan selected environmentally friendly practices as the top factor in determining whether a company was socially responsible. Respondents in the United States reported "contributing to the community" as their top factor. These studies suggest that there is a sizable percentage of consumers willing to pay more (or, at least, who say that they will pay more) for goods labeled as made under ethical conditions.

Stage 2: Discursive commitments

The anti-sweatshop network has contributed to both consumers and corporations acknowledging their responsibilities to support better working conditions in the industry. Macdonald and Macdonald suggest that by adopting codes, firms are institutionalizing their acknowledgment of the power and responsibility they bear within their supply chains. They note that this acknowledgment is often in an abstract sense, without empowering workers in specific factories to take action, since workers are often unaware of the specific retailers and their codes. Nevertheless, they suggest that anti-sweatshop activists' abilities to identify retailers as "actors wielding direct power over workers in developing countries" and to communicate this information to wide audiences, have been significant achievements of the anti-sweatshop network (2006, 105). Indeed, activists' abilities to use the media to link major retailers to inadequate working conditions—and get retailers to respond—is evidence of the network's influence.

One of the most significant shifts came in the late 1990s, when many corporations began to acknowledge some responsibility for working conditions in their supply chains and adopted codes of conduct. Rodríguez-Garavito cites a study by the World Bank that found there were more than one thousand corporate codes in existence. In a survey of five hundred companies, Wilson and Gribben found that 98 percent of the companies had a code of ethics, with nearly two-thirds adopting such codes in the 1990s (Rodríguez-Garavito 2005). In the garment industry most major clothing and footwear retailers have now adopted codes of conduct.

As with voluntary codes of conduct, the proliferation of corporate social responsibility discourse has given activists greater tools with which to exercise accountability politics. In recent years corporate social responsibility has become a focus of debate among activists, scholars, business executives, and public officials. Corporate social responsibility is a way to extend the responsibility of businesses beyond their shareholders. This might include workers, consumers, the public good, and also the environment. Many, however, are justly skeptical. Chang and Wong contend that corporate social responsibility fits within a neoliberal frame and is ineffective at restructuring labor relations. They argue that it is essentially a way for corporations to gain a positive public image without making any significant changes to the way they do business (2005). Reich also argues that the push for greater corporate social responsibility is misguided, but for a different reason. He claims that it distracts corporations from doing what they are designed to do—increase shareholder wealth. He argues that trying to get corporations to adopt corporate social responsibility practices positions businesses as self-regulators and undercuts government regulation for better labor standards (2007).

Corporations develop corporate social responsibility programs for a variety of reasons, but often in reaction to, or in an attempt to avoid, negative publicity. Clark suggests that TNCs react to consumer campaigns, even those that do not ultimately do much to their bottom line, for the following reasons. First, they may have a long-term view of their corporate image. Second, they may be aware of the growing role of ethical investors who screen their investments based upon social and environmental criteria. Last, and Clark suggests most important, consumer campaigns have the ability to negatively affect staff and management morale. He cites an example of campaigns targeting Nestle and the sale of baby formula in Africa, where corporate staff were increasingly uncomfortable (and therefore less productive) with the revelation of their employer's contribution to infant malnutrition and even death. For all of these reasons, corporations respond to advocacy campaigns by adopting codes of conduct and implementing corporate social responsibility programs (2003, 202).

The same language about workers' rights and corporate responsibilities, which activists use in their campaigns, now appears on websites and annual reports of the corporations they target. As the discourse of the anti-sweatshop movement has moved into the mainstream, ideas associated with corporate responsibilities and workers' rights have also changed. This can be seen through various phases of anti-sweatshop advocacy. During the first phase, retailers refrained from using language associated with workers' rights. In the second and into the third phase, many companies made claims of respecting workers' rights, pointing to their codes of conduct and participation in MSIs as evidence.

In some instances retailers position themselves as taking on a watchdog role, monitoring and admonishing suppliers for breaches of core labor standards. An example of this comes from the Adidas Group, regarded as one of the better companies in terms of its internal social auditing, participation in MSIs, and engagement with NGOs. Adidas's own workplace standards include a limit on working hours of sixty hours a week and a period of continuous twenty-four hours for rest within every seven days. However, even in its own reports Adidas acknowledges that suppliers regularly do not meet these standards (Adidas Group 2007b). Adidas's admission is commendable, since few companies make such information public. Nevertheless, these are extremely low standards, and the fact that they are not met does not reflect well on Adidas's own sourcing practices. Like the other retailers, Adidas does not acknowledge its pricing structure and required delivery times as contributing factors to its suppliers' poor rate of compliance with its code. Such a system puts additional pressure on suppliers to meet the code without retailers changing their own practices, further contributing to inadequate wages and forced overtime.

Stages of influence rarely follow a linear path in anti-sweatshop advocacy. Goals and values are transmuted through the stages so that by the time targeted actors make procedural or policy changes, the outcome may differ from what activists intended. This is most clearly seen in the gap between the codes promoted by activists (such as the WRC code), which include provisions for a living wage, and most company codes, which pledge to adhere to domestic minimum wages. This gap has led activists to criticize codes of conduct as a form of "fair-washing" (Conroy 2007, 24), providing hollow public-relations opportunities for corporations to tout their commitment to social causes without actually changing their own practices in any meaningful ways.

Another critique of codes of conduct concerns the ways in which emphasizing codes places TNCs in a monitoring role. Commenting on the impact this has on women workers, Elias argues, "Placing the multinational firm as a central agent in the promotion of labor standards (via codes of conduct), is highly problematic, because it represents a failure to acknowledge how firms themselves play an active role in the construction of global systems of gender inequality" (2007, 57). Elias's critique of codes of conduct raises some important questions about whether placing such emphasis on retailers ignores their roles in creating structural inequalities in the industry. Lengthy supply chains and subcontracting enable retailers to distance themselves from garment workers and off-load significant risks associated with production. These chains of production make it difficult for workers to seek redress from factory management, or from retailers at the far end of a lengthy chain. It is clear that codes of conduct do not radically alter the structure of the industry. Yet with few alternatives available, activists use retailers' discursive commitments, in the form of codes of conduct, for their symbolic value. When reality does not live up to stated ideals, such commitments provide activists with tools to be used in future campaigns.

Stage 3: Policy changes by retailers and universities

Anti-sweatshop advocates face particular challenges in achieving the third stage of influence: getting retailers or universities to put discursive commitments into practice. This process involves activists' external pressure on targeted actors as well as struggles from within the company or university to define its role in the industry. Policy changes by U.S. universities are evident in their participation in the WRC and the FLA. Participation in either organization links university licensing contracts to labor standards monitored by the MSIs.

USAS has also been successful in getting universities to disclose the factory locations where their licensed apparel is produced. Outside the university apparel market, the disclosure of factory locations to the public has been limited. Instead, some companies participate in a shared database, the Fair Factories Clearinghouse, which allows retailers to share factory audit findings on a confidential basis. As of August 2009, the database contained information on over twenty-three thousand factories in 129 countries (FFC 2009). CCC organizer Jeroen Merk said in an interview that the disclosure of factory locations was necessary and the establishment of the Fair Factories Clearinghouse's database was beneficial. Yet, he argued that the information must be made available to the public rather than being held in confidential databases, in order for companies to be held to account for working conditions in their supply chains (Merk, personal communication, February 16, 2007).

Many retailers and industry bodies simultaneously adopt the language of responsibility while rejecting the influence of anti-sweatshop NGOs. One example of this comes from the World Federation of the Sporting Goods Industry report, *Official Handbook of the Sporting Goods Industry: CSR and the World of Sport.* In the report a letter from Michel Perraudin, WFSGI president, refers to the Play Fair campaign:

> The Beijing Games more than ever will be used by the sport industry detractors to push the CSR agenda. . . . I am convinced that "ethical production" as well as "ethical buying" will become more and more important to the consumers of our products at the same time to all our members. Next to the quality of the products, the reliability of the suppliers and economic considerations, the corporate social responsibility compliance will become an element of differentiation and be part of strategic and operational considerations for the brands when making decisions on their suppliers' base. This has just been documented in a very clear way by the decision made by Nike to stop buying from one of its major suppliers in Pakistan for such reasons. (WFSGI 2007)

What is most interesting about this report, and is perhaps indicative of the move to adopt corporate social responsibility policies and practices, is the simultaneous resignation about those "sport industry detractors" along with the celebration of corporate social responsibility as an integral part of the sportswear industry. For example, the Play Fair at the Olympics campaign is noted in the report as being a sport-industry detractor. Yet, under the WFSGI's list of corporate social responsibility progress made in the last three years, the report cites WFSGI's engagement with the very same campaign.

In the same report an article from the International Olympic Committee (IOC) exalted the importance of ethical sourcing in Olympic gear and suggested that ethical sourcing may become a part of the bidding process for future Olympic Games. Ironically, the IOC had previously ignored the Play Fair campaign and had refused to engage in dialogue with activists. However, this report, aimed at industry executives, has actually adopted many of the Play Fair goals and discourse. It remains to be seen whether the IOC will actually implement any of these actions leading up to the 2012 London Olympics.

Although much of the adoption of corporate social responsibility language is not accompanied by policy changes, several retailers have made policy changes that affect their sourcing practices. One such change is the participation in MSIs.[1] The very existence of MSIs is a testament to anti-sweatshop advocacy. As described in Chapter 4, governments, industry executives, and NGOs created garment industry MSIs as a result of negative publicity from anti-sweatshop campaigns. For all of their faults, MSIs helped extend retailers' responsibilities through their supply chains. MSIs provide NGOs with an alternative form of governance in which NGOs are involved, in a limited way, in monitoring the actions of transnational retailers. Although MSIs allow NGOs to participate in the governance of the industry, many activists—with much justification—view corporate participation in MSIs as a mere public-relations exercise. Corporate-led MSIs allow retailers to absorb critiques without making any substantive changes in their sourcing practices. Whether or not they support MSIs, activists face significant challenges in getting corporations' discursive commitments realized in policy changes.

Stage 4: Behavioral changes by manufacturers

Securing genuine behavioral changes in targeted actors has proven to be elusive. Although anti-sweatshop advocates have achieved limited policy changes in many of the targeted corporations, these have not led to significant changes for workers. For example, many of the companies that have been the targets of anti-sweatshop campaigns have established internal mechanisms to monitor supply chains. Some of the larger companies, like Nike and Reebok, have corporate social responsibility departments dedicated to addressing working conditions in their supply chains.[2] Universities targeted by USAS have joined the WRC and altered their contracts with licensees. Yet these changes have not led to significant improvements for those who work in the industry.

One way to illustrate the gap between stages three and four is through reports of one company's compliance. Nike was the target of some of the first anti-sweatshop campaigns in the early 1990s. Although many activists still criticize the company's labor practices, it is widely recognized as one of the more engaged companies, participating in numerous MSIs, maintaining an internal staff of one hundred focused on social compliance, and publishing an annual report of corporate social responsibility. Unlike many of its competitors, Nike discloses its factory locations and regularly conducts and reports the findings from a variety of supply chain audits. In 2008, Nike reported record revenue of US$16.3 billion, which was an increase of US$1.3 billion over the previous year (Nike 2008a). As one of the world's largest athletic-shoe companies, Nike controls more than 33 percent of the world market. The main difference between Nike and other companies is that Nike, to its credit, actually conducts audits and makes the results public.

Locke et al. analyzed audits of eight hundred factories in fifty-one countries that produce goods for Nike. Many of the top retailers use the same factories, so their assessment most likely captures conditions pertaining to many of the other top companies as well (2007). Nike developed a compliance rating program to grade suppliers based on management audits, FLA audits, SHAPE (safety, health, attitudes of management, people investment, and environment) assessments, and factory visits. According to Nike's own compliance rating program, Locke et al. report, "Workplace conditions in almost 80 percent of its suppliers have either remained the same or worsened over time" (2007, 31). Locke et al. found that working conditions and management-labor relations varied dramatically among factories and varied by region, with factories located in countries with a strong rule of law (measured by perceptions of the incidence of crime, the effectiveness and predictability of the judiciary, and the enforceability of contracts) performing better. They also found that factories with stronger and more stable links to Nike exhibited better compliance. Locke et al. claimed that these findings demonstrate that codes of conduct are most effective in countries with strong labor laws, suggesting that company codes are complementary to national legislation rather than a replacement for it (2007, 24). Findings from Locke (2007), as well as reports from targeted companies, suggest that the anti-sweatshop network has been successful in getting sweatshops on retailers and universities' agendas and achieved discursive commitments from retailers. These have led to some policy changes on the part of targeted retailers and universities, but these policy changes have been insufficient to lead manufacturers to improve conditions on the factory floor.

This does not, however, mean that the anti-sweatshop network has been completely ineffective. In fact, some analysts have surmised that the constant campaigns of the anti-sweatshop network, along with retailers' participation in MSIs, have prevented further abuse in the industry. In an interview Katie Quan gave an example from Foxcon, an electronics factory in Shenzhen, China (Quan, personal communication, December 12, 2008). The electronics industry has many parallels with the apparel industry in terms of recruitment, wages, and structure, but it lacks a vocal advocacy network like the anti-sweatshop network. Foxcon, a Taiwanese TNC, sued reporters individually for exposing abuses at its factories in Shenzhen. Quan suggests that this would not have happened in the clothing industry because of the international attention on apparel companies. It is reasonable to assume that, without pressure from the anti-sweatshop network, retailers in the garment industry could have moved all of their orders to non-unionized factories or to locations where garment workers were unable to organize. Slowing such movement may have prevented further deterioration in working conditions and the erosion of workers' rights. If so, this would suggest that anti-sweatshop activists have had a certain level of influence on retailers, albeit a far cry from their goals as laid out in the WRC code.

Case studies

There are other aspects of NGO effectiveness that may not show up when assessing their influence on retailers and universities. These include influencing other NGOs in the advocacy network or building alliances for future campaigns. The case-study NGOs engage in garment-industry advocacy from positions of relative weakness in the global economy. Their experiences result in similar outcomes in some ways and different outcomes in others, depending on their particular position and strategies pursued. This section addresses the unique aspects of the case study NGOs and the results of their particular efforts, with emphasis on types of influence not covered in the previous section.

Clean Clothes Campaign

The goals of the CCC are to "improve working conditions and to empower workers in the global garment industry, in order to end the oppression, exploitation and abuse of workers in this industry, most of whom are women" (CCC 2008b). These goals embody the standards outlined in the WRC code, embracing the needs to address conditions as well as the enabling rights of freedom of association and collective bargaining. The CCC differs from the other NGOs in its transnational composition. It reaches across fourteen European countries, connecting European NGOs and unions across European national borders in support of workers who are predominantly located in Asia, Central America, and parts of Europe.

The CCC has influenced targeted actors by getting issues on retailers' agendas and securing discursive commitments. It has also garnered substantial media attention and was cited in over three hundred newspaper articles in major English-language newspapers in Asia, the United States, the UK, and Australia from 1999 to 2009. According to the FWF website, the CCC secured policy changes from targeted companies in Europe and contributed to fifty-one companies joining the FWF, the MSI in which CCC participates. Despite securing these policy changes by retailers, the CCC has had difficulty achieving widespread behavioral changes among manufacturers.

The CCC is most effective in cases where flagrant abuses have taken place, such as violence against trade unionists, and particularly those that include a high-profile brand that has already been a target of campaigns. In these cases the CCC disseminates requests for action through its urgent appeals system, which generates information about a particular campaign and then sends it to the CCC network, asking supporters to take particular action, usually contacting factory owners, retailers, and relevant government officials. Each chapter encourages its supporters to write letters and sign petitions. For example, the French affiliate of the CCC, Peuples Solidaires, recently conducted a campaign in support of Indonesian workers at two factories, Spotec and Dong Joe. Within four weeks, seven hundred people emailed to express their support for the workers, reporting that they had contacted Adidas in response to the campaign (Oxfam Australia 2008b). Approximately 30 percent of the urgent appeals cases between 1994 and 2004 were fully or partially successful (Sluiter 2009). The success rate was measured by workers' statements about whether or not their demands were met. Sluiter summarizes the factors that contributed to a successful outcome, "strong organisations on the ground; a good working relationship between them and international campaigning organisations; a variety of tactics, tools and actions directed at multiple pressure-points; easy ways for consumers to express their support, and regular updates to motivate them" (2009, 184). These cases resulted in improved conditions in particular factories. However, these successes have not yet translated into securing widespread improvements in working conditions or ensuring workers' rights.

The CCC's other programs, such as legislative and procurement initiatives, are less visible and grab fewer headlines, but are more proactive and represent a collaborative approach to working with governments (as opposed to targeting governments). For example, the Clean Clothes Communities initiative, which aims to get local municipalities to commit to procuring clothing that meets various labor standards, has met with varying success. In Belgium, sixty communities have adopted such ordinances, and in France, 250 have done so (CCC 2005b). In addition to individual procurement policies, the initiative encourages companies that secure government contracts to enact a code of conduct and join MSIs like the FWF.

In addition, the CCC has been successful in providing information and resources to allied organizations. It has also helped build coalitions among European unions and NGOs, linking these organizations to CCC's allies in the global South. This helps extend responsibilities beyond European organizations to create greater cross-national solidarity. One example of this is its involvement in, and support of, the Asia Floor Wage Campaign. Union leaders and labor activists in Asia launched the Asia Floor Wage Campaign to establish a minimum living wage in each country that can be standardized and compared across countries (Merk 2009). The CCC supports the campaign by providing information and analysis and by linking its European network to the network of Asian activists and unionists involved in the campaign.

United Students Against Sweatshops

USAS has been particularly successful in mobilizing university students to pressure university administrators to join the WRC. This represents a policy change for universities, correlating to stage three of advocacy effectiveness. The significance of USAS getting over 150 universities to join the WRC is twofold. First, it shows that USAS has raised awareness and opened up dialogue about sweatshops on university campuses. Second, it shows that USAS has made universities establish lines of responsibility through their contracts and supply chains. USAS has played an integral part in shifting transnational advocacy from phase one to phase two, getting companies to acknowledge their responsibilities for labor conditions in their supply chains and persuading companies that produce goods for the university apparel market to implement corporate social responsibility programs. While these internal corporate programs may not meet the WRC standards or USAS's ideals, they do signify a change in the position taken by TNCs that had previously denied any responsibility for labor conditions in their supply chains.

Like CCC's, USAS's campaigns rely on exposing abuses at factories producing goods for high-profile retailers. This is a point of leverage, but it also limits USAS's ability to exert influence on less well-known companies. USAS also tends to focus on cases with the most flagrant abuses, particularly those targeting activists, such as the arrest of Mehedi Hasan, a WRC investigator, in Bangladesh. Because of the actions of USAS, CCC, and dozens of other NGOs and unions, Hasan was released several days later. The international pressure and media attention, and Hasan's connection with an international NGO, contributed to his quick release. Other activists in Bangladesh have not been so fortunate, and the CCC reports continued surveillance and arrests of labor activists in Bangladesh (2008a).

USAS has been effective in several other ways that are not reflected in the stages of influence in the previous section. For example, the USAS network has been adapted for other uses on several occasions. USAS mobilized its supporters for immigrant rights in California and anti-war protests in the lead up to the 2003 U.S. invasion of Iraq. Another often overlooked aspect of USAS's work is the impact it has had on the broader labor movement. As noted earlier, labor analyst Katie Quan suggests that the anti-sweatshop network has helped spawn a new generation of labor activists in the United States and that USAS, in particular, has helped to populate U.S. unions with a new group of young people committed to social justice (Quan, personal communication, December 12, 2008).

FairWear

FairWear's domestic campaigns have successfully linked with the TCFUA to contribute to the development of Ethical Clothing Australia. In May 2008 then deputy prime minister Julia Gillard announced that the Australian Commonwealth government would allocate AUS$4 million over four years to the Homeworkers' Code of Practice/Ethical Clothing Australia to sign on more companies and improve compliance (DEEWR 2008). While Ethical Clothing Australia is still a voluntary initiative, federal funding may bolster the code's standing and improve its implementation capabilities.

FairWear is seeking to secure local ordinances requiring the procurement of goods certified as sweat free. Similar to the Clean Clothes Communities program, the Fair Council campaigns urge local governments to put procedures in place to ensure that workwear purchased by the council meets basic labor standards. For example, the Kogarah Local Council in New South Wales endorsed the FairWear campaign and committed to purchasing its uniforms from suppliers accredited by Ethical Clothing Australia. Hundreds of workers, mainly Chinese women, work out of their homes in Kogarah, so this procurement policy has direct implications for the local community (FairWear 2007a). These initiatives are slowly gaining momentum in Australia, the United States, and Europe.

Despite FairWear's successes in terms of achieving stage three policy changes, including voluntary regulations and procurement legislation, a recent report by the Brotherhood of St. Laurence, one of the founding members of FairWear, found that conditions for outworkers in Australia had worsened in the past five years. Workers reported that they often went weeks without any work, and when work was available they worked long hours for just AUS$2–3 per hour (Diviney and Lillywhite 2007). It is clear from FairWear's work in recent years that simply having access to an independent union does not guarantee better conditions for homeworkers in Australia, let alone workers manufacturing goods overseas for the Australian market. There are several reasons. One is because a conventional model of union membership based on consistent factory work does not apply to home-based workers, many of whom do not want to have their work moved into factories. Second, the trend of production moving offshore means that a nationally based union holds little sway over companies that can relocate elsewhere. For this reason FairWear has not focused on unionizing homeworkers and has sought to make Ethical Clothing Australia inclusive of all homeworkers, whether they are union members or not.

FairWear provides solidarity with transnational campaigns by encouraging their supporters to sign petitions, write letters, and participate in protest actions. The tools that have proven to be effective in domestic campaigns, namely, the establishment and enforcement of Ethical Clothing Australia accreditation, are unavailable in transnational campaigns. Therefore, FairWear is in the process of developing alternative tools for international campaigns. In 2006, FairWear developed a Fair Work Standard for Australian companies sourcing overseas. According to its website, FairWear's international focus developed "in recognition that the conditions of homeworkers in Australia is a function of the exploitation rife in the international garment industry." This increased international outlook is a function of the changing nature of the industry and reflects a recognition of the gains made by European and American activists in achieving policy changes in targeted companies (Gardener, personal communication, November 21, 2006).

STITCH

STITCH's goals are to empower women in the labor movement and bring marginalized women's voices to global debates on globalization, trade agreements, and immigration. Assessing STITCH's effectiveness in terms of the WRC code, it is clear that STITCH organizers prioritize the enabling rights of freedom of association and collective bargaining, believing that without these fundamental rights, no outside actors can ensure workers' long-term well-being (Myers, personal communication, January 5,

2007). STITCH's emphasis on workers' rights led the organization to focus on building independent union movements in Central America.

Some international labor solidarity campaigns emphasize workers in multiple locations with the same employers. In contrast to these campaigns, STITCH emphasizes the broader identity of women workers. This is in part because the women STITCH works with are primarily employed in small factories far down the subcontracting supply chain. STITCH is unable to rely on association with high-profile companies to generate international awareness; instead, it focuses on other ways to generate support for women workers.

Of the case-study NGOs, STITCH works most closely with garment workers and other women workers. Through its worker exchanges, training, and leadership development, STITCH works with women workers in Central America to support the slow process of building a movement from the ground up. In this way STITCH exercises significant political responsibility to the women it works with, perhaps more so than some of the other U.S.-based NGOs. Yet, exercising high levels of political responsibility does not guarantee effective outcomes in garment-industry advocacy, where workers themselves have little power over retailers.

In December 2007, STITCH, the ILRF, and the U.S. Labor Education in the Americas Project convened anti-sweatshop NGOs in Washington DC to discuss the future of anti-sweatshop activism in the United States. In an interview STITCH executive director Beth Myers explained that the purpose of the meeting was to discuss the state of the industry and the state of anti-sweatshop advocacy. Despite the success of various consumer campaigns, conditions for workers remained largely unchanged—or had even worsened in the previous few years. Myers argued that this was not only due to structural challenges in the garment industry but also to the network's overemphasis on consumer campaigns (Myers, personal communication, October 22, 2008).

Director of the AMRC, Sanjiv Pandita, expressed a similar frustration during an interview in 2008. Instead of acting as one point in triangular solidarity (workers' organizations, unions, and consumers), he said, consumer campaigns had become the dominant mode of labor activism among Northern-based NGOs (Pandita, personal communication, October 8, 2008). He argued that consumer campaigns position Northern groups as the driving force for change, because these groups can negotiate with TNCs, something that workers and unions are unable to do. He suggested that these campaigns may change consumers in the United States, but they do not change Americans' and Europeans' imperialistic attitudes toward workers in the South. What is most needed, he said, is a cultural shift in which Northern-based advocates stop talking about helpless workers and start talking about, and analyzing, inequality. Rather than focusing on consumer campaigns, Northern-based labor advocates should focus their energies on strengthening their own labor movements and creating equal exchanges among advocates.

These critiques apply to some of the Northern-based anti-sweatshop NGOs more than others. Most of the case-study NGOs are moving in the direction proposed by Pandita. The only one of the case-study NGOs that this critique applies to directly is the CCC, since it is explicitly a consumer campaign. Even though the CCC network includes many unions in Europe, its goal is not to strengthen European labor movements but rather to support garment workers worldwide through consumer campaigns. The other three case-study NGOs are seeking to strengthen their connections to domestic labor movements, as well as their transnational advocacy. In recent years USAS has begun to engage more directly in domestic campaigns through its campus-based campaigns to ensure a living wage for custodial and food-service workers on university campuses. FairWear is closely aligned with the Australian labor movement through the TCFUA. STITCH aims to strengthen labor movements through its worker exchanges, delegations, and workshops of union women from the United States, Honduras, Nicaragua, and Guatemala.

Anti-sweatshop campaigns

The main way that NGOs in the anti-sweatshop network influence change in the industry is by waging campaigns on behalf of workers in specific factories. The Gina Form and BJ&B campaigns are profiled next. Each is focused on a specific factory, one in Thailand and the other in the Dominican Republic, and both involved numerous anti-sweatshop NGOs. These campaigns illustrate the challenges activists face in relying on consumer-oriented campaigns and factory-level organizing. The Gina Form and BJ&B campaigns reflect the structural challenges facing the broader anti-sweatshop network. Activists initially hailed both cases as successes. Later, the cases showed the difficulty of sustaining improvements in working conditions. The CCC and USAS were involved in the campaigns, as were many other actors in the anti-sweatshop network. STITCH and FairWear were not as involved with these two particular campaigns. Nevertheless, these campaigns are included here because they demonstrate changes in the industry over the past fifteen years as well as the particular limits of consumer campaigns.

Gina Form Bra campaign

Between 2002 and 2006 workers protested in the streets of Bangkok, activists picketed retailers in London, North American consumers sent thousands of letters and emails, and Thai workers negotiated with management, all in the campaign to secure due compensation for workers at the Gina Form Bra factory in Thailand. The Gina Form workers' campaign lasted several years and included thousands of people in Thailand, North America, Europe, Hong Kong, and Australia. At issue were claims by the Gina Relations Workers Union (GRWU) that workers did not receive minimum wages, were forced to work overtime, and were harassed by management for being involved with the union. With assistance from the Solidarity Center in Bangkok, the union sought international support through the Transnational Information Exchange–Asia and the CCC. After investigating the claims, the CCC distributed the workers' requests as part of its urgent appeals system. Activists around the world responded with a deluge of letters and emails to factory management and retailers that bought their lingerie from Gina Form. They also sent messages to the U.S. Government and the Thai prime minister (MSN 2005; WRC 2006).

As a result of local and international pressure, Gina management entered into a collective agreement with the GRWU in 2003 that reinstated workers dismissed for union involvements and paid them back wages. Robertson and Plaiyoowong noted that the Gina Form campaign resembled a three-ring circus, with actions taking place simultaneously at the factory level, at the Thai national level, and internationally. Ongoing activities in each ring were linked together by NGOs, and the GRWU acted as the ring master. Robertson and Plaiyoowong considered the agreement between management and the GRWU to be a successful outcome and cited the campaign as an example of solidarity among local labor advocates and international allies (2004).

However, this success did not last long. The Clover Group announced the closure of its Gina Form factory in September 2006. Workers once again reached out to the anti-sweatshop network, setting in motion a public campaign that aimed to prevent the factory from closing its doors. It soon became clear that with the end of the MFA, the closure was inevitable, and the factory would be moving elsewhere, possibly to China or Cambodia. The Gina Form workers resigned themselves to the closure of the factory and sought to secure compensation due to them under Thai law, as well as some additional severance benefits.[3] Once again, activists in Europe, North America, and Asia sent letters to Gina Form, the retailers and the Thai and U.S. governments, urging them to intervene in the case.

In October 2006 workers held a protest in front of the U.S. Embassy in Bangkok urging the U.S. Government to take action, particularly with U.S.-based buyers from Gina Form. Meanwhile, activists in Canada, the United States, and Europe held protests targeting Gina Form's buyers. USAS sent alerts to its members, encouraging them to contact buyers of Gina Form, and students held protests outside Victoria's Secret stores (USAS 2006b). According to the CCC website, the UK chapter of the CCC, Labour Behind the Label, protested in front of Calvin Klein stores. By November 2006 the Clover Group entered into an agreement with the GRWU granting outstanding bonuses, legally required severance under Thai law, and an additional payment for workers equivalent to three-and-a-half months of wages. The agreement was worth US$1.6 million. Although this was a fairly good outcome for the displaced workers, they were left with few employment alternatives (Mather, Eyskoot, and Ascoly 2007). The Gina Form case shows that even amid all the pressure from NGOs and the union, the Clover Group chose to close the unionized Thai factory and move production to a lower-cost location. It also shows that extensive international pressure was needed to get severance pay for workers.

BJ&B campaign

In 2001, BJ&B was one of the largest manufacturers of baseball caps in the Western Hemisphere, employing more than two thousand workers. The factory was located in the Villa Altagracia EPZ in the Dominican Republic and wholly owned by a Korean company, Yupoong. BJ&B customers included Nike, Reebok, Quiksilver, Gap, and Gear. According to reports by the CCC, USAS, and the WRC, employees were forced to work overtime and regularly faced verbal abuse and harassment. According to one BJ&B employee, Yenny Perez, "we worked sometimes from 7 in the morning until 11 at night. And it was obligatory, always, the extra hours. When people fell sick, they didn't let them leave the factory to go to the doctor. No one had any way to defend themselves" (CCC 2007c). Despite resistance from management, Perez and others began to organize a union in 1998 with the help of the Federacion Nacional de Trabajadores de Zonas, which contacted the U.S. union UNITE for additional support.

At that time UNITE was also involved with the students responsible for founding USAS. In response to requests from BJ&B workers, UNITE conducted its own investigation and brought two BJ&B employees to the United States to tour university campuses (Ross 2004b). By 2001, USAS chapters began pressuring their universities to join the WRC and to investigate the workers' claims of abuse, forced overtime, and violations of workers' rights to form a union. Members of the CCC put pressure on European retailers to investigate the allegations by issuing an urgent appeal to supporters and staging protests in front of retail shops. Nike, Reebok, and Adidas-Salomon launched a third-party investigation through the FLA in January 2002 (Ross 2004b). Even though they are often at odds, the FLA and WRC agreed to work together on this case.

The FLA report, along with subsequent factory visits by the WRC, found that managers continued to intimidate workers and prevent them from joining a union (Ross 2004b). Once again, buyers wrote to Yupoong urging it to remedy the situation. Eventually, in March 2003, management recognized the union and signed a collective agreement. The agreement included a 10 percent wage increase, educational scholarships, paid holidays, and the establishment of a workers' committee to deal with health and safety concerns at the factory (FLA 2008). The agreement was the first of its kind in the EPZ and represented a victory for the workers and the international campaign organized to support them. It was hailed by many as a sign of the success of transnational organizing, particularly the strategic role played by USAS in exerting pressure on universities to take action through the WRC (Garonzik 2005; Ross 2004b).

Perez claimed that conditions improved in the factory once the union, called the Sindicato de Trabajadores de la Empresa BJ&B S.A., was formed. "The verbal mistreatment stopped. The extra hours changed, so that it was voluntary. There were also many benefits we gained with the collective-bargaining agreement. For example, we got a market basket for pregnant workers. We got paid leave. We fixed many problems that came up with management," such as conflicts about workers who were illegally fired (CCC 2007c). Another BJ&B worker, Sebastian Garcia, thought that international pressure on the factory owners helped him get his job back after he was fired for his involvement with the union (CCC 2007c). In relation to the role of students in the campaign, Ignacio Hernandez, general secretary of the Federacion Nacional de Trabajadores de Zonas, said: "I never thought a group of students, thousands of them, could put so much pressure on these brands. We were determined to win, but without them it would have taken five more years" (quoted in Gonzalez 2003).

The collective agreement was to be renegotiated in 2004, and workers once again found themselves in a precarious position. Yupoong threatened to close the BJ&B factory in the Dominican Republic and move production to its factories in Vietnam and Thailand. Yupoong's customers, including Nike, simultaneously touted a commitment to "responsible competitiveness" and support of workers' rights at BJ&B (Hauser 2007, 1), while also putting downward pressure on the factory to produce cheaper goods more quickly. According to a USAS report, "During the same period in which the factory has made strides to respect labor rights, Nike and Reebok have been paying lower and lower prices for their hats. Instead of increasing its orders at one of the few factories that has actually respected our codes of conduct, Nike and Reebok are slowly squeezing the factory and forcing it out of business" (USAS 2006a, 17). Once again, activists in the United States and Europe put pressure on BJ&B buyers to use their influence to encourage BJ&B management to negotiate with the union. The factory stayed open, but it began cutting back its workforce.

International pressure continued. In 2006 the CCC disseminated an appeal to supporters to contact Yupoong and its buyers. Actions included letter writing, leafleting, and protests. The German chapter of the CCC presented the case of BJ&B workers to the Adidas shareholders meeting (CCC 2007d). In February 2007 Yupoong announced the closure of the BJ&B factory, claiming it could no longer remain competitive (Cha 2007). By this time the workforce had shrunk to 234 employees. A report by the FLA stated, "Not surprisingly, the closure was highly controversial, partly because so much effort had gone into establishing freedom of association at the company that its closure was regarded by many as a setback for workers rights in general and in the Dominican Republic in particular" (FLA 2008, 166).

At this time Nike announced that it would be moving its orders to Yupoong's other factories in Asia, saying that BJ&B was no longer competitive in producing caps (Hauser 2007). Anticipating the closure of BJ&B, Garcia said, "If I was younger, I could move away to try to find a job. But I have a family, so I can't do that. Of course, I will look for work. But not only am I of an advanced age, I am also a known trade unionist. The times coming would be very hard. I am worried the children could go hungry." He went on to say, "We put our care into making these hats. The brands and Yupoong, they owe it to our community to stay here" (CCC 2007d). But of course there was no formal contract among the retailers, Yupoong, and the local community. Once BJ&B was considered to be uncompetitive, Nike placed its orders elsewhere.

Once again BJ&B employees worked closely with American and European allies to put pressure on Yupoong and its buyers to keep the factory open. If that was not possible, workers at least wanted severance payments and assistance finding new jobs. After extensive discussions among BJ&B

management, Yupoong, WRC, FLA, the union, and buyers such as Nike, BJ&B management met with union officials. Management presented individual agreements for union officials in exchange for their assurance that they would drop all further demands on behalf of BJ&B employees. Some of the union officials accepted the agreement, which gave them one year of severance pay. Several of those who signed the agreement claimed that this was done under coercive circumstances and later rescinded their individual agreements (WRC 2007). Eventually, the rest of the BJ&B employees received one month of severance pay in addition to the two months of pay legally required under Dominican Republic law. Pregnant employees were given six months of severance pay. Benefits for pregnant employees were the result of the involvement of female trade unionists. This agreement, while in some ways better than what was legally required of BJ&B, was considered by some activists to have undermined the union because certain aspects, such as obtaining one month's severance payment, were done outside of negotiations with the union (WRC 2007). Following this payment, Yupoong, Nike, and the FLA claimed the settlement was a sign of BJ&B's good faith, while the WRC claimed that the settlement was simply a payoff to silence the union (WRC 2007).

These two campaigns illustrate the overwhelming challenges activists face in trying to improve working conditions and workers' rights, given the structure of the garment industry. In each campaign, activists initially fought for and helped secure better conditions for workers and the right to unionize. Several years later they were again campaigning in the same factories, but this time they struggled to secure severance packages for unemployed workers when the factories moved to cheaper locations in the post-MFA environment. The power of retailers and manufacturers over small contractors and workers, the prevalence of short-term contracts, demands for quick turnaround times, and the absence of enforcement of labor standards all contributed to a situation where improvements beyond individual factories have been difficult to secure and maintain, particularly in relation to workers' right to organize. Even when independent unions were established and improvements were made in a particular factory, as in BJ&B, the shifting nature of the industry made those changes unsustainable. In both campaigns, activists ended up focusing on how best to help workers who were left unemployed once the factories closed. This process is a far cry from activists' overall goals of empowering workers and securing better conditions, as set out in the WRC code. However, given the existing environment, activists were left with few alternatives and struggled to make a bad situation a little bit better for those left unemployed.

Conclusion

This chapter assessed the effectiveness of anti-sweatshop advocacy by examining the stages of influence of the anti-sweatshop network, reviewing the case-study NGOs, and analyzing campaigns in the Dominican Republic and Thailand. The anti-sweatshop network has been successful in achieving the first level of influence, raising awareness and agenda setting. The network has also influenced the industry's adoption of the discourse of responsibility and workers' rights, the second level of influence. The network has achieved mixed results with the third level of influence of policy change. As a result of anti-sweatshop advocacy, some targeted corporations have implemented internal social auditing programs and joined MSIs. However, the anti-sweatshop network has been unable to achieve the fourth level of influence—behavioral change by manufacturers. This means that workers' rights and working conditions, as articulated in the WRC code, remain largely unfulfilled. This was not due to the bad faith or weak efforts of anti-sweatshop advocates but rather to the power of retailers in the industry.

Although the case-study NGOs have been confronted with similar structures, their approaches have differed slightly. The CCC developed a systematic approach to consumer campaigns throughout Europe, coordinating the actions of European NGOs and unions to act in support of garment workers in the global South. FairWear developed a unique mechanism for the Australian context with Ethical Clothing Australia, providing support to the union and allowing the industry to avoid additional regulation. USAS built a large network of student-run groups acting locally on their university campuses in support of a coordinated action to get universities to join the WRC. STITCH conducted workshops and provided training for workers without accessing high-profile media campaigns. These strategies intervened at different points in the garment industry. They helped raise awareness about working conditions in the industry; achieved discursive commitments from universities, retailers, and governments; and secured some policy changes. They also built strategic alliances, bolstered local labor movements, and adapted the network for other uses. In spite of this, these NGOs and the rest of the anti-sweatshop network have been unable to achieve transformative change in the industry.

The Gina Form and BJ&B campaigns were initially heralded as success stories of local and transnational advocacy. More recently, these campaigns have come to exemplify the challenges of advocacy campaigns, as factories close and production is moved to another city or country. Despite the international pressure from consumer campaigns and locally based organizing, gains made were not maintained. This was fundamentally due to the ability of companies easily to shift orders to non-unionized factories, with little recourse for workers. In each new location labor activists will begin again the process of organizing workers and reaching out to international allies to improve conditions in the factories. Although these particular campaigns are over, the stories of the workers and factories continue. In 2010 the BJ&B factory became the site of the Altagracia Project. Established by Knights Apparel, the Altagracia Project was set up to operate as a model factory, showcasing that a factory could pay a living wage (three times the average wage for garment workers in the region), respect workers' rights to join a union, and at the same time turn a profit (Greenhouse 2010b). The factory employees 120 people, including some former BJ&B employees. In July 2010 the WRC conducted an initial assessment of the project and found that it was meeting all of its initial promises to pay a living wage and respecting workers' rights to unionize (WRC 2010b).

The network, case studies, and campaigns point to the structural challenges advocates face in attempting to influence powerful retailers and universities. Advocates have been effective at extending retailers' and universities' responsibility through supply chains. Although this sense of responsibility is only in the form of a discursive commitment from corporations, it provides activists with tools to use in future campaigns to highlight the gap between retailers' stated commitments and the conditions in factories where their goods are produced. This certainly falls short of activists' goals, yet it is perhaps the most that activists can hope to achieve given the current structure of the industry, its uneven regulatory environment, the power of retailers in controlling lengthy subcontracting chains of production, and the unwillingness of states to enforce regulations.

Chapter 8

Conclusion

The anti-sweatshop NGOs examined in this book are part of broad transformations under way in global civil society. As NGOs proliferate, they participate in networks that traverse political boundaries and use a variety of tools to influence states and corporations and to create cultural change. In recent years international relations scholars have begun to examine these changing roles of NGOs in world civic politics. This book contributes to that growing literature by positioning anti-sweatshop NGOs as political agents seeking to improve working conditions and ensure workers' rights in the global garment industry. It has combined analysis of the structural power of states and corporations in the global economy with more subtle forms of power including discursive and communicative power. Through examination of the material as well as the ideational realms, it has demonstrated both how these NGOs are surprisingly influential for their small size and scant resources and how they are severely constrained in what they are able to accomplish when confronted with powerful retailers and governments resistant to change.

These small Northern-based NGOs have been creative, dynamic, and largely unrecognized political actors that focus their campaigns on North American, European, and Australian consumers in the belief that these consumers can pressure name-brand retailers to improve working conditions in their supply chains. In doing so, they engage in political action that seeks to change the behavior of consumers and retailers in order to improve the quality of life for garment workers worldwide. The TANs they enact, through consumer campaigns and new technologies, have created new spaces for political action, which in turn have caused retailers to implement programs to address labor conditions in their supply chains. As a result of anti-sweatshop campaigns, most major retailers now acknowledge some level of responsibility for the working conditions under which their goods are produced. Many of these companies have adopted

187

codes of conduct and implemented internal social responsibility programs. Some have also joined private regulatory initiatives that monitor working conditions in the industry. These are significant victories for the anti-sweatshop network in an era of widespread deregulation and growing corporate power.

At the same time, consumer-based campaigns alone contain inherent limits to effecting structural changes to the governance of the industry. Despite the success of individual or even collective campaigns, conditions for garment workers have remained difficult. The threat of factory closures and the persistent unwillingness of governmental agencies to enforce good working conditions have proven bigger obstacles than these networks could surmount. This shows that while consumer campaigns can be a useful strategy for activists aiming to improve working conditions in the garment industry, they must be complemented by other approaches that strengthen labor movements and bolster enforcement of international labor standards.

Several themes emerged in the writing of this book: (1) networked activism and world civic politics, (2) factors that facilitate or constrain NGOs' actions as transnational political actors, (3) opportunities and limitations of consumer campaigns, (4) agency and power in the garment industry, and (5) developing alternative forms of governance.

Networked activism and world civic politics

The effectiveness of small NGOs has been enhanced by their location in a networked structure with allied organizations. Reliance on the network is especially pronounced for anti-sweatshop NGOs because of their limited resources and small staff. The NGOs in this study are highly dependent on networked allies to support and disseminate their work. This was demonstrated in the Fibre & Fabric International campaign. The CCC disseminated information from NGOs and unions in Bangalore, first about conditions in the FFI factory and then later about a gag order placed on activists. Information was sent to dozens of anti-sweatshop, labor, and human rights NGOs, which led to hundreds of people signing online petitions and extensive international news coverage. This helped gain the attention of government officials. As part of its resolution, FFI addressed all of the workers' original concerns and dropped all charges against the Dutch and Indian activists. In exchange, the activists agreed to cease their campaign against FFI. This case showed the capacity of activists to bring about positive changes. Activists were successful in the campaign against FFI because of the media attention generated by the lawsuit against the activists and, subsequently, the intervention of the Dutch government. This case is an example of NGOs using a variety of tactics to pressure retailers and government to take action to protect activists' freedom of speech and improve conditions for garment workers. Activists were able to apply such pressure by calling on a broad range of actors in the anti-sweatshop network. This pressure helped raise the profile of the case and garner media attention, demonstrating the importance of networked activism in resolving the case.

Anti-sweatshop advocates use various forms of civic politics aimed at the private sector, due in large measure to a lack of political will among states to enforce existing regulations. Yet, states are still important actors in the garment industry. Chapter 1 included analysis of actions by the United States and the European Union to influence the industry through trade policies. Chapter 4 showed how states determine the channels available to anti-sweatshop NGOs through funding, taxation, and other regulations. Chapter 5 highlighted government action—or lack of action—in specific campaigns, such as the limited success of activists in the Yoo Yang campaign pressuring the Honduran Department of Labor to recognize the SITRAIMASH union. Some of the most effective anti-sweatshop campaigns combined civic politics with politics focused on the state. This was clear in the FFI case, which was finally resolved when activists pressured both retailers and the Dutch government. When one approach was insufficient, activists were able to use the broader network to combine tactics and pressure targeted actors from multiple angles.

Factors that facilitate or constrain NGOs' actions as transnational political actors

Many factors influence anti-sweatshop NGOs' ability to achieve their goals. The book has addressed some of the most important, including NGOs' use of information politics, financial resources, frame resonance, and organizational structure. Analysis of NGOs' relationships within the broader anti-sweatshop network demonstrated the profound significance of the network in enhancing individual NGOs' capacity. This form of networked activism influenced issue framing, the dissemination of information, and the NGOs' capacity to exercise political responsibility to garment workers. Networked activism played a key role in the anti-sweatshop NGOs' abilities as transnational political actors. An example comes from the campaign targeting Russell Athletic. In that case USAS was successful in getting Russell Athletic to reinstate dismissed workers after one hundred universities severed their contracts with Russell Athletic. This was the first time that anti-sweatshop activists convinced a company to reopen a factory and rehire workers. Activists were successful in this case because of the networked activism of university students pressuring their university administrators to sever their contracts with the retailer. Activists were able to advocate for a boycott of Russell Athletic (something most anti-sweatshop campaigns do not usually do) because the factory was already closed and, therefore, a boycott did not risk harming workers. In addition to the presence of the vast network of student activists, this case depended on having a mechanism in place to resolve the issues. Such a mechanism existed through the WRC, which investigated workers' claims and mediated between the universities and Russell Athletic. The success of this campaign was due to USAS's work over the previous decade of building a network of student activists and helping establish the WRC. This case demonstrated the NGOs' use of communicative power, combined with the material leverage of university contracts, to influence powerful actors in the industry.

Macro-level factors also shape transnational anti-sweatshop advocacy. These include the political economy of the garment industry, and political institutions. The structural power of states, coupled with governments' unwillingness to constrain transnational capital, have supported the structure of the garment industry, which condones widespread disregard for international labor standards. The fact that there is such widespread neglect of ILO standards among governments, retailers, and manufacturers demonstrates both the extent of the challenge facing anti-sweatshop activists and the structures at work in maintaining the existing system.

At the commencement of this research in 2005, many anti-sweatshop activists expressed a sense of cautious optimism. There was a feeling that years of activism were beginning to pay off as a result of several factors, including the launch of government procurement initiatives in the United States and Europe, the fact that numerous retailers had joined multi-stakeholder initiatives, and activists having secured several campaign victories in specific factories. The mood has changed since then. Current campaigns, such as the Grupo Navarra campaign, tend to focus on how to slow down plant closures and obtain severance payments for workers, rather than on establishing living wages and obtaining freedom of association, as was the focus of earlier campaigns. USAS's recent victories against Russell Athletic and Nike may contribute to a renewed sense of optimism among activists. The establishment of the Altagracia Project in the former BJ&B factory is also sure to provide inspiration and fuel activists in their continued struggles.

Opportunities and limitations of consumer campaigns

The anti-sweatshop network provides a clear example of how activists mobilize through transnational networks to challenge corporate-led globalization. The anti-sweatshop network has focused much of its energy on raising consumer awareness about the conditions under which goods are produced, with the goal of exposing how the production and consumption of clothing is fundamentally a relationship among people rather than a relationship among things. While the anti-sweatshop NGOs in this study are relatively weak compared to retailers and manufacturers, they can and do influence the global garment industry by identifying and accessing strategic points of leverage.

Anti-sweatshop NGOs identified and exploited one point of leverage in particular: retailers' reliance on brand image. By exposing labor abuses in factories that produce goods for well-known retailers, activists were able to use symbolic politics to draw attention to the gap between retailers' claims and the reality of how their goods were produced. As seen in the Hytex case against Nike or the Russell Athletic campaign, activists used this information to mobilize supporters and pressure companies to change their behavior. Given a limited range of options, NGOs exercise the power they do have to influence targeted retailers and universities. However, they face tremendous difficulties in transforming their limited influence into real change for garment workers.

Consumer campaigns are necessary, but not sufficient, to address the widespread abuse in the garment industry. Consumer campaigns are still needed, given the current structure of the industry. Yet, these campaigns need to be joined by a multi-pronged strategy that includes strengthening labor movements and ensuring adequate regulatory frameworks. There are several ways to think about such an approach. One comes from Leong and Ka-wai (2007), who refer to triangular solidarity—workers' organizations in the South, consumers in the North, and the trade union movement. In a different conceptualization Ross refers to three pillars of decency, which include rebuilding union strength, government policy, and reformers and consumers. All three pillars are needed since even the strongest unions will have little bargaining power with retailers that can easily move orders to non-unionized factories (2004b, 322). This was evident in the BJ&B and Gina Form campaigns, which involved both unions and consumer campaigns. The combination of consumer campaigns and union activities was not enough to sustain the gains that activists and workers had previously made. In these two cases the activists and workers were relatively effective

at achieving improved working conditions, particularly in the most flagrant cases where workers were not receiving wages due to them or were
forced to work extreme overtime. Yet, even when the anti-sweatshop NGOs
were successful at getting targeted actors to influence suppliers, changes
were short-lived. Achievements were unsustainable and did not have the
desired effect on the rest of the industry. This illustrates the limitations of
consumer campaigns when not accompanied by strong labor unions and
adequate regulations.

Agency and power in the garment industry

Despite identifying and exploiting brand image as a key feature of the
garment industry, anti-sweatshop NGOs have been unable to compel corporations to adhere to existing labor standards. Consumer campaigns have
won short-term gains in terms of changes in declared corporate policies.
These are significant and should not be easily dismissed. Given their size
and lack of political influence, anti-sweatshop NGOs have been surprisingly effective at pressuring corporate actors to make these policy changes.

The anti-sweatshop NGOs in this study exhibit rooted cosmopolitanism as they use their particular local and national contexts to engage in
transnational advocacy. Rooted cosmopolitanism helps explain the achievements and limitations of the anti-sweatshop NGOs. Chapter 3 explained
how USAS activists invoke their identities as students of particular universities to mobilize other students to pressure university administrators to
join the WRC. It also showed how each chapter of the CCC is rooted to its
national context and adapts its campaigns to appeal to a local audience.
Yet, all of the CCC chapters are unified in their goal to promote better
working conditions for garment workers beyond their national borders.
The connections the NGOs have to their geographic locations and political positions shape their advocacy strategies and the tools available to them.

It is no surprise that the anti-sweatshop NGOs have been unable to
directly challenge powerful economic and political actors that benefit from
the low wages and poor working conditions in the industry. The current
state of workers' rights and conditions in the industry is not necessarily a
reflection of the ineffectiveness of NGOs and unions, but rather an example of structural asymmetries in the industry. Political decisions such as
the implementation and phaseout of the MFA, additional bilateral quota
restrictions, structural adjustment policies favoring export-oriented production in developing countries, and the absence of labor standards in
trade agreements all contribute to the current structure of the garment

industry. These aspects of the industry do not provide much promise for activists and workers. On the other hand, these features of the industry show that change is possible. The current structure is neither natural nor inevitable, but the result of human action, and human actions today have the potential to influence structures in the future.

Developing alternative forms of governance

Targeted companies have changed their responses to anti-sweatshop campaigns over the years, with many companies now adopting codes of conduct and joining MSIs. These policy changes by corporations indicate activists' success in getting retailers to accept their responsibility for decent working conditions through their supply chains. Through their membership in an MSI, retailers (or universities in the case of the WRC) adopt standardized codes of conduct, make their supply chains more transparent by disclosing factory locations, and consent to monitoring suppliers' factories. However, MSIs rely on voluntary participation, and they conduct audits of a relatively small percentage of factories. Some MSIs, like WRAP, are controlled by the same corporations they are designed to monitor.

Esbenshade (2004) offers an extensive critique of MSIs engaged in private versus independent monitoring. She suggests that the WRC is an example of an organization that supports independent monitoring. It does not include retailers as members and relies on NGOs and unions to conduct audits. The WRC, in connection with USAS, has been particularly effective at identifying and investigating labor abuses in factories producing for the North American collegiate market. Its membership is made up of universities, which have joined as a result of anti-sweatshop activism on their campuses. Universities use their leverage with licensees to address labor abuses in particular factories. In cases like this, MSIs may present an opportunity for NGOs to influence retailers by exposing misconduct and highlighting inconsistencies between factory conditions and MSI codes.

Despite the opportunities for NGOs, MSIs are a poor substitute for state regulation. Lipschutz states that corporate regulation of working conditions in the industry is limited and stronger state regulation is needed. He argues that the state must be central to the reduction of labor abuses in the industry, since "only the state has the power, legitimacy, and authority to regulate market activities" (Lipschutz 2005, 104). Greater enforcement of existing labor laws is needed, yet governments where garments are increasingly produced have few incentives to enforce labor laws. While greater pressure on governments to adhere to international labor standards and enforce existing regulations is necessary, the economic pressure on governments to resist such change is significant. This is especially so in countries highly dependent on the industry, where government officials are eager to hold on to garment manufacturing as a source of foreign investment. Northern consumers have little sway with national governments in garment-producing countries, and they have been unable to get their own governments to tie labor standards into trade agreements. Given these circumstances, consumer campaigns and the establishment of MSIs might be one of the few tools at their disposal.

In addition to MSIs, Northern-based anti-sweatshop activists need to find ways to galvanize the public to pursue government policies in support of workers in their own countries and in the global South. This could include legislation like the Decent Working Conditions bill or in trade agreements that support the enforcement of labor standards. The Better Factories Cambodia project is a notable success in this regard. The BFC project provides an example of linking working conditions to a trade agreement between the United States and Cambodia. The exact conditions of the BFC project are not available to other countries because it was tied to increasing quotas, which no longer exist, but there may be other similar approaches that involve governments providing incentives for manufacturers to comply with existing standards, combined with a greater monitoring role for the ILO. This approach involves states showing a commitment to labor standards, providing incentives for manufacturers to adhere to those standards, and the ILO acting as a coordinator and monitor. The BFC project may provide a model for similar programs elsewhere.

MSIs that involve independent monitoring, such as monitoring by the WRC, are one way for anti-sweatshop activists to improve working conditions on a factory-by-factory basis. Developing adequate governance of the whole industry, however, would require enforceable regulations monitored by states or an international body such as the ILO, combined with strengthening and linking workers' organizations and external pressure and media attention from NGOs. Even though it is difficult to get states to act and ensure workers' rights and enforce legislation, this does not mean that activists should abandon the regulatory process altogether in favor of private systems of governance, which rely on corporations to police the industry.

No single approach will improve working conditions in the industry on its own. Many different approaches are needed, simultaneously, to pressure manufacturers, retailers, and governments while providing workers with the resources they need to advocate for themselves. Without significant changes to the regulatory structures and differential power relations among workers, manufactures, and retailers, any optimism about the future of working conditions in the industry must be cautious, at best.

Many of the phenomena relating to NGOs and world civic politics in this book can be observed across other issues and industries. The conditions that push migrants into garment factories are evident in the coffee, flower, toy, and cocoa industries, where workers face harsh conditions driven by global competition and concentrated power among retailers. Like the garment industry, these industries are the focus of advocacy campaigns that have contributed to budding governance and certification programs.

At the heart of such campaigns are questions about expanding notions of responsibility beyond political jurisdictions and beyond relationships built on formal contracts. With this in mind, I conclude with a remark from Young who said that "each of us must look to our own institutional positions, skills and capacities, and the other responsibilities that come to us, to assess our tasks that will most effectively coordinate with others to help bring about more just outcomes" (2004, 384). This book sought to do that by expanding understandings of civil society actors in international politics and by contributing to the community of scholars and activists working to bring about more just outcomes in the global garment industry.

Appendix

Organizations involved in transnational advocacy and the global garment industry

Asia Floor Wage Campaign
Asia Monitor Resource Center
Association for Women's Rights in Development

Business and Human Rights Resource Centre

Campaign for Labor Rights
China Labor Watch
Chinese Working Women Network
Clean Clothes Campaign
Coalition for Justice in the Maquiladors
CorpWatch

Ethical Trade Action Group
Ethical Trading Initiative*

Fair Labor Association*
Fair Wear Foundation*
Fairtrade Labelling Organizations International
FairWear Australia
Focus on the Global South

Global Exchange
Global Unions

Note: This is a partial list and may not include all of the organizations engaged in transnational anti-sweatshop advocacy.

Homenet
Homeworkers Worldwide
Human Rights Watch

Interfaith Center on Corporate Responsibility
International Confederation of Free Trade Unions (ICFTU)
International Gender and Trade Network
International Labor Rights Forum
International Textile, Garment and Leather Workers' Federation
International Trade Union Confederation
IRENE

Joint Initiative on Corporate Accountability and Workers' Rights (JO-IN)

Labour Behind the Label
Labourstart

Maquila Solidarity Network
MFA Forum*

National Labor Committee
No Sweat

Oxfam Labor Rights/Nike Watch

Self-Employed Women's Association (SEWA)
Social Accountability International SA8000*
Solidar
Solidarity Center/American Center for International Labor Solidarity
SOMO
STITCH
Students and Scholars Against Corporate Misbehaviour (SACOM)
SUDWIND
SweatFree Communities
Sweatshop Watch/Garment Workers Center

Textile, Clothing and Footwear Union of Australia
Thai Labor Campaign
The Third World Network
Transnational Information Exchange

UNITE
United Students Against Sweatshops
U.S. Labor Education in the Americas Project (US/LEAP)

Verite

War on Want
Women in Informal Employment: Globalizing and Organizing (WIEGO)
Women Working Worldwide
Workers Rights Consortium*
Worldwide Responsible Accredited Production Certification Program
    (WRAP)*

---

* These organizations are multi-stakeholder initiatives.

Notes

Introduction

1. Nevertheless, the term *non-state actor* remains and is used at times in this book to be consistent with the broader international relations literature.

2. For notable exceptions, see Hobson and Seabrooke (2007) and Uvin, Jain, and Brown (2000).

3. While an exact definition of a small NGO may be difficult, it often is easier to define what it is not. Eight of the two thousand international NGOs engaged in humanitarian aid and development control 50 percent of the US$8 billion aid market (Uvin 2000). Access to this level of resources makes large organizations atypical rather than representative of the thousands of NGOs worldwide.

4. I conducted a total of thirty-five interviews in Shenzhen, China; Amsterdam; Washington DC; Anthony, New Mexico; San Francisco; Melbourne; and, via telephone, with activists in Sydney and New York.

5. The following studies emphasize workers' perspectives in the garment industry in China (Pun 2005), Sri Lanka (Lynch 2007), and New York City (Chin 2005).

1. Political economy of the garment industry

1. I generally follow Gereffi's terminology. However, for simplicity and clarity, I refer to firms oriented toward consumers through retailing, branding, marketing, and design as retailers. This includes traditional retailers such as Gap as well as branded marketers like Nike and Reebok that rely on brand images to sell their products through third parties. Some activists refer to the latter group of companies as brands or branded retailers. I refer to companies engaged in assembly and production as manufacturers.

2. Since the ATC is less widely known, I follow the general practice of referring to this period under the ATC as inclusive of the MFA, and therefore refer to the period after 2005 as post-MFA, even though the MFA technically ended upon the inception of the ATC in 1994.

3. The reason that the United States was able to activate these safeguard measures was because of China's accession to the WTO in 2001. At that time, China agreed to conditions that allowed WTO members to apply safeguards against Chinese clothing and textiles if the importing government could demonstrate market disruption.

4. For example, see the Jo-In (2004) report on Turkey; Chan (2003) on conditions in China; Marshall, Iritani, and Dickerson (2005) reporting from Lesotho; and Oxfam Australia and CCC (2008) in Indonesia. In contrast, see Jung-ok (1998, 17), which cites considerable improvements in the conditions for South Korean workers in Gumi and Masan EPZs. Jung-ok attributes these improvements to trade union movements in South Korea in the late 1980s.

5. This indicates a weakness with the ILO declaration and, by extension, many corporate codes of conduct based on it. By focusing on the most flagrant types of abuse, the less sensational, more-routinized aspects of exploitation tend to be overlooked, minimized, and indeed not even counted.

6. The International Confederation of Free Trade Unions (ICFTU) merged with the World Federation of Trade Unions to become the International Trade Union Confederation (ITUC) on November 1, 2006.

7. On the gendered dimensions of the industry and constructions of the ideal worker, see Kabeer (2000) and Oxfam (2004b).

2. Development of the anti-sweatshop network

1. The loosely coordinated, highly decentralized structure of the anti-sweatshop network has proven to be frustrating at times for activists. Increasing coordination among those in the network would help address some of these issues, yet none of the activists I spoke with during the course of the research for this book expressed a desire for an overarching structure with greater centralization. The activists are faced with the challenge of determining how to create greater coordination without losing the benefits of a decentralized network.

2. Advocacy related to the garment industry exists in other regions as well, mainly through unions, industry organizations, or development NGOs. For example, see the Apparel Lesotho Alliance to Fight AIDS (ALAFA 2008).

3. Legal action is rarely an option for anti-sweatshop activists because factories do not often share political jurisdictions with retailers. However, Saipan is a U.S. protectorate. This is the reason much of the production was located there in the first place, because manufacturers could attach Made in USA labels without having to meet other labor obligations for doing business within the United States.

4. In an interview Abad described her role in the case, including how she sewed a camera into her clothing in order to film the inside of the factory where she worked. Some of that footage appeared on U.S. television on ABC News' *20/20* on March 13, 1998, and later became part of the documentary "Labor behind the Labels" (Lessin 2001).

5. Corporate responses depend on many factors, including corporate culture, resources, and allies within targeted organizations. In the course of my interviews several people mentioned the important role of individual staff members within

targeted companies pushing from within the company for greater social-auditing programs.

6. For example, beyond several NGOs like STITCH and Working Women Worldwide, few of the Northern anti-sweatshop NGOs discuss ways to ensure that unions are truly democratic and adequately represent women workers. This particularly relates to homeworkers, who make up a significant portion of the workforce in the garment industry but are often excluded from traditional unions.

3. Places and practices of four anti-sweatshop NGOs

1. An example of a different, nationally based approach can be found on the website of All USA Clothing, a company that sells union-made apparel produced in the United States. Its homepage says: "Have you thought about how other countries are developing now? They are riding the wave of our appetite for cheap goods. Our money is going to places that often times do not like us, our money is building their infrastructure, our money is building their military, our money is raising their quality of life and education. Of course, some of this is good. But what about us? We need to bring some balance back on our side." This illustrates how pleas to support union-made products are often couched in national terms rather than in support of workers globally.

4. Structures of governance and anti-sweatshop NGOs

1. This chapter focuses on Northern states because the case-study organizations interact most directly with Northern states. Other Northern-based anti-sweatshop NGOs such as the ILRF have more direct, and sometimes contentious, contact with states in the global South. For example, the government of the Philippines placed ILRF lawyers on a terrorist watch list and denied them access to the country following their involvement in researching violence against trade unionists (Waterman 2007).

2. UNITE (now UNITE HERE) is the U.S. union of workers in hospitality, gaming, food service, manufacturing, textile, laundry, and airport industries.

3. For the full text of the Senate bill, see Govtrack.us (2008b). Similar legislation has been introduced in the UK through amendments to the Companies Bill that would require corporations to report on their supply chains in their annual business review.

4. The private actors targeted by NGOs are not completely separate from the state. For example, many U.S. universities are publicly and privately funded, and many corporations in the United States receive significant grants and tax breaks from the government. Nevertheless, the state is not the primary target of NGOs' actions.

5. Retailers have embraced MSIs as a way to diffuse activist pressure and avoid state or intergovernmental oversight. Nonetheless, Merk (2008b) argues, MSIs have opened up space for transnational regulation of the industry, which has the potential to benefit workers.

5. Consumer campaigns and the use of civic politics

1. The risk with consumer campaigns is that by focusing on consumers as political agents, such campaigns can overstate consumer choices while overlooking structural changes needed in the industry and regulatory bodies, such as national governments or the WTO. For more on the politics of consumerism, see Shah et al. (2007).

2. Alliances among activists in the North and South are particularly important in situations where workers in the South are unable to pressure their own state directly because of the presence of a weak state infrastructure to deal with such abuses or out of fear of repression.

3. Activists continued to organize Play Fair campaigns surrounding the 2008 Olympic Games in Beijing and in preparation for the 2012 Olympic Games in London.

4. As a result of the campaign, Asics joined the FLA. Puma, Umbro, Asics, and Mizuno made commitments to improve their labor policies. Fila, Lotto, and Kappa were less cooperative (Merk 2005).

5. The campaign also involved direct pressure on retailers, pressure on secondary retailers and subsidiaries of Russell Athletic, and letters to universities. Several universities cut their contracts with Russell Athletic even though there was not an active USAS chapter on campus (Rod Palmquist, personal communication, April 10, 2011).

6. In June 2009 the WRC issued two reports on the status of Russell Athletic's remediation plan. One of the reports summarized the results of interviews with more than one hundred workers. The WRC found that most workers were either unaware of Russell Athletic's pledge to freedom of association or were told that while they had the right to join a union, there was no need to since the company-controlled union was sufficient. The WRC claims that this is in direct violation of ILO Convention 98 on the freedom of association, which Honduras has ratified (WRC 2009c; WRC 2009d).

7. In February 2010 the WRC reported on the implementation of the November 2009 agreement between workers and Russell Athletic. They found that Russell Athletic was taking action on many of the terms of the agreement, including rehiring Jerzees de Honduras workers at the new factory, establishing a workers' welfare fund, recognizing SITRAJERZEESH as the representative of workers at the new factory, disciplining managerial staff engaged in anti-union activity, and establishing an oversight committee. Russell Athletic had not yet implemented

the training program for staff on freedom of association but indicated that there were plans to do so (WRC 2010a).

8. Many companies authorized to use the label choose not to do so. FairWear organizers believe this is in part because it would draw attention to the companies' other products that are not certified as sweat-free merchandise (Gardener, personal communication, November 21, 2006).

6. NGO accountability and political responsibility

1. Collingwood explains that one line of argument critical of NGOs claims that NGOs rely on high-profile stunts to gather media attention; this exaggerates problems and ignores the complexity of issues and undermines their legitimacy in global politics (2006).

2. Some NGOs' codes of conduct now include statements about the organizations' duties to respect the dignity, culture, and values of the people they work with in their communications to the public. For an example of this, see the Australian Council for International Development code of conduct, available on its website.

3. In an interview Nina Ascoly of the CCC's International Secretariat explained that the criteria include whether the violation has taken place in the garment sector, the seriousness of the violation, the potential impact that the case could have on the whole sector in a country or in a specific EPZ, links to the European market, and the capacity of CCC at the time of the request (Ascoly, personal communication, February 7, 2007).

7. Effectiveness of anti-sweatshop advocacy

1. For example, as a result of campaigning by the CCC, Dutch retailer C&A implemented a policy requiring that any of its suppliers that employed children continue paying the children's salaries while they attended professional or vocational training (Sluiter 2009).

2. It is unclear what impact the global financial crisis will have on corporate social responsibility programs. According to a recent report by the MSN, some analysts predict that corporations will cut their corporate social responsibility programs extensively, except for those activities that can be shown also to decrease other costs. This could include reducing energy costs, decreasing staff turnover, or collaborating with other retailers to share the costs of social auditing. Other analysts predict that corporate social responsibility programs will remain intact because with increased competition, retailers cannot afford the bad publicity that comes with decreasing attention on social auditing (MSN 2009b).

3. In many countries, including Thailand, employers are required to pay displaced workers severance payment in lieu of a state-run unemployment benefit scheme. Even though severance payments are required under Thai law, few employers set up funds in escrow to pay severance and often disregard the legal requirements to pay severance (WRC 2006).

References

Adidas Group. 2007a. "Giving 110%: Our Efforts to Be a Responsible Business in 2007." Herzogenaurach, Germany: Adidas Group SEA Team and Corporate Communications.

———. 2007b. *Striving to Improve Performance: Corporate Responsibility Report 2007*. Herzogenaurach, Germany: Adidas Group.

Ahmed, S., and D. M. Potter. 2006. *NGOs in International Politics*. Bloomfield, CT: Kumarian Press.

AIDWATCH. 2007. "Backgrounder: ATO's Removal of AID/WATCH's Charity Status." AIDWATCH website.

ALAFA. 2008. "Apparel Lesotho Alliance to Fight AIDS." ALAFA website.

Anheier, H. 2001. "Measuring Global Civil Society." In *Global Civil Society 2001*, edited by H. Anheier, M. Glasius, and M. Kaldor, 221–24. New York: Oxford University Press.

Anheier, H., M. Kaldor, and M. Glasius, eds. 2005. *Global Civil Society 2004/5*. London: Sage Publications.

Anheier, H., and L. Salamon. 2006. "The Nonprofit Sector in Comparative Perspective." In *The Nonprofit Sector: A Research Handbook*, edited by W. W. Powell and R. Steinberg, 89–116. New Haven, CT: Yale University Press.

Anner, M. 2001. "The Paradox of Labor Transnationalism: Northern and Southern Trade Unions and the Campaign for Labor Standards in the WTO." Cornell University Working Paper. Ithaca, NY: Cornell University.

ATNC. 2006. "ATNC Monitoring Network 2005 and Before." Asian Transnational Corporation Monitoring Network website.

Bandy, J., and J. Smith, eds. 2005. *Coalitions across Borders: Transnational Protest and the Neoliberal Order*. Lanham, MD: Rowman and Littlefield.

Bendell, J. 2006. *Debating NGO Accountability*. Geneva: UN NGO Liaison Service.

Bender, D. 2004. *Sweated Work, Weak Bodies: Anti-Sweatshop Campaigns and Languages of Labor*. New Brunswick, NJ: Rutgers University Press.

Benjamin, M. 2001. "Foreword." In *Can We Put an End to Sweatshops?* edited by A. Fung, D. O'Rourke, and C. Sabel, vii–xi. Boston: Beacon Press.

Bennett, W. L. 2006. "Branded Political Communication: Lifestyle Politics, Logo Campaigns, and the Rise of Global Citizenship." In Micheletti, Follesdal, and Stolle 2006b, 101–26.

BFC. 2007. *Nineteenth Synthesis Report on Working Conditions in Cambodia's Garment Sector*. Kingdom of Cambodia and International Labour Organization. Better Factories Cambodia website.

Bob, C. 2004. "Contesting Transnationalism: Anti-NGO Mobilization and World Politics." Annual Meeting of the American Political Science Association. Chicago. September 2–5.

———. 2005. *The Marketing of Rebellion: Insurgents, Media, and International Activism*. Cambridge: Cambridge University Press.

Boyenge, J-PS. 2007. *ILO Database on Export Processing Zones*. Revised edition. International Labour Organization website.

Braun, R., and J. Gearhart. 2005. "Who Should Code Your Conduct?" In Eade and Leather 2005, 203–21.

Brecher, J., T. Costello, and B. Smith. 2002. *Globalization from Below: The Power of Solidarity*. Cambridge, MA: South End Press.

Brooks, E. 2005. "Transnational Campaigns against Child Labor: The Garment Industry in Bangladesh." In Bandy and Smith 2005, 121–41.

———. 2007. *Unraveling the Garment Industry: Transnational Organizing and Women's Work*. Ann Arbor: University of Michigan Press.

Brown, S. 2006. *Congressional Record: Support the Decent Working Conditions and Fair Competition Act*. House of Representatives. June 22.

Burger, A., and P. Dekker. 2001. *The Nonprofit Sector in the Netherlands*. Working Paper 70. The Hague: Sociaal En Cultureel Planbureau.

Burger, A., P. Dekker, and S. Toepler. 1999. "The Netherlands: Key Features of the Dutch Nonprofit Sector." In *Global Civil Society: Dimensions of the Nonprofit Sector*, edited by L. Salamon, H. Anheier, R. List, S. Toepler, and S. W. Sokolowski, 145–62. Baltimore, MD: Johns Hopkins Center for Civil Society Studies.

Castells, M. 2000. *The Rise of the Network Society*. Oxford: Blackwell Publishers.

———. 2005. "Grassrooting the Space of Flows." In *The Global Resistance Reader*, edited by L. Amoore, 363–70. London: Routledge.

CCC. 2000. "Maquila Workers Ask for Your Support." Clean Clothes Campaign website.

———. 2005a. *Made by Women: Gender, the Global Garment Industry, and the Movement for Women Workers' Rights*. Amsterdam: CCC.

———. 2005b. "Clean Clothes Communities: Ethical Public Procurement of Work Wear." Clean Clothes Campaign website.

———. 2007a. *Annual Report 2006*. Amsterdam: Clean Clothes Campaign.

———. 2007b. "Clean Clothes Campaign Summoned to Indian Court in Alleged Defamation Case." Clean Clothes Campaign website.

———. 2007c. "Sportswear Workers in the Dominican Republic Need Your Support." Clean Clothes Campaign website.

———. 2007d. "Country Reports." February–June. Clean Clothes Campaign website.

———. 2008a. "Price Mark-Up of a 100 Euro Sportshoe." Clean Clothes Campaign website.

————. 2008b. "Growing Public Concern." Clean Clothes Campaign website.

————. 2008c. "FFI Case Closed." Clean Clothes Campaign website.

————. 2008d. "Settlement Reached by A-One Factory Workers in Bangladesh 6 February." Clean Clothes Campaign website.

————. 2008e. "FAQs—What Does the Clean Clothes Campaign Do?" Clean Clothes Campaign website.

————. 2008f. "Factory Investigator Mehedi Hasan Released; Urgent Action Still Needed in Bangladesh." Clean Clothes Campaign website.

Cha, J. 2007. Email from WRC to Parties concerned about the Announced Closure of BJ&B: English Translation of Letter from General Manager of BJ&B to Employees. Washington DC: Worker Rights Consortium. February 22.

Chan, A. 2003. "A Race to the Bottom: Globalisation and China's Labour Standards." *China Perspectives* 46 (March/April): 41–49.

Chang, D., and M. Wong. 2005. "After the Consumer Movement: Toward a New International Labour Activism in the Global Garment Industry." *Labour, Capital, and Society* 38, nos. 1, 2: 127–56.

Chin, M. 2005. *Sewing Women: Immigrants and the New York City Garment Industry*. New York: Columbia University Press.

Clark, J. D. 2003. *Worlds Apart: Civil Society and the Battle for Ethical Globalization*. Bloomfield, CT: Kumarian Press.

Cohen, M. 1992. "Rooted Cosmopolitanism." *Dissent* 39, no. 4: 478–83.

Cohen, R., and S. Rai, eds. 2000. *Global Social Movements*. London: The Athlone Press.

Collingwood, V. 2006. "Non-Governmental Organisations, Power, and Legitimacy in International Society." *Review of International Studies* 32: 439–54.

Collins, J. 2003. *Threads: Gender, Labor, and Power in the Global Apparel Industry*. Chicago: University of Chicago Press.

Colwell, M. A. C. 1996. "The Potential for Bias When Research on Voluntary Associations Is Limited to 501(c)(3) Organizations." Working Paper. Washington DC: The Aspen Institute.

Compa, L. 2003. "Workers' Freedom of Association in the United States: The Gap between Ideals and Practice." In *Workers' Rights As Human Rights*, edited by J. A. Gross, 23–52. Ithaca, NY: Cornell University Press.

Connor, T. 2005. "Time to Scale Up Cooperation? Labor Unions, NGOs, and the International Anti-Sweatshop Movement." In Eade and Leather 2005, 69–81.

————. 2007. "Rewriting the Rules: The Anti-Sweatshop Movement; Nike, Reebok, and Adidas' Participation in Voluntary Labour Regulation; and Workers' Rights to Form Trade Unions and Collective Bargaining." PhD thesis. University of Newcastle.

Connor, T., and K. Dent. 2006. *Offside! Labour Rights and Sportswear Production in Asia*. Oxford: Oxfam International.

Conroy, M. 2007. *Branded! How the "Certification Revolution" Is Transforming Global Corporations*. Gabriola Island, British Columbia: New Society Publishers.

Croeser, S. 2006. "The Global Justice Movement: Providing Human Security to the Least Secure?" International Society for Third Sector Research Seventh International Conference. Bangkok. July 9–12.

DEEWR. 2008. "Homeworkers' Code of Practice Program-Launch." Media release. Department of Education Employment and Workplace Relations website.

Diani, M. 2003. "Networks and Social Movements: A Research Programme." In *Social Movements and Networks*, edited by M. Diani and D. McAdam, 299–319. Oxford: Oxford University Press.

Diokno-Pascual, M. T. 2002. "Development and Advocacy." In Eade 2002b, 1–6.

Diviney, E., and S. Lillywhite. 2007. *Ethical Threads: Corporate Social Responsibility in the Australian Garment Industry*. Fitzroy, Victoria: Brotherhood of St. Laurence.

DSP Working Group. 2006. "The Designated Suppliers Program (Revised)." United Students Against Sweatshops website.

Duffy, M. 2008. "Nike Contractor Using Forced Labour." Yahoo Channel 7.

Eade, D. 2002a. "Preface." In Eade 2002b, ix–xvi.

Eade, D., ed. 2002b. *Development and Advocacy*. Oxford: Oxfam Publishing.

Eade, D., and A. Leather, eds. 2005. *Development NGOs and Labor Unions: Terms of Engagement*. Bloomfield, CT: Kumarian Press.

The Economist (editorial). 2000. "Angry and Effective." *The Economist* 356, no. 8189: 85–87. September 23.

Edelman. 2009. *Edelman Trust Barometer*. Edelman website.

Edwards, M. 2002. "'Does the Doormat Influence the Boot?' Critical Thoughts on UK NGOs and International Advocacy." In Eade 2002b, 95–11.

———. 2006. "Foreword." In *NGO Accountability: Politics, Power, and Innovation*, edited by L. Jordan and P. Van Tuijl, vii–ix. London: Earthscan.

Eitzen, D. S. 2006. *Fair and Foul: Beyond the Myths and Paradoxes of Sport*. New York: Rowman and Littlefield.

Elias, J. 2007. "Women Workers and Labour Standards: The Problem of 'Human Rights.'" *Review of International Studies* 33: 45–57.

Elliot, K. A., and R. Freeman. 2005. "White Hats or Don Quixotes? Human Rights Vigilantes in the Global Economy." In Freeman, Hersch, and Mishel 2005, 47–98.

Esbenshade, J. 2004. *Monitoring Sweatshops: Workers, Consumers, and the Global Garment Industry*. Philadelphia: Temple University Press.

Escobar, A. 1995. *Encountering Development: The Making and Unmaking of the Third World*. Princeton, NJ: Princeton University Press.

Fairwear. 2007a. "Local Council Setting the Example." Fairwear website. October 12.

———. 2007b. "Over 100 Mexican Jean Workers Fired for Supporting Independent Union." Fairwear website. December 4.

Featherstone, L. 2002. *Students Against Sweatshops*. New York: Verso.

Ferenschild, S., and I. Wick. 2004. *Global Game for Cuffs and Collars: The Phase-Out of the WTO Agreement on Textiles and Clothing Aggravates Social Divisions*. Vienna: SUDWIND.

FFC. 2009. "FFC Software Statistics." Fair Factories Clearinghouse website.

Fisher, W. 1997. "Doing Good? The Politics and Antipolitics of NGO Practices." *Annual Review of Anthropology* 26: 439–64.

FLA. 2008. *2007 Annual Report*. Washington DC: Fair Labor Association.

Florini, A. ed. 2000. *The Third Force: The Rise of Transnational Civil Society*. Tokyo: Japan Center for International Exchange; Washington DC: Carnegie Endowment for International Peace.

Forero, J. 2005. "Report Criticizes Labor Standards in Central America." *The New York Times*. July 1.

Freeman, R., J. Hersch, and L. Mishel, eds. 2005, *Emerging Labor Market Institutions for the Twenty-First Century*. Chicago: University of Chicago Press.

Garment Worker Center and Sweatshop Watch. 2004. *Crisis or Opportunity? the Future of Los Angeles' Garment Workers, the Apparel Industry, and the Local Economy*. Los Angeles: Garment Worker Center and Sweatshop Watch.

Garonzik, B. 2005. "El Sindicato Unido De Trabajadores De BJ&B: A New Vision Realized in the World of International Labor Organizing." United Students Against Sweatshops website.

Gereffi, G. 2002. *The International Competitiveness of Asian Economies in the Apparel Commodity Chain*. Manila: Asian Development Bank.

Ghiase, M. 2007. "Memorandum of Complaint under S.200 of the Criminal Procedure Act in the Court of the 7th Additional Chief Metropolitan Judge at Bangalore Cc no. 11593/2007." Clean Clothes Campaign website.

Giddens, A. 1991. *Modernity and Self Identity: Self and Society in the Late Modern Age*. Stanford, CA: Stanford University Press.

GMI. 2005. "GMI Poll Finds Doing Good Is Good for Business." Media release. Global Market Insite website.

Gonzalez, D. 2003. "Latin Sweatshops Pressed by U.S. Campus Power." *The New York Times*. April 4.

Govtrack.us. 2008a. "Decent Working Conditions and Fair Competition Act H.R. 1992." Govtrack.us (database of federal legislation).

———. 2008b. "Decent Working Conditions and Fair Competition Act S.367– 110th Congress." Govtrack.us (database of federal legislation).

Greenhouse, S. 2000. "Sweatshop King: Nike Exec Reneges on $30 Million Pledge." *The New York Times*. April 25.

———. 2009. "Labor Fight Ends in Win for Students." *The New York Times*. November 18.

———. 2010a. "Pressured, Nike to Help Workers in Honduras." *The New York Times*. July 27.

———. 2010b. "Factory Defies Sweatshop Label, But Can It Thrive?" *The New York Times*. July 18.

Hale, A., and M. Burns. 2006. "The Phase-Out of the MFA from the Perspective of the Workers." In Hale and Wills 2006, 210–33.

Hale, A., and J. Wills, eds. 2006. *Threads of Labour: Garment Industry Supply Chains from the Workers' Perspective*. Oxford: Blackwell.

Hannerz, U. 2003. "Being There . . . and There . . . and There! Reflections on Multi-Site Ethnography." *Ethnography* 4, no. 2: 201–16.

Hauser, F. 2007. Email from WRC to Parties concerned about the Announced Closure of BJ&B: Statement from Nike to Stakeholders. Washington DC: Worker Rights Consortium. February 22.

Hearson, M. 2009. "Cashing In: Giant Retailers, Purchasing Practices, and Working Conditions in the Garment Industry." Clean Clothes Campaign website.

Hobson, J., and L. Seabrooke, eds. 2007. *Everyday Politics of the World Economy.* Cambridge: Cambridge University Press.

Hookway, J. 2008. "Inflation Fuels Vietnam Strikes: Workers Demand Hefty Pay Increases from Foreign Firms." *Wall Street Journal.* June 3.

Hurley, J., and D. Miller. 2006. "The Changing Face of the Global Garment Industry." In Hale and Wills, 16–39.

Hurrell, A. 2005. "Power, Institutions, and the Production of Inequality." In *Power in Global Governance*, edited by M. Barnett and R. Duvall, 33–58. Cambridge: Cambridge University Press.

ICFTU. 2000. *Annual Survey of Violations of Trade Union Rights.* Brussels: International Confederation of Free Trade Unions.

———. 2006. *Annual Survey of Violations of Trade Union Rights.* Brussels: International Confederation of Free Trade Unions.

ILO. 2005. *Promoting Fair Globalization in Textiles and Clothing in a Post-MFA Environment.* Geneva: International Labour Organization.

Incite! Women of Color against Violence, ed. 2007. *The Revolution Will Not Be Funded: Beyond the Non-Profit Industrial Complex.* Cambridge, MA: South End Press.

ITGLWF. 2000. "Complaint against the Government of Honduras Presented by ITGLWF, International Textile, Garment and Leather Workers' Federation." ILO website.

———. 2006. *Bangladesh Employers Told to Stop Destroying Garment Industry.* Brussels: International Textile, Garment and Leather Workers' Federation.

———. 2008. *Bargaining for a Living Wage: A Trade Union Guide.* International Textile, Garment and Leather Workers' Federation website.

ITUC. 2008. *2007 Annual Survey of Violations of Trade Union Rights.* Brussels: International Trade Union Confederation.

Johns, G. 2003. "The NGO Challenge: Whose Democracy Is It Anyway?" Conference: We're Not from the Government, But We're Here to Help You. American Enterprise Institute. Washington DC. June 11.

Jo-In. 2004. *Background Study on Turkey: Basic Information on Labour Conditions and Social Auditing in the Turkish Garment Industry.* Joint Initiative on Corporate Accountability and Workers' Rights.

Jordan, L., and P. Van Tuijl. 2000. "Political Responsibility in Transnational NGO Advocacy." *World Development* 28, no. 12: 2051–65.

Josselin, D., and W. Wallace, eds. 2001. *Non-State Actors in World Politics.* New York: Palgrave.

Jung-ok, L. 1998. "Export Processing Zones in South Korea." In AMRC 1998, 7–26.

Kabeer, N. 2000. *The Power to Choose*. London: Verso.

———. 2002. *Globalisation, Labour Standards, and Women's Rights: Dilemmas of Collective Action in an Interdependent World*. Brighton: Institute for Development Studies.

Kahler, M., ed. 2009. *Networked Politics: Agency, Power, and Globalization*. Ithaca, NY: Cornell University Press.

Kahn, R., and D. Kellner. 2004. "New Media and Internet Activism: From the 'Battle of Seattle' to Blogging." *New Media and Society* 6, no. 1: 87–95.

Kaldor, M. 2003. *Global Civil Society: An Answer to War*. Cambridge: Polity.

Kaldor, M., H. Anheier, and M. Glasius. 2005. "Introduction." In Anheier, Glasius, and Kaldor 2005, 1–25.

Kearney, N., and J. Gearhart. 2005. "Workplace Codes As Tools for Workers." In Eade and Leather 2005, 249–60.

Keck, M., and K. Sikkink. 1998. *Activists beyond Borders*. Ithaca, NY: Cornell University Press.

Kidder, T. 2002. "Networks in Transnational Labor Organizing." In *Restructuring World Politics: Transnational Social Movements, Networks, and Norms*, edited by S. Khagram, J. V. Riker, and K. Sikkink, 269–93. Minneapolis: University of Minnesota.

Klein, N. 2000. *No Logo*. London: Flamingo.

Krugman, P. 1997. "In Praise of Sweatshops." *Slate*. March 21.

Krupat, K. 2002. "Rethinking the Sweatshop: A Conversation about United Students Against Sweatshops (USAS) with Charles Eaton, Marion Traub-Werner, and Evelyn Zepeda." *International Labor and Working Class History* 61 (Spring): 112–27.

Kuper, A. ed. 2005. *Global Responsibilities: Who Must Deliver on Human Rights?* New York: Routledge.

Leong, A., and C. Ka-wai. 2007. *Critical Reflections on CSR: A Labour's Perspective*. Hong Kong: Asia Monitor Resource Centre.

Lessin, T. 2001. "Labor behind the Labels: Garment Workers on Saipan." Video, 46 minutes. New York: Witness.

Lipschutz, R. 2005. "Global Civil Society and Global Governmentality: Or, the Search for Politics and the State amidst the Capillaries of Social Power." In *Power in Global Governance*, edited by M. Barnett and R. Duvall, 229–48. Cambridge: Cambridge University Press.

Lipschutz, R., with J. K. Rowe. 2005. *Globalization, Governmentality and Global Politics*. London: Routledge.

Lloyd, R. 2005. *The Role of NGO Self Regulation in Increasing Stakeholder Accountability*. London: One World Trust.

Locke, R., T. Kochan, M. Romis, and F. Qin. 2007. "Beyond Corporate Codes of Conduct: Work Organization and Labour Standards at Nike's Suppliers." *International Labour Review* 146, no. 1/2: 21–37.

Lynch, C. 2007. *Juki Girls, Good Girls*. Ithaca, NY: Cornell University Press.

Lyons, M. 1998. *Defining the Nonprofit Sector: Australia*. Baltimore, MD: Johns Hopkins Institute for Policy Studies.

Macdonald, T., and K. Macdonald. 2006. "Non-Electoral Accountability in Global Politics: Strengthening Democratic Control within the Global Garment Industry." *European Journal of International Law* 17, no. 1: 89–119.

Maddison, S., R. Denniss, and C. Hamilton. 2004. *Silencing Dissent: Non-Government Organisations and Australian Democracy*. Manuka, ACT: The Australian Institute.

Manheim, J. 2003. "Biz-War: Origins, Structures, and Strategy of Foundation-NGO Network Warfare on Corporations in the United States." Conference: We're Not from the Government, But We're Here to Help You. American Enterprise Institute. Washington DC. June 11.

Marcus, A., Dabindu Collective, Women's Center, Joint Committee of Workers' Councils in the FTZ, and Institute of Occupational Health and Safety. 1998. "Free Trade Zones and the 'Transnationalisation' of the Sri Lanka Economy." In *We in the Zone: Women Workers in Asia's Export Processing Zones*, 135–73. Hong Kong: Asia Monitor Resource Centre, 1998.

Marcus, G. E. 1995. "Ethnography in/of the World System: The Emergence of Multi-Sited Ethnography." *Annual Review of Anthropology* 24: 95–117.

Margasak, L. 2005. "U.S. Blocked Release of CAFTA Reports." Associated Press. June 29.

Marshall, T., E. Iritani, and M. Dickerson. 2005. "Clothes Will Cost Less, But Some Nations Pay." *Los Angeles Times*, January 16.

Martin, M. F. 2007. *U.S. Clothing and Textile Trade with China and the World: Trends Since the End of Quotas*. Washington DC: Congressional Research Service.

Mather, C., M. Eyskoot, and N. Ascoly. 2007. *Newsletter*, no. 23 (May). Amsterdam: Clean Clothes Campaign.

McAdam, D., J. D. McCarthy, and M. N. Zald, eds. 1996. *Comparative Perspectives on Social Movements*. New York: Cambridge University Press.

Mendez, J. B. 2002. "Creating Alternatives from a Gender Perspective." In *Women's Activism and Globalization*, edited by N. Naples and M. Desai, 121–41. New York: Routledge.

Merk, J. 2005. "The Play Fair at the Olympics Campaign: An Evaluation of the Company Responses." Amsterdam: CCC, ICFTU, and Oxfam.

———. 2008a. "The Structural Crisis of Labour Flexibility: Strategies and Prospects for Transnational Labour Organising in the Garment and Sportswear Industries." Amsterdam: Clean Clothes Campaign.

———. 2008b. "The Private Regulation of Labour Standards: The Case of the Apparel and Footwear Industries." In *Transnational Private Governance and Its Limits*, edited by J. C. Graz and A. Nolke, 115–26. London: Routledge.

———. 2009. *A Decent Wage across Borders*. New Delhi: Asia Floor Wage Alliance.

Micheletti, M., A. Follesdal, and D. Stolle. 2006a. "Introduction." In Micheletti, Follesdal, and Stolle 2006b, ix–xxvi.

Micheletti, M., A. Follesdal, and D. Stolle, eds. 2006b. *Politics, Products, and Markets: Exploring Political Consumerism Past and Present.* London: Transaction Publishers.

Micheletti, M., and D. Stolle. 2008. "Fashioning Social Justice through Political Consumerism, Capitalism, and the Internet." *Cultural Studies* 22, no. 5: 749–69.

Miller, D. 2005. "A Play Fair Alliance Evaluation of the WFSGI Response to the Play Fair at the Olympics Campaign." Amsterdam: CCC.

Mohanty, C. T. 2003. *Feminism without Borders.* Durham, NC: Duke University Press.

MSN. 2005. "Brand Campaigns and Worker Organizing: Lessons from Lesotho, Thailand, and Honduras." Toronto: Maquila Solidarity Network.

———. 2008. "Grupo Navarra Closes Factory to Punish Workers for Joining Union." Maquila Solidarity Network website.

———. 2009. "How Will the Global Financial Crisis Affect the Garment Industry and Garment Workers?" Maquila Solidarity Network website.

Munck, R. 2002. *Globalisation and Labour: The New "Great Transformation."* London: Zed Books.

Murthy, L. 2004. "Play Fair at the Olympics." Infochange News and Features.

Nash, A. 2001. *People.Dot.Comm Unity: A Resource for Effective Community Activism.* Geelong: Villamanta Legal Service.

Nelson, P., and E. Dorsey. 2008. *New Rights Advocacy.* Washington DC: Georgetown University Press.

Nike. 2006. "Innovate for a Better World: Nike FY05–06 Corporate Responsibility Report." Beaverton, OR.

———. 2008a. "Company Overview." Nike website.

———. 2008b. "Nike Inc. Statement Regarding Hytex Contract Factory." Nike website.

NLC. 2006. "Homepage." National Labor Committee website.

Nordas, H. K. 2005. *Labour Implications of the Textiles and Clothing Quota Phase-Out.* Geneva: ILO.

Nova, S. 2009. *WRC Update: Russell and Union Conclude Historic Agreement.* Worker Rights Consortium, via email, Washington DC, 18 November.

O'Brien, R., A. M. Goetz, J. A. Scholte, and M. Williams. 2000. *Contesting Global Governance.* Cambridge: Cambridge University Press.

O'Rourke, D. 2006. "Multi-Stakeholder Regulation: Privatizing or Socializing Global Labor Standards?" *World Development* 34, no. 5: 899–918.

Oxfam. 2004a. "Play Fair at the Olympics: Respect Workers' Rights in the Sportswear Industry." Amsterdam: Oxfam GB, CCC, and ICFTU.

———. 2004b. *Stitched Up: How Rich Country Protectionism in Textiles and Clothing Trade Prevents Poverty Alleviation.* Oxford: Oxfam.

Oxfam, CCC, and Global Unions. 2004. *Play Fair at the Olympics: The Tae Hwa Indonesian Factory*. Oxfam website.

Oxfam Australia. 2008a. "Nikewatch Newsletter August." Sydney: Oxfam Australia.

———. 2008b. "Nikewatch Newsletter May." Sydney: Oxfam Australia.

Oxfam Australia, and CCC. 2008. *Sector-wide Solutions for the Sports Shoe and Apparel Industry in Indonesia*. Amsterdam: Oxfam Australia and Clean Clothes Campaign.

Pearson, R. 1998. "Nimble Fingers Revisited: Reflections on Women and Third World Industrialisation in the Late Twentieth Century." In *Feminist Visions of Development: Gender Analysis and Policy*, edited by C. Jackson and R. Pearson, 171–88. London: Routledge.

Pederick, B., and J. Pederick. 1998. *Twenty Pieces: Outworkers Tell the Real Fashion Story*. Melbourne. Produced for the Fairwear Campaign.

Peled, M. X. 2006. *China Blue*. Teddy Bear Films.

Piper, N., and A. Uhlin. 2004. "New Perspectives on Transnational Activism." In *Transnational Activism in Asia: Problems of Power and Democracy*, edited by N. Piper and A. Uhlin, 1–25. London: Routledge.

Prugl, E. 1999. "What Is a Worker? Gender, Global Restructuring, and the ILO Convention on Homework." In *Gender Politics in Global Governance*, edited by M. Meyer and E. Prugl, 197–209. Lanham, MD: Rowman and Littlefield.

Pun, N. 2005. *Made in China*. Durham, NC: Duke University Press.

Qiang, L. 2009. *A Refutation of the Argument That China's Labor Contract Law Hurts the Working Class*. China Labor Watch website.

Quan, K. 2007. "Women Crossing Borders to Organize." In *The Sex of Class*, edited by D. S. Cobble, 253–71. Ithaca, NY: ILR Press.

Read, R. 2008. "Nike Looks into Workers Rights Breaches." *The Oregonian*. August 2.

Reich, R. B. 2007. *Supercapitalism: The Transformation of Business, Democracy, and Everyday Life*. New York: Alfred A. Knopf.

Risse-Kappen, T. 1995. "Bringing Transnational Relations Back In: Introduction." In *Bringing Transnational Relations Back In: Non-State Actors, Domestic Structures and International Institutions*, edited by T. Risse-Kappen, 3–33. Cambridge: Cambridge University Press.

Rivoli, P. 2005. *The Travels of a T-Shirt in the Global Economy*. Hoboken, NJ: John Wiley and Sons.

Robertson, P. S., and S. Plaiyoowong. 2004. *The Struggle of the Gina Workers in Thailand: Inside a Successful International Labour Solidarity Campaign*. The Southeast Asia Research Center. Hong Kong: City University of Hong Kong.

Rocheleau, D. 2005. "Political Landscapes and Ecologies of Zambrana-Chacuey: The Legacy of Mama Tingo." In *Women and the Politics of Place*, edited by W. Harcourt and A. Escobar, 72–85. Bloomfield, CT: Kumarian Press.

Rodríguez-Garavito, C. A. 2005. "Global Governance and Labor Rights: Codes of Conduct and Anti-Sweatshop Struggles in Global Apparel Factories in Mexico and Guatemala." *Politics and Society* 33, no. 2: 203–33.

Rosen, E. I. 2002. *Making Sweatshops: The Globalization of the US Apparel Industry*. Berkeley and Los Angeles: University of California Press.

Ross, A. 1997. *No Sweat: Fashion, Free Trade and the Rights of Garment Workers*. New York: Verso.

Ross, R. 2004a. "From Antisweatshop to Global Justice to Antiwar: How the New New Left Is the Same and Different from the Old New Left." *Journal of World-Systems Research* 10, no. 1: 287–319.

———. 2004b. *Slaves to Fashion*. Ann Arbor: University of Michigan Press.

SEWA. 2007. "Homepage." Self Employed Womens Association website.

Shah, D. V., D. M. McLeod, L. Friedland, and M. R. Nelson. 2007. "The Politics of Consumption/The Consumption of Politics." *Annals of the American Academy of Political and Social Science* 611: 6–15.

Sluiter, L. 2009. *Clean Clothes: A Global Movement to End Sweatshops*. New York: Pluto Press.

Smith, J. 2005. "Globalization and Social Movement Organizations." In *Social Movements and Organization Theory*, edited by G. Davis, D. McAdam, W. R. Scott, and M. Zald, 226–48. Cambridge: Cambridge University Press.

Smith, J., C. Chatfield, and R. Pagnucco, eds. 1997. *Transnational Social Movements and Global Politics*. Syracuse, NY: Syracuse University Press.

Snow, D. 2004. "Framing, Processes, Ideology, and Discursive Fields." In *The Blackwell Companion to Social Movements*, edited by D. Snow, S. Soule, and H. Kriesi, 380–412. Oxford: Blackwell.

Solidarity Center. 2009. "Where We Work." Solidarity Center and AFL-CIO. Solidarity Center website.

Stienstra, D. 1999. "Of Roots, Leaves, and Trees: Gender, Social Movements, and Global Governance." In Meyer and Prugl 1999, 260–72.

STITCH. 2002. "Trainings and Exchanges." STITCH website.

———. 2008. "The Other Immigrants/Los Otros Inmigrantes: Women Workers in the U.S. Labor Movement." Washington DC: STITCH.

Symington, A. 2004. *Intersectionality: A Tool for Gender and Economic Justice*. Washington DC: Association for Women's Rights in Development.

Tarrow, S. 2005. *The New Transnational Activism*. New York: Cambridge University Press.

TCFUA. 1995. *The Hidden Cost of Fashion: Report on the National Outwork Information Campaign*. Sydney: Textile, Clothing and Footwear Union of Australia.

Tran, D. 2006. "Outworkers Scared to Speak on Plight." *Australian Financial Review*. November 22.

Tuan, N. 2008. "Vietnam: Strike Action Hits 112 Apparel Plants This Year." Just Style website.

Udayagiri, M. 1995. "Challenging Modernization: Gender and Development, Postmodern Feminism, and Activism." In *Feminism/Postmodernism/Development*, edited by M. H. Marchand and J. L. Parpart, 159–78. London: Routledge.

UNCTAD, and R. Appelbaum. 2005. *TNCs and the Removal of Textiles and Clothing Quotas*. Center for Global Studies. Santa Barbara: University of California.

The Urban Institute. 2007. "National Center for Charitable Statistics Quick Facts about Nonprofits." Urban Institute website.

USAS. 2006a. "International Intern Report 2005." United Students Against Sweatshops website.

———. 2006b. "Support Gina Workers in Thailand." United Students Against Sweatshops website.

———. 2009a. "Twenty-Five Universities Cut Contracts with Russell Athletics, a Serial Abuser of Workers Rights!" United Students Against Sweatshops website.

———. 2009b. "We Won! Honduran Union Signs Historic Agreement with Russell Athletic!" United Students Against Sweatshops website.

USLEAP. 2007. *Just Garments Closes: Forced to End Efforts As Sweat-Free Producer*. U.S. Labor Education in the Americas Project website.

Uvin, P. 2000. "From Local Organizations to Global Governance: The Role of NGOs in International Relations." In *Global Institutions and Local Empowerment: Competing Theoretical Perspectives*, edited by K. Stiles, 9–29. London: Macmillan.

Uvin, P., P. S. Jain, and L. D. Brown. 2000. "Think Large and Act Small: Toward a New Paradigm for NGO Scaling Up." *World Development* 28, no. 8: 1409–19.

Vakil, A. 1997. "Confronting the Classification Problem: Toward a Taxonomy of NGOs." *World Development* 25, no. 12: 2057–70.

Van de Donk, W., B. D. Loader, P. G. Nixon, and D. Rucht, eds. 2004. *Cyberprotest: New Media, Citizens and Social Movements*. London: Routledge.

Verite. 2004. *Excessive Overtime in Chinese Supplier Factories: Causes, Impacts, and Recommendations for Action*. Verite website.

Wapner, P. 1996. *Environmental Activism and World Civic Politics*. Albany: State University of New York Press.

Waterman, P., and J. Timms. 2005. "Trade Union Internationalism and a Global Civil Society in the Making." In Anheier, Glasius, and Kaldor 2005, 175–202.

Waterman, S. 2007. "Americans Placed on Filipino Watch List." *United Press International*. October 12.

Wells, D. 2006. "Best Practice in the Regulation of International Labor Standards: Lessons of the US-Cambodia Trade Agreement." *Comparative Labor Law and Policy Journal* 27, no. 3: 357–76.

WFSGI. 2007. *Official Handbook of the Sporting Goods Industry: CSR and the World of Sport*. Lausanne, Switzerland: World Federation of the Sporting Goods Industry.

Wills, J., and A. Hale. 2006. "Threads of Labour in the Global Garment Industry." In Hale and Wills 2006, 1–15.

WRC. 2006. "Factory Assessment Update December 19, 2006." Worker Rights Consortium website.

———. 2007. "Memorandum to Parties concerned about the Announced Closure of BJ&B." Email. Washington DC: Worker Rights Consortium.

———. 2009a. "Affiliate Schools." Worker Rights Consortium website.

———. 2009b. "Russell Corporation's Rights Violations in Honduras." Worker Rights Consortium website.

———. 2009c. "WRC Assessment re Rights of Association of Russell Athletic and Fruit of the Loom Employees in Honduras: Analysis of 'Collective Pacts.'" Worker Rights Consortium website.

———. 2009d. "WRC Assessment re Rights of Association of Russell Athletic and Fruit of the Loom Employees in Honduras: Analysis of Employee Interviews." Worker Rights Consortium website.

———. 2010a. "Progress Report re Implementation of Russell Athletic/Fruit of the Loom Remediation Agreements for Operations in Honduras." Worker Rights Consortium website.

———. 2010b. "Verification Report re Living Wage Compliance at Altagracia Project Factory." Worker Rights Consortium website.

WTO. 2008. International Trade Statistics Tables Ii65 and Ii70. World Trade Organization.

Yimprasert, L. 2006. "Dignity Returns—A Workers' Brand Is Possible!" Thai Labour Campaign website.

Young, I. M. 2004. "Responsibility and Global Labor Justice." *Journal of Political Philosophy* 12, no. 4: 365–88.

———. 2006. "Responsibility and Global Justice: A Social Connection Model." *Social Philosophy and Policy Foundation* 23, no. 1: 102–30.

Index

About the Author

SHAE GARWOOD has worked with numerous NGOs in the United States, Nepal, and Australia on issues including civil rights, girl trafficking, and community development. She received a master's degree in gender and development studies from the London School of Economics and a PhD in political science and international relations from the University of Western Australia. She is currently a researcher with Shelter WA, where she focuses on affordable housing, homelessness, and housing policy. She is also an honorary research fellow at the University of Western Australia.

Kumarian Press, located in Sterling, Virginia, is a forward-looking, scholarly press that promotes active international engagement and an awareness of global connectedness.